SECOND David

TRIALS AND TRIBULATIONS

SECOND
David
TRIALS AND TRIBULATIONS

A Biblical historical novel

BY JOSEPH GANCI

AUTHOR'S PAGE

God wears a double bow on his shoulder. Each color has a particular wave, depth, and light length, representing his intelligence's vastness. The high priest's Ephod has gold, blue, purple, scarlet, and white fine-twined linen. The twelve stones on the breastplate of judgment are different colors and represent the birthstones of the twelve sons of Jacob. Consider Joseph's coat of many colors or Tamar and all of King David's virgin daughter's apparel of diverse colors. I had witnessed a breathtaking double bow that had fallen on the sheer shale face of Mount Crested Butte as I approached where the end of the rainbow rested. It looked like the rock was on fire but not being consumed. I believe this is what Moses witnessed in the burning bush on Mount Sinai. (Sinai means: The bush in the clay desert, the place of enmity)

Since the Glory of God is intelligence, and Israel is the chosen people, they are natural heirs to intellect.

Ignorance that refuses to learn is no better off than stupidity that is unable.

Pain is the touchstone of spiritual growth. You can't be comfortable and grow spiritually at the same time.

Priestcraft: the art of awing the laity, managing their consciousness, and diving into their pocket.

Pride is the number one sin because it disavows the existence of God or the need thereof.

Ridicule is death to the ego, and the ego will sacrifice the body on the altar of pride in a vain attempt to stay alive. The preacher said vanities of vanities all is vanity.

What does not kill you makes you less edible. A little tougher and harder to swallow.

Check your side view mirrors. Beliefs may be closer than they appear, causing us to become blind to the obvious.

Belief, by any of the limited senses, may be merely emotional or intellectual, while faith implies such confidence and conviction as it will compel you to act.

FOREWORD

Garrison Wynn, CSP

Bestselling author and internationally known speaker

This latest offering from Joseph Ganci, like all his books that precede it, is the work of a biblical detective who uncovers truths we never saw to tell a story we only thought we knew. For many, it will bring enlightenment and a new understanding of the surprisingly important details of the world's most influential book. For others, it will bring to life the dramatic, action-filled story of David, the great unifier, led by God into a world that Ganci expertly paints in vivid detail. This book miraculously draws unexpected connections between seemingly unrelated events, giving us a familiar narrative we feel comfortable following. For believers and skeptics alike, an intriguing journey awaits.

Thank You, Garrison. It's a win, Wynn.
Joseph Ganci

TABLE OF CONTENTS

Table of Contents

Table of Contents

PROLOGUE
Second David, Trials and Tribulations

This book covers Second Samuel 12:31 through

First Kings 2:11

This book picks up where David God's Chosen Crucible leaves off. There is a natural break in his story at this point. David is at the height of his power and acclaim. He has married his soulmate Bathsheba, who is pregnant with his unborn child. He made the child legitimate by killing Bathsheba's husband, Uriah the Hittite, and marrying her when she became an available widow. David believes he has eluded both the judgment of men and God's Judgment. Stating that since it was the sword of Amon and not him directly, claiming that "The sword of war devours one as well as another," allowing him to proclaim innocence.

He is now the master of a huge domain, the empire of Israel. This feat surpasses his imagination of greatness.

At a feast celebrating all that he had accomplished. Nathan the Prophet enters and asks David for a judgment. Nathan tells of two men, one rich with flocks and herds and a poor man with one ewe lamb that he treated like family and ate at his table. The rich man took the poor man's one ewe lamb and dressed it for the stranger. He asks David, "What would you do to this rich man who took the poor man's one ewe lamb."

In self-righteous anger, David proclaimed, "I would have him killed and make him pay it back four times."

Nathan looks David squarely in the eyes, points to him, and accusingly announces, "You are the man, and the sword will never leave your house."

Nathan's fable tricks David, and he Judges himself and sets his punishment. Is this not how, when standing in front of God with our perfect knowledge of our sins, we judge ourselves and announce the punishment to set the scales of justice right, For mercy cannot rob justice?

Vast wealth and greed!... Envy, trickery, lust, murder, and underhanded power grabs! Assassination attempts, Incest!, and deadly family plotting. An unwitting party to human sacrifice and contending with fierce battling giants.

As a novelist, I use poetic license to depict events I imagine could have happened. I use well-researched details consistent with the human mind, will, and emotions for the era: geography, local customs, rumors, legends, and the ever-dark spin of power politics.

In King Solomon's immortal words, "There is nothing new under the sun."

The beginnings and the endings remain consistent with the Biblical narrative. This work and all my works are for the sole purpose of glorifying God. I hope this story will encourage you to search out the Scriptures for yourself and delve deeper into the mind of God.

CHAPTER ONE

A Gift from God, and the Cruelest Cut

It was nine months and one week to the day, the same day that marked the death of the poisoned fruit of David's adulterous affair. On that day, God took David's unnamed and uncircumcised son back to heaven. Yet, on that fateful day, Bathsheba gave birth to a healthy man-child. This was the natural outcome of comfort so tenderly offered by David, her soulmate and lover. Expectations ran high that the robust new infant blessed by God might signal a reprieve and that no further punishments would be forthcoming.

The infant hungrily fed on Bathsheba's milk-swollen breasts. The greedy boy suckled insatiably until her nipples bled. In time, she overcame the pain, thanks to the joy of producing a new life, perhaps by God's will, the future king of Israel.

The darkened chamber was bright and hopeful, even with the weatherworn cedar shutters tightly closed to ward off chilling drafts. The unmistakable smells of powders and soiled wrappings wafted high above the flickering candlelight. Nursing mothers stood in attendance, ready and waiting to assist, but Bathsheba denied all offers of a stranger's nourishment for her beloved offspring. Instead, she insisted on bonding with her infant son, thus proving that she cared little about personal sacrifice. The baby was tranquil, yet his eyes never stopped moving.

He constantly tried to penetrate the gray fog of shapes and colors. The curious infant tried to make sense of unfamiliar sounds through dancing shadows. His tiny world consisted of his mother's embrace, a sweet, milky nipple, and a soothing voice that lulled him into a dreamless sleep.

Still tender from the previous loss, David visited the nursery every day. He doted on Bathsheba and the new baby with fondness, generosity, and love. Bending over the cradle, he filled his son's vision with his beaming, grateful, and smiling face. Bathsheba chuckled, "Aren't you a world of surprises?"

David beamed, "I'm just so delighted and fulfilled in the fathering of a healthy son issued by my most beloved wife."

He kissed her cheek. "I have summoned Nathan, the prophet, to bless the child. The eighth day of naming and God's covenant of circumcision quickly approaches. I am excited about the ceremony and the prospect of declaring our child a son of God and Israel. My dear wife, have you thought of a name?"

Bathsheba responded sincerely, "I have long reflected on a proper name befitting the new prince. He is peaceful and quiet; you would not know he was alive. He only stirs when hungry or irritated from lying too long in his dirt. So, I would name him Solomon, meaning ‹Peaceful One.'"

David's ears perked as if he had heard the name from some distant past.

He instantly resounded, "Yes, my dear madam, that will be his name. It is as if it was already ordained."

"My husband, you can hear his name from the past. I can hear his name echoed in the palace halls in the not-so-distant future: King Solomon!" said Bathsheba, feeling pleased with herself and giddy with delight.

David winced a bit and gently chided, "Madam, it is by God's will, a very long time from now, and besides, many sons will make their challenge. When the time is right, I will count on the spirit of God to name my heir apparent. If I announce my choice too soon, it could bring murder afoot. Bloody civil war can find its menacing uproar if I wait too late and beyond my grave. No, God will pick the time and the place. I can show no favoritism, even in the slightest; besides, it keeps all the boys on their toes and vying for my favor."

The eighth day fell on the Shabbat, a sacred time to fulfill God's ritual circumcision. David's and Bathsheba's love child and the newest prince of Israel would be named and consecrated to God by a holy prophet on the coming Shabbat. So, David set about seeing to all the hallowed arrangements. He called forth Ebed, his dutiful manservant who always remained within earshot, day or night, whim or wish. He stood at the ready to fulfill the king's every request.

David excitedly directed, "My good man, it is the prince's time to be named and circumcised. The Shabbat and the prince's eighth day of precious life is the day after tomorrow.

Consequently, all must be in place before sundown without exception or hesitation. My oldest brother Eliab will carry the baby to the child's maternal grandfather Ahithophel, who will act as the sandek and hold the baby still during the cutting. The prophet Nathan has agreed to do the dividing. A minyan must witness this for it is God's commandment, 'I will spare Sodom and Gomorrah for the sake of ten righteous men,' and so ten righteous men are required to sanctify the occasion."

Unusually for Ebed, the itch for knowledge forced his hand, and he found himself speaking his mind. "Forgive my curiosity, Your Majesty. I am personally and painfully familiar with that ancient ritual. Unfortunately, I have never quite understood the purpose of such harshness on an infant. Or, for that matter, the pain and cruel mutilation endured by any man to become a sanctified Hebrew."

Strong in God's knowledge, David explained, "Ebed, we circumcise because it is a covenant of possession. God said to Abraham, 'I will give unto you, and to your seed after you, the land wherein you are a stranger, all the land of Canaan, for an everlasting possession; and I will be your God, and you shall be my people. So that every man child among you shall circumcise the flesh of your foreskin, and it shall be a token of that covenant between you and Me. It will take place on the eighth day of his new life. It is the undeniable evidence of God's everlasting promise.' Ebed listened carefully as David continued, "Remember, Ebed, the foreskin is a blemish, and by its removal, it enables a man to achieve bodily perfection by fulfilling a divine commandment. If it were not for circumcision, heaven and earth would not exist. Therefore, the performance of this duty is proof of God's acceptance."

"Thank you, my king; I understand the sacred purpose of this ritual marking. It is like a deed of trust for the land of Canaan written in blood." Ebed chuckled, his eyes twinkling with enlightenment. "Um, if I might be bold, sire?"

"Speak on, Ebed, and make this your last query, for I grow weary of your endless childlike questioning."

As he hovered on the edge of provoking a royal irritation, Ebed braced himself. "Thank you for your infinite patience. But why is it eight days?"

David paused and pondered the question before saying, "God, in His infinite wisdom, knows that the infant had suffered great shock at birth and is in a delicate and fragile condition. At the very soonest, it would take eight days for the infant to become strong enough to endure the insult and readily heal from the stress placed upon his flesh. Before entering the covenant of circumcision, the infant needs to pass through, at least, one Shabbat. Any animal sacrifice needs to be, at least, eight days old before being accepted by God as holy." David took a pause.

"So, too, the child's mother remains unclean for seven days after giving him life. Then, on the eighth day, she is clean and so is the fruit of her womb. Then, and only then, does the child become available to God. Lastly, we circumcise our children when they are eight-day-old babies because eights are supernatural. The Brit Milah, or covenant circumcision, symbolizes Israel's mystical bond with God. It is a spiritual connection beyond perfection found in the natural world. Enough said, I tire of your inquiries and of my telling explanations."

David then reluctantly suggested, "Oh, yes, and lest I forget, and for the sake of politeness, invite Eliam, Bathsheba's father, and her grandfather Ahithophel. I hope that their enmity has subsided. Eliam and Ahithophel might hold a seething hostility against me for killing Uriah and marrying his widow. Abiathar will hold the prince steady during the ceremony.

The Shabbat and the time of the princes' circumcision commenced at sundown. David's brothers and his nephews Joab and Abishai, his two fearsome military commanders, were in attendance. Unfortunately, but not unexpectedly, there were some noticeable absentees. This included David's in-laws Eliam, one of his esteemed Mighties, and Ahithophel, his prime minister, seer, and counselor.

The last of the sun's dying rays bathed the receiving hall when Nathan crossed the threshold. With God's always-perfect timing, the prophet was able to make it undercover before sundown.

Eliab hurried to the king's private apartments to fetch David and the baby. A manly knock on the door was proceeded by a familiar voice, "It is time, brother, to name the baby and present him to God and obtain the promised possession of the land of Israel."

The door opened to the sight of Bathsheba nursing her baby. She turned towards Eliab and, as a comforting mother, uttered, "Please give me a moment. A full belly and clean wrappings will comfort the prince before his painfully slicing ordeal."

"Certainly, madam, take whatever time you need to comfort

the child. But, David, can I see you outside and give Bathsheba some privacy?" Eliab began jerking his head towards David, indicating the need for some privacy to allow for a private discussion. The brothers left the room and closed the door firmly behind them.

"What is it, Brother?" David inquired.

"As you had suspected, neither Eliam nor Ahithophel are in attendance," replied Eliab. "I thought it best not to speak of their absence in front of Bathsheba. I do not wish to dash her hopes of reconciliation, especially on the day her son seeks admittance into the Kingdom of God."

David nodded in agreement with his brother's compassion before whispering, "Then so be it; the honor falls upon you, my dear and oldest brother. You will bring the prince into the room and deliver him to Abiathar, the acting sandek or the child's comforting companion—while Nathan, the prophet, removes the foreskin."

There was a gentle tapping on the chamber door, and Bathsheba whispered, "Enter; the prince is ready to meet his first public challenge." David took the baby in his arms, kissed Bathsheba on the cheek, and proceeded out the door with Eliab.

Before entering the hall, David gave the baby to Eliab and took his place next to Abiathar.

Nathan began, "Blessed is the one who arrives. David, what name have you given the child?"

David proudly responded, "Solomon is his familiar name."

"Very well, and God also requires me to give him his new name only to be used in holy ordinances and when he passes through the angels to attend the throne of God."

Nathan began, "Blessed art Thou, O Lord our God, king of the universe, who hast sanctified us with Thy commandments and has given us the command concerning circumcision." He then took the sharp, thin blade and pinched the foreskin tight before deliberately slicing it. The infant screamed, and blood spilled from the open wound. Nathan blotted the cut with wine-soaked wipes.

David then recited, "Blessed art Thou, O Lord our God, king of the universe, who hast sanctified us with Thy commandments, and commanded us to make our sons enter the covenant of Abraham, our father."

The men responded in unity, "Even as this child has entered into the covenant, so may he enter into the Torah, the nuptial canopy, and good deeds."

Nathan then took a cup of wine and started to speak over it, "Blessed are You, our God, ruler of the world, Creator of the fruit of the vine."

Nathan sipped the wine as the blessing giver and uttered, "Our God and God of our fathers, preserve this child for his father and mother, and his name in Israel shall be called Solomon, son of David. God has directed me to give the child a new name that can only be spoken at a particular place and time, Jedidiah, meaning 'beloved of the Lord, friend of God.'" Nathan then proceeded to drip two drops into the infant's mouth, signifying that the child had received the blessing. Solemnly he continued, "May the father rejoice in his offspring, and his mother is glad about the fruit of her womb.

May your father and mother rejoice, and she who bore you be delighted." To which all present said, "Amen."

Solomon cried out from the sharp pain, and while still whimpering from his injury, David picked him up and whispered in his ear, "Life is painful, and joy is fleeting, so enjoy your moment in the sun, little prince. The sooner you accept this reality, the sooner you find strength and purpose in wisdom." Then, the freshly circumcised child was off to his mother's loving arms for the sweet milk of kindness and a badly needed change from soiled and bloody wrappings.

CHAPTER TWO

A Son-in-Law of Alliances

David's first wife, Princess Michal, still loved David as he was her first love and one of the three prizes granted to the slayer of Goliath. King Saul promised that he would provide the slayer with great riches, give the victor his daughter, and make his father's house free of taxes forever in Israel. Since David was there to collect pledges to help pay his father Jesses's back taxes, he felt he was on a mission from God to fulfill his destiny.

Michal was not delivered as promised, for King Saul had placed an additional bounty on her affections of 100 Philistine foreskins. Nevertheless, David surpassed the challenge with 200 foreskins—proving that God's anointing is a mark of divine power.

But all too soon, Saul's envy erupted into anger. David always did the next right thing and honored and respected the king. The young man's charm and likeability enraged Saul, who viewed his humility as a cunning plot to undermine his authority—at dinner one fateful night and being playful and charming and strumming his liar. Every chord plucked struck Saul's nerves; he had had enough and, in a fit of rage, sought David's life with a well-placed javelin throw barely missing David's head. David fled for his life. Michal helped him escape, saving his life but leaving his loving princess far beyond his reach.

Saul gave Michal away to another, Palti, son of Laish. After Saul's death, she became a political bargaining chip. Ish-bosheth, Saul's son and heir, became the next king of Israel. His war with David was going badly. Ish-bosheth relented to David's demand and returned to him his wife, Michal, as a sign of respect and to open a negotiated peace settlement. Palti was so distressed over his loss that he followed her back to David like a lost puppy dog seeking comfort, but he turned back at the king's death-defying boundary. Michal later ridiculed David for dancing with joyful immodesty during the Ark of the Covenant's entrance into Jerusalem. The argument was so hateful that David sent Michal away to live as a widow and never knew her again carnally, thus ensuring that Saul's seed would never taint his lineage.

Ahinoam, or pleasantness herself, had a delicate and refined temperament. David's lovely second wife hailed from Jezreel Valley.

The beautiful and wealthy Abigail the Carmelite, the widow of Nabal, was David's third wife. The hostility from a grievous insult from Nabal brought David to the verge of his murder. God stepped in and slew Nabal, using his appetite for riotous living to ensure his downfall. However, David repented his evil intention and reaped the rewards of a desperately-needed fortune and the comfort of a beautiful wife.

In the days of Ziklag, the town was given to David by Prince Achish in the Philistine province of Gath. Here, David had a reprieve from Saul's unrelenting, maddening, and murderous pursuit. Needing to feed his six hundred vagabond warriors, they raided the Gershurites, the Gezrites, Amalekite towns, and villages. These ancient peoples inhabited the land of Canaan soon after the Great Flood.

David went as far as Shur. He even raided the land of Egypt. His forays were against heathens and allies of the hostile Philistines or Canaanites nations. For the most part, some lived peaceably without fear of attack or violence, thus making them easy prey. But David was sure never to attack any Judean or Israeli settlements.

He and his band massacred whole villages, including men, women, and even children. He left none alive. David was not one to give away his lethal plot, thus shielding this knowledge from his benefactor, Prince Achish of the Philistine.

When Achish inquired, "Where did you raid today?" David often replied by saying, "The south country of Judah," "The south country of the Jerahmeelities," or "The south country of the Kenites." The tribute Achish received was bountiful, and so he never questioned further. On the contrary, he readily believed David and thought, He hath made his people of Israel utterly to hate him; therefore, he shall be my servant forever.

Ziklag was David's home and stronghold. David and his

six hundred were constantly on the prowl into the heart of Canaanite territory. Upon their return, and after a meager haul, only to find that Ziklag, David's pride and joy and home to his six hundred vagabond mercenaries, had been burnt to the ground. His wound was made more grievous by the abduction of his two wives, Ahinoam and Abigail, who went missing. Amalekite bandits likely kidnapped them, seeking plunder, enslaving people, and bartering hostages.

David, a self-appointed privateer, only destroyed the enemies of Israel, unlike the Amalekites, who attacked any targets of opportunity. The Amalekites sought out signs of weakness regardless of politics. They were a powerful and well-organized army of gypsies, pirates, and cutthroats.

David and his outlaw army pursued and attacked the Amalekite shapeshifters, resulting in a fierce all-day and all-night battle. Some Amalekites turned into animals and fled, barely escaping David's vengeance.

After rescuing his two wives, David found an Amalekite treasure cave and seized vast stores of wealth, flocks, and herds. He gathered an incredible mountain of wealth and generously gifted the Judean chieftains. In return, they made him their king. Nothing can ensure goodwill as much as gifted gold and silver.

David settled in Hebron, where the cave Machpelah [or the place of The Double Tombs] resides. This was the revered burial place of the three patriarchs, Abraham, Isaac, Jacob, and their wives, Sarah, Rebeka, and Leah. Rachel was buried in her ancestral tomb in Sachem.

King David dwelt in Hebron on a throne set upon a

marble pedestal. But it was only on the rarest of occasions that he actually rested upon it. For the most part, his scepter remained idle. He constantly battled Ish-Bosheth, the king of Israel, and Saul's seasoned Chief Captain Abner, son of Ner.

On one of those rare occasions that saw a lull in fighting, David called forth his brother Shimeah, Joab, his nephew, and chief captain, and Abiathar, his high priest. Joab was the last to arrive, having just returned from a skirmish with Abner and the Israeli forces. Glad to see his nephew still alive and not bloodied, David gleefully rose to meet him, "Welcome, Joab. Seeing you victorious and unharmed is always a gladness to my eyes. Before you tell me about your recent encounter, I have prepared some food and wine to wash down the dust in your throat. Let us praise God for your safe return and the bounty he sets before us." Joab nodded the acclaim before replying, "Thank you, uncle, and thank God. I thirst and starve. I need to regain my strength. Let us partake."

The esteemed high priest and family engaged in light chatter and sat in the comfort of slurps, bites, and the chew of good-natured conversation. King David was anxious to express his plan for his newest conquest. He began, "Nephew, how goes the war with Israel and chief captain Abner?"

Joab put down his goblet and confidently responded, "It is going better than expected. We have some hard fighting ahead of us. But for now, we are holding our own. The good news is that Abner's resolve seems to be weakening. If I keep up the pressure, it will only be a matter of time. Abner will relent when forced to face the inevitable. His defeat will set aside the last obstacle in making you the future king of Israel and Judah."

"That is reassuring news, Chief Captain Joab. Chief Captain Abner is well-experienced, crafty, and cunning. I wish he were on our side instead of having to fight against him. But no matter, we will beat that old fox with resolve and courage."

David then continued with a more pressing and personal matter. "My most trusted friend and family, I need some aid and counsel. While traveling to battle, I recently came upon a beautifully tall and willowy woman with a crown of hair that touched the ground, and all at once, she touched my heart. The princess had graceful hands and elegant fingernails. The long nails imply nobility, as she was unaccustomed to toiling with her hands in manual labor. I must admit I could barely look away. I hastily inquired and discovered that her name is Maacah (meaning crushed), a favored Geshurite princess. She regularly sacrifices to their gods, seeking the favor of finding a suitable husband. I would have her for myself and seal an alliance with King Talmai, her father. The Geshurite army could very well turn the tide against Chief Captain Abner and end the reign of Ish-bosheth." The gathered men listened intently as David continued.

"I propose we go to Geshur, all but you, Joab. It is vital to intensify your unrelenting attacks on Abner and Israel. Your actions will also benefit me by keeping Abner distracted and not inquiring about my whereabouts.

"I must be especially cautious in my approach to the Geshur capital. I had often ransacked Geshurite towns and villages. If somebody might have recognized me and word of my raids got back to King Talmai, Maacah's father, I could be walking into a pit of vengeful vipers. As king of Judah, I intend to send envoys to safeguard my arrival. They will make my offer of marriage and negotiate the mohar or bride's ransom. Such a proposal would be expected and considered proper etiquette. As emissaries from a more powerful kingdom, Talmai would not harm or even dare to insult my representatives. He knows that it would be considered an act of war. However, suppose suspicion of my earlier raids has come to his ears, and he finds the proposition deplorable, he will likely dismiss you immediately with a stern warning never to return." David stiffened, fearing that one day his bloody forays would be discovered and an accounting would be forthcoming.

"Abiathar, the Priest, and my brother Shimeah—well-known for his negotiating skills—will act as my goodwill ambassadors. We will take fifty men, enough for protection but not so many to suggest a hostile intention or a prelude to invasion. Also, an ox cart loaded with a gold talent agrees that Maacah is worth her weight in gold. Lastly, it would be best to emphasize that our marriage will seal an alliance with Judah's reigning monarch and Israel's future anointed king with the unbreakable bonds of matrimony. King Talmai, if he agrees, will be expected to break his allegiance to King Ish-bosheth of Israel. Talmai must pledge to us his army. We will then enjoy mutual protection, and he will join our ever-widening circle of allies." The moment David found out that Maacah was a royal princess, his plan to acquire both the beauty and a much-needed alliance took shape.

"I will camp with my forty men just outside of the Geshurite border. Ten men will accompany Shimeah, my brother, and you, too, Abiathar, across the forty miles to the stronghold of Et-Tell. I prefer to distance myself until I know there are no hostile intentions against my person. Once there is an agreement about my marriage, send a messenger stating all is well, and you can then herald my arrival. In this way, you remain the king's guests while giving him the confidence of valued hostages. We do this only to confirm our honorable intentions and that this is not a ploy in plotting an invasion. Of course, I will bring gold and give Talmai the bride's ransom. But remember, brother, offer them her weight in gold—a generous offer, even for a beautiful Geshurite princess."

Abiathar cleared his throat to avoid a raspy croak. What he had to impart could quash David's best-laid romantic intentions and darker political objectives.

"A delicate matter, my king, requires your obedience."

"Speak on, learned high priest." David urged.

"Maacah will be an eshet yefat to'ar or a non-Hebrew wife. The law is strict as to the conditions of such a marriage. In humility, the woman must first shave her head and pare her nails because long and luxurious nails are the province of nobility, who have been spared the tedium of physical labor from birth. Then she must wear mourning clothing and lament for her parents' home for thirty days."

Stiffening his backbone, David looked Abiathar squarely in the eyes before speaking in a sullen voice, "Thank you, high priest, for that piously challenging obstacle. Those religious measures must be considered only after both parties approve the nuptial contract. I will be the one to broach the subject if we get that far. By then, Talmai will be counting his new-found wealth and relishing the security and power that will come with a Hebrew son-in-law potentially gifted with two kingdoms. He will not break his word for an ancient cultural ritual. Unless we forget, her hair and nails will eventually grow back; it is, at best, a temporary setback. If Princess Maacah cringes at the proposition, I will soothe her injured vanity with loving kindness. I plan to marry the princess in Bethesda, the Geshurite capital, so her family and friends can attend the festivities." David paused for a moment as he continued to fixate his gaze in Abiathar's direction.

"Abiathar, now you know why I need you there. It is your priesthood authority to make it a legitimate wedding in the eyes of God and all the twelve tribes."

"I am honored, sire, and remain your faithful servant."

"We will carry the wedding canopy and all the necessary trappings. Even if reluctantly, I need you to cooperate if Princess Maacah insists that one of her pagan oracles assists in the wedding ceremony," David added.

The priest quickly replied, "I must object to any heathen mischief, as it would not be proper and, in fact, even an insult to our God."

"That is a sharp barb of reason, priest. Therefore, I will propose a second and separate ceremony. But only if Maacah demands the need to satisfy her pagan practices."

Now focusing on the eyes of all in attendance, David asked, "Are there any questions, misgivings, or suggestions? Speak up now, for we leave at first light. I do not want whispered rumors. The trade of spies is in helping Abner to catch me vulnerable in the wilderness."

The room remained silent until Joab, with a knowing smile, replied, "No, not at all, uncle. As usual, you have thought of every possibility. I do not doubt you are truly the Lord's anointed and the future king of Israel."

Hours before dawn, sparking torches crisscrossed the mansion. The king's house bristled with scurrying servants and men at arms yelling orders to secure the required provisions. All was made ready for the king's departure. A talent of gold was carefully and secretly loaded in the dark. The company's destination and its objective remained a mystery. The two oxen lowed as the wedding canopy and all holy accessories were loaded, covered, and securely lashed down. Food and skins of wine overflowed from another cart as the back gate slammed shut. The sun peaked over the Hebron horizon. The ninety-four miles to a new wife and a much-needed ally lay before the strong-willed king and his handpicked crew. The excitement of a new adventure spurred David to challenge a realm of giants.

CHAPTER THREE
A Tall and Willowy Beauty, Maacah

Talmai was the son of Ammihud and the reigning king of Geshur. He was a direct descendant of the Nephilim race: the fallen ones, giants in their own right. The Nephilim knew human women, and together they produced a race of Rephaim giants. Talmai's kingdom had bled wealth and power. The Gezrites and Amalekites' kingdoms suffered greatly under ruthless assaults from yet an unknown power. Luckily, David's raids remained shrouded in secrecy. Marauders that seemed to come out of nowhere and vanish just as mysteriously. A dark power that left its mark with fire and massacre. All that was left after they passed were dead bodies and smoldering embers. Most thought it was Amalekite pirates, but these massacres were even too brutal for them. They enslaved people and ransomed the highborn wealthy, as dead bodies had no value.

How to stop this carnage was on Talmai's mind day and night. He was at a loss for a solution. Then, at that very moment, fate and luck stepped in. Still panting from his urgent news, a gate guard presented himself to King Talmai.

"Sire, two envoys from David ben Jesse, the recently anointed king of Judah, arrived at the entrance, seeking an audience with the king."

Very little surprised Talmai, but this unexpected intrusion was an exception. Talmai questioned, "Are they alone, and do these strangers have names?"

"It does appear so, all alone, and one says they come in peace. He is unarmed and says to be Shimeah, brother of King David of Judah, and his companion is a Hebrew high priest named Abiathar. He claims to be on a delicate and personal mission for the Judean King. So, they request a private audience with King Talmai of the Gershurite."

"Bring them to my anteroom and post extra guards. I will speak to them there."

Entering the room, Shimeah bowed and waited for a nod of acknowledgment from the king.

After a brief pause, Talmai then spoke, "Speak your business, emissaries of David."

Shimeah began, "We have come to you at the bidding of my brother David, the king of Judah. If your Majesty permits, I will get right to it."

"Speak on," said the king as he waved his hand.

"When my brother went to war, he saw your beautiful daughter Maacah. He desires her so much that he wishes to make the princess his bride. He believes an alliance between our two houses would benefit both kingdoms. After my brother's conquest of the Amalekites and his anointing as king of the Jews, he can afford a generous dowry to fill your coffers for the privilege of your daughter's hand in marriage."

Listening closely, Talmai then turned his attention to Abiathar while digesting this unexpected alien proposal, "What is your part in this high drama, priest?" Abiathar proceeded to address the king with the simple truth, "Your majesty, I am here to assure the king of my sovereigns' honorable intention, and if a priest is required, I stand ready to serve."

Talmai remained quiet and unmoving, considering this proposition. Then, gathering his wits, he replied, "There is much to consider, and I must consult with my dutiful daughter before making such a decision. Therefore, Shimeah and Abiathar, you will remain our guests until I can sort this out and decide what is best for our daughter and our kingdom and in that order. Hebron is nearly a hundred miles away, so I assume you have the full authority to negotiate for the bride's ransom and any consequential alliance."

"Yes, I do. I have my brother's every confidence not to come home empty-handed." Shimeah was then escorted away to a massive room with an oversized bed.

Talmai contemplated an alliance with the newly appointed Hebrew king. According to the oracles, was this not David, the anointed king of Israel? He might have been a shepherd, mercenary, and outlaw, but now he is Judah's king and has done this by his own will and mind. Moreover, if the stars align and the battles yet to fight go right, he would be the next chosen sovereign of Israel, a wealthy and powerful nation. Although

Talmai would have to bear Israel's military vengeance if he cast his lot with David, King Ish-bosheth and his Chief Captain Abner could prove a daunting adversary.

King Talmai sent for Princess Maacah, known for her tall, willowy figure and hair draped to the ground in a cascade of long, luxurious blond waves.

The princess crossed the receiving hall threshold, and every eye immediately fixed upon her breathtaking beauty. She curtsied respectfully to the king. Her practical-minded father extended his hand, inviting her to sit beside him on his large throne, befitting his stature. King Talmai was a big man—in keeping with his ancestry. He whispered to his daughter, "My dear child, you look especially radiant this morning. Your hair is the envy of every woman in the kingdom."

Maacah replied, "Father, it seems you always start with compliments and niceties just before you lay down the law of what service I need to perform to help protect and enrich your kingdom."

With a wry smile, her father replied, "I am afraid you know me too well, my wise and learned daughter." To which Maacah remained silent, awaiting her father's bidding.

"As you know, we have been unable to find you a suitable husband. But I think your pilgrimages to the high places, prayers, and sacrifices to the moon god and the aroused bull have born the most unlikely fruit."

Intrigued by the prospect of finding a suitable match, Maacah pressed her father, "I know there is a snare to this catch. Please speak on so that I can fathom your hidden agenda."

Talmai swallowed hard and sputtered, "It is David ben Jesse."

Maacah's ears perked up, "Who?" She exclaimed with disdain. "That is a Hebrew name. Do you want me to marry one of those short little Hebrew people? Are you making light of me? I am in no mood for such a jest, even as little as you suggest, as it has no humor."

Talmai knew his proposition was going to be an uphill battle. Nevertheless, he exerted his best logic and reasoning. "Hear me now, and be open to my plea, my dutiful daughter. This David is now the king of Judah and the commander of a formidable army. He can, at a whim, destroy our lightly defended kingdom." Both duty and intrigue piqued Maacah's interest in this Hebrew prince

"David is becoming more daring and formidable with every conquest, and his influence grows daily. He was, after all, Prince Achish's vassal and maintained many dangerous friends. We find ourselves in the middle of political intrigue requiring a diplomatic solution. Suppose we can quiet these uncertainties by allying with this newly made king and inviting him into the family. Besides, I have it from a reliable source that a Hebrew prophet has anointed this David to be the future king of Israel and that his name and house will last forever. He will know greatness and glory. In short, he could become one of the world's wealthiest and most powerful men, surpassing Egyptian Pharaohs and all the Eastern kings combined.

"I have investigated the man, who is taller than most of his Hebrew race and allegedly handsome and cunningly clever. He is truly a man of destiny and a fitting future son-in-law. Our timing for this proposed alliance aligns perfectly with both of our desires. For you, a husband and, for me, a bulwark of protection in securing a formal coalition."

Wary of her father's impassioned plea, Maacah suspiciously questioned, "What has prompted this sudden interest in this foreign Hebrew prince?"

"Well, my dear girl, it seems fate and chance have aligned themselves with our needs, mine for an ally and you for want of a husband."

"Speak plainly, Father!"

Taking a deep breath, Talmai said, "Two emissaries from King David of Judah, representatives, have come to me today with a declaration of matrimony. One is King David's brother, and the other is his high priest. Both men have respected positions of honor. They seek my permission and your agreement to marry this Hebrew prince, David ben Jesse, king of Judah. This union will unite our two kingdoms in an unbreakable family bond. Furthermore, we will mutually pledge to come to the other's assistance, thus ensuring protection from our deadly enemies. Before I speak to David's emissaries and weigh their proposal, I will tell you what I know of this would-be suitor and highly regard your opinion and woman's intuition." The king, making sure he still had his daughter's attention, took a pause before continuing his plea.

"When a shepherd boy named David defeated the Rephaim giant Goliath, he stood only armed with a rock and a sling. This David, your suitor, has made himself the king of Judah by his own hand and soon, with our help, the king of Israel. He was anointed as a mere youth to fulfill this destiny. He is a cunning desert fighter who lives for a challenge. David relishes the chase and revels in conquest. The rumor is that he suffers from the lust of the eyes and cannot restrain himself when he sees a beautiful woman. He has proven that he will go to any length to accomplish his task once he sets his mind to the outcome."

"Tell me, Father, what makes you think he will favor me?"

"He has already seen you and found you alluring. David probably saw you when you were up at Gath, and he was going out to battle. Sending his ambassadors, one of them his brother, to secure our consent is evidence of his sincerity. I know he will find you pleasing, for you have wit and charm. Therefore, I pray that you find him acceptable as your prince and the future father of your children."

Maacah considered every word. Her silence hung in the air like a circling bird of prey; then she finally began, "Father, what if I find this little David Hebrew distasteful, or when he meets me in person and finds his ardor was merely just lust in passing? Of course, any soldier going to war sees every maiden as the last chance to spread his seed before entering the uncertain cauldron of combat. But, Father, he could very well find my height intimidating."

Talmai replied with wisdom and uplifting flattery, "Had you considered that your elegant stature could be why he finds you so attractive? You are so different from the petite and slight Hebrew woman. My dear Maacah, remember that political alliances through marriages are often void of emotions but what is best for our affected people. Your birthright of nobility obliges you to make this sacrifice. But I am a practical man. The pact between David and Geshur might not hinge on accepting a new bride to seal the bargain but solely on mutual benefit and protection. Therefore, my dear daughter, do not allow the unsettling wind of expectations to control your every passion. Instead, put your trust in practical good sense and, by doing so, ensure a more pleasing outcome." Maacah pondered her father's sage wisdom. Talmai continued, "To ease your mind, and if the amount of the bride's ransom honors your station and the treaty is favorable, I will not commit until David comes to sign the final documents. On the other hand, if you find this warrior king unsuitable or the least likely of husbands, I will see if the treaty alone is still possible. In any event, I will not force my will upon your decision, my free-spirited daughter."

CHAPTER FOUR

The Politics of Love and Marriage

Ministers, sages, and seers took their familiar places around a large oaken council table. The morning fare was bitter barley bread, cold meat, new wine, and heated debate. The collective wisdom deliberated the benefit and cost of an alliance with David, the king of the Jews, between sips and chews. This David was also a friend and a vassal of Prince Achish, heir apparent of the Philistine Empire. Most agreed as to the strategic advantage of such a treaty. But then, a fearsome-looking fellow and captain of the host named Gedrite stood head and shoulders above the assembly. He challenged, "Is this not the David whispered to be the leader of a band of massacring outlaws that destroyed countless outlying towns and villages?"

Talmai was aware of the stories and countered. "Yes, that rumor persisted. But there is no proof as no one remained alive—neither men, women, nor child to confirm or deny."

So finally, all in attendance dismissed the story as unfounded gossip. Eventually, although reluctantly, even Gedrite decided it was probably the shape-shifting Amalekite pirates. After all, David is Prince Achish's vassal, and Achish would never sanction raids against his Canaanite allies.

King Talmai agreed and ordered, "Let us examine the Hebrew's offer and weigh the amount of the bride's ransom. A generous amount may help fill our all but near-empty coffers. Next, call forth the two Hebrew emissaries to the council chamber. We will gauge their sincerity, evidenced by the generosity of the marriage ransom. Princess Maacah is another hurdle; she will only consent if she finds this little Judean appealing. But, if required, I am confident she will submit to safeguard the kingdom and ensure our people's well-being."

An insistent knock woke Abiathar and Shimeah from their much-needed sleep. The king's servant ducked down to enter the darkened chamber and asked, "By your leave and pardon, esteemed ambassadors, the king, and his councils request your attendance as soon as you can manage. I will show you to the summer parlor and bring a water pitcher to freshen up your faces. The council room has meat, bread, cheese, and wine. I remain at your disposal to guide and see to your every need. But we do need to get there as soon as possible, like most monarchs. King Talmai is impatient and hates waiting; I suggest we hurry with all dispatch to avoid his displeasure."

A quick turn at the water closet and the promise of a needed meal to ease the growl of empty stomachs put speed in the steps of both Abiathar and Shimeah.

The two Hebrew emissaries appeared at the great hall and were dutifully ushered in by two brutishly large palace guards. Noticing their arrival, King Talmai broke off mid-sentence. He stood exceptionally tall, even for a Geshurite. Rising, he towered over the assembled nobles. He began by addressing Abiathar and Shimeah, "Welcome, gentlemen, to our kingdom, most trusted and learned ministers. I long to hear your proposition of a political alliance sealed by the marriage of our highly valued and beautiful daughter, Princess Maacah. Would you please relax and refresh yourself with some food and new wine? First meetings seem more productive when informal, making it easier to cut through all the political posturing and get quickly to the heart of the matter. I trust that you both slept well." Abiathar and Shimeah bowed in respect.

Shimeah began, "Thank you, King Talmai, for your generous hospitality and concern. We slept well and look forward to a long and mutually beneficial relationship."

Shimeah, after his dutiful statesman-like posturing, spoke up next, "As you know, we are King David's emissaries. I am his older brother and have full authority to act on his behalf." Listening intently, King Talmai motioned for him to continue.

"My Lord, we were sent by King David to convey his heartfelt longing to wed your daughter Maacah and seal an agreement of mutual protection and assistance in these uncertain times. King David confided that he stopped in Gath while going off to battle. He beheld your comely daughter's face and noble stature in the bustling marketplace. He told me he was smitten and knew he would have her for his wife. David immediately inquired of Prince Achish and was told she was of royal blood—and even a princess of the Geshurite nation. He then confided in me that he would have this beauty and that their union would forever seal an alliance between our two great kingdoms with strong family ties of blood."

Abiathar grunted and nodded in agreement but stayed busy eating and drinking the sweet new vintage. He thought it best to keep his opinions to himself and not disrupt Shimeah's delicate negotiations with distracting chatter.

Shimeah continued, albeit more tactfully, "I see two small hurdles to conclude our successful coalition. One is the sensitive and practical negotiation of coming to an acceptable bride's ransom. The other would be if Princess Maacah would find David a suitable husband and her children's future father.

"I think you would agree that political practicality often overrides emotional needs in favor of the kingdom's greater security. But to ensure a happy and enduring marriage, it also requires a meeting of the hearts and minds. But as many a man to his chagrin, our great king discovers that matters of the heart are subject to a woman's wilds and wistful inclination. Therefore, allow me to proceed first with my king's generous offer of the bride's ransom-"

Talmai quickly interrupted, "As long as it is understood that I had promised the princess the freedom to choose her destiny. Therefore, we can proceed, but only with the understanding that no bargain binds us until the princess consents to the union."

"Very well, wise king. My brother King David proposes an offer fitting Maacah's elevated station: her full weight in gold, for she will be more precious to him, even greater than rubies and pearls."

Talmai was visibly impressed by what he heard; he was almost at a loss for words. He did not expect such an honoring and extravagant offer. He looked around at his counselors, witnessing delighted head-bobbing, smiles, and grins. The esteemed advisors rose in unison and huddled in an adjacent alcove. They remained out of earshot, whispering their suspicions and objections. But finally, as a body, as was the Geshurite custom, each laid their ceremonial daggers flat upon the table. None struck the table upright in defiance, affirming their agreement that the financial and political alliance was in the kingdom's best interest.

Shimeah spoke once again, "Well done, most noble king, and a salute to your wise and esteemed ministers. I now see only one small hurdle remaining—the consent of the princess to marry my brother and seal the bargain with matrimony." The king nodded in agreement.

Shimeah continued, "My farsighted brother King David, at the very outset of his proposal, realized that you, great king, would be reluctant to send your daughter, Princess Maacah, a hundred miles away from her home, even with my best proper guarantees and assurances of her safety. She would still be a stranger in a strange land, forced to suffer stress by navigating an alien landscape of language and culture. Then she is expected to marry a man she hardly knows with few or no family members attending. This proposition would be unsettling for any young woman, even a strong and noble princess.

The obvious solution would be for David to journey here to your domain. He had already considered that if our negotiations were fruitful, he could then sally forth and present himself with the ransom of marriage. I have some excellent news, majesty. David, with a small entourage, has encamped on the southern border of Geshur. He did this, foreseeing that our negotiations would be fruitful and finalizing our mutually beneficial alliance with Princess Maacah's hand in marriage.

"Upon his arrival, David can court the princess in safe and familiar surroundings. If he can gain her trust and affection, the ceremony can be performed in the great hall with friends and family to celebrate the joy-filled occasion."

Talmai responded, "I do not know whether to applaud David's assured confidence or to be disturbed by his premeditated audacity."

To which a wise minister then offered his opinion, "Your majesty, these traits speak highly of a potential future son-in-law. Let us applaud our possible future ally's insight and invite King David to partake in our hospitality."

King Talmai paused in reflection before abruptly standing, "Very well then. Let us invite this Hebrew upstart to the table and see what he has to say. We will see if he is bold enough to tame my daughter's appetite for living life to the fullest."

Shimeah strengthened the agreement further, "I will stay here as your guest and belay any misgivings of guile or hostile intentions. Abiathar ben Ahimelech, David's best friend and high priest, will summon David immediately with our great news."

Abiathar nodded his approval. "Make haste, priest, and tell him he has King Talmai's permission to approach Maacah, inviting him to begin his courtship earnestly. Also, suggest that my brother bathe, bring flowers, and tune his wooing lyre to a fine pitch and polish." The room erupted in laughter, easing the diplomatic tension.

CHAPTER FIVE

A Measured Invitation

"Have you ever ridden a she-mule?" King Talmai prodded Abiathar.

"No, your majesty, not ever," Abiathar answered. "For the law of our God makes it plain, 'Do not mate with different kinds of farm animals. We are not allowed to create she-mules.' Although a few beasts find their way from other lands to indulge a few of our noblemen. Horses are for pulling wagons, chariots, plows, and threshing stones, not for mounting. Our God prefers that we keep our feet to the earth; doing so keeps us grounded and reminds us that we are born of dust, and to dust we shall return. Lastly, it puts us in a lofty position looking down on our fellow travelers, for we are all equals in God's eyes," he concluded.

"That is a quaint religious philosophy, priest. However, we have observed that a rider on a she-mule can carry a dispatch over longer distances at twice the speed of your fleetest messenger. Therefore, I will have a saddled mule and a few armed guards to accompany you to inform your king of our gracious invitation." King Talmai announced.

"Thank you for your kind offer, but since I have never ridden a beast, I prefer to walk as is our custom."

The king, however, didn't seem convinced by the priest's response. "If we are to be allied by family ties, engaging in our she-mule culture would be best for future relations. Besides, I do not wish to wait on the speed of feet when a mule's strides put wings on time. Even an accomplished rider is thrown to the ground seven times before mastery of the beast. Therefore, I will also include an extra mule for your King David. He will be able to leave his men at arms and come alone. He can then order his men to bring up the 'bride ransom.' They will arrive separately and give David enough time to state his case. We can then measure the man being defenseless and lacking protection. We will expect your king by week's end."

Considering it best not to dispute Talmai's request, Abiathar reluctantly agreed so as to avoid an unwinnable argument.

Shimeah reassured him, "You will do well and become an accomplished rider. As a high priest, consider it as expanding your horizons. Tell my brother that all is well, and I await his speedy arrival."

At high noon, Abiathar found himself confronting a tall, stout mule named Raven. The creature was stubbornly coaxed to a nearby rock, providing Abiathar with a step up. Unsure and wobbly, Abiathar finally made peace with his hard leather seat, and then just as abruptly, they were off at a brisk trot over the snickering chuckles of his escort. As Abiathar bobbed and bounced, his bottom was taking an unforgiving pounding as he held onto the bridle and saddle for dear life. Finally, after three hours and twelve miles, Abiathar could withstand this bottom battering no more as he abruptly bristled in agony, "Enough, my bottom is bruised and burning. You can slaughter me right here on this spot. But I cannot and will not endure another second of this jarring torment." Abiathar then clumsily slid down, suffering the ridicule of his braying mule and thanking God for the steady ground beneath his bowlegged feet.

Concerned for the Hebrew priest's anguish, the host's captain called out, "You are a valued guest of our king, and we will keep pace with your steps. If it gives you any comfort—all beginner riders suffer from the same insult. I am sure your king is familiar with the riding of a she-mule. We will accomplish King Talmai's command for the swift retrieval of your king, no matter how long it takes."

Abiathar was relieved to hear this. He began to slowly walk at a snail's pace until his kinks and blisters were reduced to a dull throb, and his tempo readily increased. Finally, after five more miles, the Geshurite captain announced, "Sundown approaches. It is time to dismount and set up camp. We will make the border by sunset tomorrow and hopefully approach your Hebrew king's encampment by nightfall."

Tucked down tight between two outcrop boulders, Abiathar passed the night faced down, ignoring the grandeur of the cosmos in favor of his aching bottom.

He awoke to a traditional Geshurite breakfast of dried meat, barley bread, and a skin of sweet new wine to wash it all down with. "Would you like another try on the beast, Hebrew priest?" the Geshurite Captain jokingly chided. Then, still aching and bow-legged to boot, Abiathar silently turned his back and trudged on foot. The captain took frequent breaks to give the determined saddle soar plodder breaks throughout the day.

Meanwhile David waited anxiously, too much time that had passed without word from his two emissaries. His mind darkened with foreboding possibility that he had been discovered as the phantom raider. Were his brother and high priest executed as spies only to send the message that he was next on the chopping block? Was there an army of vengeful Gershurite giants headed his way? The haunting of his past deeds grew wings, was this the time of his reckoning?

Finally, just before sundown, the small party of Gershurite guardians spotted David's encampment atop a distant hill.

Alerted to the arrival of a small company of mounted Gershurites, David announced warily, "Every man come to the ready; this could be a Geshurite trap."

When witnessing Abiathar leaving his escort at the base and struggling to climb to the crest where David stood with the setting sun at his back, David was overjoyed and dismissed any hostile intentions. His old friend was alive and whole, excepting the pain from the bowlegged saddle soars. With a grand smile of relief David reached out a helping hand knowing all went well.

Delighted to see his old friend, David began, "Well, my esteemed high priest, I am glad you are all in one piece. But what of my brother Shimeah? Tell me all the details and leave nothing to my imagination." Then, David abruptly turned his attention to his guard captain and instructed, "Bring food and wine down to the Geshurite party and tell their captain to come up at first light. I will speak to him at that time. Now go!"

David then turned to the priest. "Abiathar, your timing is perfect. We were about to savor some freshly killed goat." The priest prayed a quick thanksgiving, savoring the smell of the sweet roasted flesh that was presented to him before swallowing his salivating drool between chomps and chews.

He then began, " Your brother Shimeah stayed behind as a voluntary hostage to ensure your honorable intentions. Some are not convinced that you were not the hated, mysterious marauder of their outlying villages. Since you were Prince Achish's vassal, you made that suggestion all but impossible."

David then prodded, "What of the marriage to Maacah and the accompanying Geshurite alliance?"

"King Talmai and his ministers agreed to her weight in gold as the bride's ransom and were pleased with your honoring and generous offer. The King's Council was also in favor of a coalition. They considered you a vassal of Price Achish and an ally of the Philistine nation. The fact that you are the king of Judea and the future king of Israel boded well for the safety and prosperity of Geshur. However, there is one small problem, or actually not so small as it regards giants."

David countered, "Speak on, priest."

"It seems that the princess is a free-spirited woman and has been given leave by her father to decide who will be her future husband. As I see it, there are two hurdles that you must overcome. One is that the princess needs the delicate courting of a seasoned hand. Secondly, and as I had counseled you before, for a Hebrew man to marry a Canaanite woman, she must perform the Eshet yefat to'ar; that is the law. Without reservations or hesitation, the princess must consent wholly on her own accord."

David listened carefully as his priest continued, "As you know, Princess Maacah has long and luxurious hair. It is her adorning crown. It won't be easy to convince her to shed her plush tresses for a naked scalp, let alone abandon her heathen ways and embrace Adonai, the true God. First, however, she must comply with our sacred rituals and become a converted Hebrew woman. All this has to be demanded before making herself available for you to marry. Your brother offered you some sage advice: 'To bathe, bring flowers, and tune your wooing lyre to a fine pitch and polish.'"

David grinned, and his eyes sparkled. The two things he loved the most were pleasing God and a challenge. "Well then, I must heed my older brother's wisdom. Is there anything else I need to know, Abiathar?"

The priest paused before responding to his king, "Yes, and most certainly, King Talmai wants you to return alone and unaccompanied, even without your bodyguards. He wants to size you up and take your measure. You will be all alone and vulnerable. This is your first test. The Geshurite escort below has brought you a she-mule so that you can arrive well before your protectors and a wagon load of gold. As for me, I will not mount that infernal beast again. Instead, I will ride the gold wagon back to Bethesda."

"Do you think it is a trap?" probed the king.

The priest responded confidently, "No, not in the slightest. Talmai is sincere and hopes you can persuade Maacah to be your wife and seal the treaty with the secure ties of matrimony. It seems that your generosity has disarmed all objections."

"Then I will go as invited. You, priest, take your ride in the ox cart, and I will get busy building confidences and pursuing Maacah."

CHAPTER SIX
Of Trust and She-mules

Dawn found Gedar, the Geshurite chief captain, climbing the hill's rocky crest. David stood unmoving at the overlook, silhouetted against daybreak's first light. There was no mistaking his commanding majesty. This towering figure was undoubtedly the king of the Jews.

Gedar, a head taller than David, immediately dropped to one knee in respect and began, "My lord, my name is Gedar, chief captain of all Geshur. My master, King Talmai, has tasked me with being your escort and welcoming party to our great nation. He offers his utmost respect and protection. My men and I will accompany you back to Bethesda, where a feast in your honor awaits your timely arrival. We have brought you a she-mule to speed up our journey. Let me put it this way, our good King Talmai is not known for his patience. So, in good faith, our king has invited you, David, king of Judea, to come along as a sign of trust and to leave behind the rest of your company. Even commanding your fearsome bodyguards to follow but only at a distance."

David stiffened his back and exhaled, "Yes, I will comply with your king's request in good faith. However, I have advised my men, who are none too pleased with my decision, to comply, thus making myself vulnerable to Geshurite foul play." David then took a brief pause before continuing, "Some have insisted on always keeping me within sight. I warn you they are fearsome and loyal and will seek a full measure of justice at the slightest hint of trouble."

"I can understand your concern, great king. However, let me assure you, your majesty, if anything happens to you even in the slightest, neither injury nor accident, my life and the lives of my men will promptly stand forfeited in the most unusual and cruelest punishment imaginable."

"Very well, Captain Gedar, I remain your reluctant guest at best. But to put your mind at ease, I am familiar with the she-mule and its passage. Unfortunately, however, it is not my preferred way to travel. So let us be off and not strain King Talmai's chafing lack of patience. Like a woman, a king left waiting can easily conjure an insult of contempt."

The security escort then surrounded David in an impenetrable wall of protection as the she-mules stood large enough to accommodate even the stoutest Geshurite warrior.

Meanwhile, Benaiah, a Mightie in his own right and David's chief bodyguard, was not pleased with his master's decision to travel unprotected with potential assassins. So, he called forth the now-idle defenders of the royal personage to assign protection countermeasures.

"Men, the king has gone off with a party of Geshurite guards, alone and unprotected. I will keep the king in sight with four of my fastest runners. The rest of you men will guard the oxcart with Abiathar and the bride's ransom of gold and start making your way to Bethesda. Be wary, as this might be an elaborate trap to kill the king and capture the gold."

The five stalwart bodyguards were off at a breakneck gait, determined to keep the king constantly in view. Below the valleys and rills, the Geshurite party disappeared but would reemerge when on the high ridges. It was forty miles from the encampment to the stronghold of Et-Tell, and even the she-mules needed time to rest and refresh with water and feed. The Geshurite escort decided to camp for the night, the moon was new, and the deep darkness could even be treacherous for the sure-footed she-mules. Moreover, they swore an oath against any harm or accident, refusing to take chances with their precious royal cargo.

Benaiah and his dedicated sprinters were weary but continued the best they could until darkness overtook their valiant efforts. Then, uneasily, they crept stealthily towards the Geshurite encampment on their bellies, where they remained prey to snakes, scorpions, and the bitter cold until dawn.

Meanwhile, the escort posted guards against prowling beasts or a cunning assassin cloaked in darkness. David enjoyed the comfort of heavy bedding, a roaring fire, succulent meats, and the best Geshurite vintage. Once the campsite was secure for the night, David thought to engage Chief Captain

Gedar in meaningful conversation.

"Captain, please tell me about Princess Maacah and be at ease, for whatever you tell me is in the strictest confidence; rest assured on that, you have my word. Your openness will help me win over the fair maiden's heart and help to ensure an alliance of protection, joining our two great nations with a family bond of marriage."

"Well, David, king of the Jews, I do not see it as my place to speak of the princess's personal life. Besides, I am unfamiliar with her private comings and goings. So, it is not my concern," Gedar replied.

"All I request is common knowledge of the princess's activities. For instance, is she loved by your people? Is she pious to your gods? Does she give freely to the poor and needy? Is she dutiful to her father's wishes? I have seen her striking beauty and grand stature. I am sure she has had many suitors. Why is she not a married woman?"

David waited patiently for his arrows of inquiry to find their mark with Gedar. The needed answers would help him create subtle levers of romance: no longer a dark stranger but a well-versed and enlightened admirer.

After allowing the questions to sink in, Gedar dutifully weighed his every word, "I can see the need for a strong alliance in these uncertain times. Therefore, I will disclose my limited observations as you are to be treated as an honored guest of the king and afforded all rights and privileges demanded by your station. To answer your question, yes, Princess Maacah enjoys our people's love and respect, and her piety to our ancient gods is a testament to our Geshurite heritage. She is pious and often makes pilgrimages to the quarries for week-long veneration.

"Moreover, the princess is known for her generosity and kindness to the ill and afflicted. When she parades through the streets, she is a vision of loveliness with long, perfumed hair that elegantly sweeps behind her. Her fingernails are long and finely manicured, attesting to her station and never participating in manual labor.

"Although she is a dutiful daughter, she is educated and independent." Gedar then paused, struggling with his following confession. "I tell you this only with your assurance that it will go no further." He finally choked out.

"Be confident that your words will die in my ears and never rise to my lips; please, captain, continue," David responded.

"Very well then, I will take you at your word, honored King. There have been many suitors that have tried, but all have failed to win her heart." David nodded in response as the captain continued, "There is one other thing that might help, she does love her she-mules and is an accomplished rider. She often travels the realm and goes even so far as Gath, the Philistine capital."

"Thank you, Captain. You can't start a romantic fire without a spark of familiarity. Curiously, you had mentioned Gath. Prince Achish had invited me to war, and that is when I first saw the princess at the Gath marketplace. Since then, she has invaded my dreams, and I knew I must have her. I know the Gershurites and Judaean kingdoms together would make steadfast allies, and what better bond than marriage and blood? But please be convinced that your honesty has restated any nagging suspicions of foul play. You have restored my confidence in this unguarded abduction. I can now rest easy, secure in your honorable intentions regarding my safety and well-being. Goodnight, Captain."

CHAPTER SEVEN

A Grand Entrance, Bethesda

The morning was brisk as the she-mules vigorously trotted, well-rested and refreshed, while the ever-eager David felt stirred by the challenge of another female conquest and a much-needed military alliance.

The Hightower of Et-Tell pierced the blue horizon like a sundial, casting no shadow, for it was high noon as the group approached the citadel.

Outpost guards had alerted the royal household far before David's arrival. As a result, the upper balconies were filled with onlookers and armed warriors lined the battlements.

King Talmai and his honoring entourage awaited the Hebrew king's entrance into the capital city. Shimeah, David's hostage/guest brother, was also there to signal that all was well on the diplomatic front. Unfortunately, Princess Maacah was noticeably absent. Her long tresses took hours of thorough brushing to untangle knots, and her long-neglected luxurious nails needed delicate attention. She tried on one dress after another, with each quickly discarded; the perfect outfit remained absent. Finally, after scanning her extensive wardrobe, she exclaimed in desperation, "I have nothing to wear that is becoming for this once-in-a-lifetime occasion!" She pondered, "Could this really be the foreign prince of my dreams?"

David entered the city filled with riotous cheering and the shrill sounding of ceremonial trumpets. He rode up to the front of the marble staircase directly below Talmai and was comforted by seeing Shimeah, his well-kept brother. He then uneasily dismounted, feeling saddle sore and slightly bowlegged. David looked up at King Talmai, standing tall on his entrance before nodding slightly, giving respect, a courtesy afforded by one monarch to another. Then Talmai beckoned David to rise and stand beside him in the place of honor given only to equals and heroes.

Next, Talmai raised his arms to quiet the mob; the uproar immediately calmed to an excited murmur. They knew that such happenings usually meant an abundance of roasted oxen and the king's bottomless wine barrels.

Talmai waited for absolute silence before speaking, "People of Geshur, my brothers and sisters of our noble Nephilim ancestors. Where we stand has been our land before time began and even remained so after the great flood. Our height and stature attest to this very fact of this inheritance. Moreover, the richness and fertility of our soil have provided food to sustain us through famine, drought, and plague and nourished our youth with height and weight. Yet, we live in uncertain times, and armed conflicts can easily threaten our borders. Therefore, I deemed it wise to have invited David, the king of Judah, to discuss a mutually beneficial alliance. Naturally, our royal guest's security and comfort are equally important, helping us to achieve mutual security. Therefore, to celebrate his timely and welcome arrival, we will have a feast, both in the great hall and the streets, that all are welcome to partake in."

A cheer resounded in anticipation of having plenty to eat, wine, and a welcomed break from the daily grind.

At that very moment, a well-groomed princess emerged from the shadows. She hurriedly moved beside her father as fast as poise, dignity, and grace could travel. Princess Maacah was elegance in motion, and even the gathered rabble stopped to take in her majestic beauty. Formal introductions were in order, "King David of Judah, as well as the anointed king of Israel, and so too an esteemed vassal to Prince Achish of the Philistine." Then turning towards his confident daughter, he clasped her hand and proudly said, "Behold, this vision of loveliness is Princess Maacah of the Geshurite. She is my pride and joy and sometimes even obedient to my wishes. But, be warned, young prince, her beauty hides a searing wit and cunning intellect."

David and Maacah's eyes met and locked instantly; neither could turn away. Maacah blushed, and David grew pale with lust. Love was in the air. There was no doubt that Cupid had plucked his heartstring bow twice, and his piercing darts had found their ready marks, it was love at first sight.

Becoming uncomfortable with the entranced moment,

Talmai, although pleased with the sudden unforeseen connection, tugged on Maacah's hand to bring her back into the moment's reality by saying, "I am sure you two will have oceans to discuss. But now is not the time. King David needs to recover from his grueling she-mule punishment." Then, jokingly turning to David, he continued, "So tell me, Hebrew King, does a hot bath and time to ease your back parts sound inviting? After all, you are the guest of honor at tonight's festivities. Would you like to rest and refresh, king of the Hebrews? Feel free to make your needs known."

Then, trying to tear himself away from Maacah's deep almond eyes, David confessed, "Your majesty, your daughter is radiant as if an angel has graced us with her presence."

Talmai smiled, proud that he had sired such a beautiful child. Maacah blushed and looked away; her heart was overflowing with emotions for this strange foreign suitor. Had she found her soulmate?

Talmai then turned to Shimeah, "I am sure you and your brother have much to discuss regarding our negotiations." David put his arm around his big brother as they walked to private surroundings.

Meanwhile, Benaiah and four exhausted bodyguards had presented themselves at the Et-Tell gate, demanding entrance to the far side of the compound just before sundown. "We are King David's sworn protectors and need to see to him and know that he is well attended to and unharmed, and at once!"

The gate quickly opened, and all five men rushed in, unnerving the guards with their fierce bravado. They were well-armed and anxious to join their sovereign in a dungeon pit or a plush guest apartment. Ultimately, the squad found their way to David's location, guarded by a contingent of giants. Benaiah burst in, taking a well-deserved sigh of relief at the sight of David looking unharmed, bathed, and dressed well. His clothes hung loosely about him; it was the smallest size his host could provide. All took a knee, and Benaiah exclaimed, "I was convinced this voluntary abduction was an enemy plot. But what pleasure it is to my lips to say I seemed wrong. Although, your majesty, I advise you to stay wary; these Gershurite giants are cunning and devilishly tall."

"Your point makes perfect sense, but for now, we will play our parts as honored guests, so I can successfully pursue the princess and seal a needed alliance with marriage. That is why we are here, is that understood?"

Benaiah, with an uneasy nod, complied with his king's wishes.

"So, there will be no feats of strength, brawls, or challenges to test one's skills or manly prowess. Speak kind words to our hosts or, better yet, speak not at all. That goes for one and all. So, I hold it to you, Benaiah, to restrain your men. Abiathar and the gold wagon should arrive late tomorrow with the rest of the attachment. Now go and refresh yourselves, eat, drink, and I thank you for your heroic efforts in seeing to my safety and welfare."

"Yes, my liege." Pleased that their king was safe and unharmed, they left with an air of satisfaction.

Turning his attention to his brother, David questioned,

"Tell me, how did we fare in the negotiations?"

"I would say, well, all in all. Talmai and his ministers are ready and ripe for an alliance. The region is in an uproar of uncertainty now that Saul is dead. They see you as a stabilizing factor, a buffer between ever higher Philistine taxes and mysterious renegades that have savaged their outlying villages."

Shimea nodded and agreed, saying, "I am sure those misdeeds will fade forever and soon pass from memory.

"It is best not to mention it again. Even your Mighties know not to breathe a word of our massacres on pain of death."

Making it clear, David expressed, "Getting between Achish and his revenue was a fool's errand. If his portion was substantial, he had no questions. So, there was no sense in letting on to the truth and the certainty of reprisal on that front. The loss of Ziklag, our home, and even worse, heads would roll on a day of reckoning. So, purge it from your mind. Now tell me of the reception of Talmai and Princess Maccha to my marriage proposal to seal the alliance?"

"The king is all for it and has agreed to the bride's ransom of her weight in gold. Or, at the very least, a talent, so we have curried favor with our generous offer. But unfortunately, he has left the final decision to the princess regarding her future husband. One other thing, and I hate to mention it."

"Go on, man; I need to know every detail!"

"If the princess rejects you, Talmai intends to keep the gold as a goodwill offering. But this is only if all parties agree to the treaty, which I believe is assured because his ministers concurred. Secondly, I feel that he needs the gold."

"I take it the princess remains unaware of the requirement of an eshet yefat to'ar for a non-Hebrew woman to marry a Hebrew man, and the king of the Jews is a must?" David asked.

"I thought it best not to breach such a delicate subject and that she would agree after you have won her heart. But undoubtedly, it will be a particularly difficult concession, especially since her long virgin hair frames her face and slender body. However, I know, brother, that you are up to the challenge with so much at stake. Once you have secured the Geshurite alliance by legally marrying a foreign princess, you will have the forces to usurp King Ish-bosheth's power and authority by defeating Abner's army. Thus, the elders of Israel will have no choice but to accept you as the rightful king of Israel."

"That is much to consider, brother, especially since time and the distance from home are not on our side. I will use my most seductive charms and allow her to woo me into her arms—the ways of a woman's heart remain a mystery to most men. So that you know, I will use every tool in my lover's arsenal to seduce this woman to be my wife and help ensure my destiny as the anointed king of Israel. Let us depart to the great hall for tonight's banquet, where I can bolster our first dreamy eye contact with the princess upon my arrival," David concluded.

A group of assigned servants swiftly ushered David and Shimea to the honoring feast. The two men entered the boisterous room, and the crier's stout staff struck the floor thrice in a call to order, then, in a booming voice, commenced, "King David of Judah."

King Talmai stood, and the room immediately followed

suit, easing the lively chatter. Then, he began, "King David, you honor our house with your presence. Please, you and your brother, join us at the royal table as befitting your stations." David respectfully nodded, acknowledging his host's gracious hospitality, but quickly focused on Princess Maacah. She was elegant, sleek, and slender next to her imposing father. Her natural sensual manner immediately roused a familiar carnal hunger in David. He confidently made his way to the empty chair, the place of honor and beside the alluring damsel. The princess was a full head taller than David, making her all the more exotic and appealing. All stood in respect of King Talmai's authority as they waited for him to sit, thus commencing the well-appointed festivities.

"Allow me," David said as he gently adjusted Maacah's chair, allowing her to settle in comfortably on her exquisite derriere.

Then, nervous as a schoolgirl, Maacah blurted out, "Thank you, kind sir, for your polite manner. I think I like you already."

CHAPTER EIGHT
Love Songs and the Courtship of Giants

The clatter echoed off the banquet hall walls as courses of succulent meats, bread, and vintage wine overflowed into nut-brown bowls. Hungry mouths chomped and slurped between bouts of heavy laughter.

David leaned in close and whispered in Maacah's ready ear, "I have a confession to make."

Maacah, delighted by his nearness, whispered, "I pray you tell me, handsome prince, why you have come so far in your difficult and dangerous romantic pursuit?"

"Then allow me, gentle lady, to reveal my heart. I first saw you at the market in Gath when I went off to war. Since then, I have been unable to think of anything else but your lovely face and form. Unfortunately, due to the Philistine uncertainty about where my loyalties lie, they refused my recruitment in their coming conflict against my former master, King Saul of Israel. As a result, angry hostility ensued among the Philistine nobility. So, I had to leave immediately to avoid the threat of violence before I could discover who you were and where I could find you."

The princess was instantly enamored by David's determination to overcome every obstacle to make her his wife.

David continued, "Nevertheless, I persisted and eventually questioned Prince Achish to disclose what vision of loveliness had invaded my fantasies. After much prodding, he recalled that you, a Geshurite princess, had been visiting Gath on a shopping expedition. Since then, I tried to find you with all the resources at my command."

Maacah cast her eyes and blushed, "I now understand that the rumors of your legendary charms are not just an idle boast. I cannot lie; I feel like I am falling, and my feet no longer touch the ground. What would you have of me, beguiling prince, now that you have found me?"

"My precious princess, I am now smitten from the crown of my head to the souls of my feet when I am in your presence. I refuse to let you go, as doing so would crush my heart into a thousand parts. But, as I am sure you already know, I have asked your father for your hand in marriage. The king has even agreed to the bride's ransom for your weight in gold. Little did he know I would have given twice as much for one of your caresses. Undoubtedly, your father holds you in great esteem and will only give his blessing by and with your consent. Your happiness is his greatest concern and mine also, gracious lady."

Maacah was utterly smitten, evidenced by her lingering silence. She was overwhelmed by the audacity and boldness of this strange foreign suitor who had taken her breath away.

David spied a lone harp nestled in the shadows. He hastily retrieved the familiar and well-practiced lyre before confidently striding around the banquet table until he stopped directly in front of the princess. Only a man stricken in love could blot out all distractions as he was seemingly oblivious to being surrounded by giants. Three picks sounded, dispelling all the noisy chatter. Instead, everyone focused on the pluck of the crooner and his impromptu serenade.

David began to play and recite a love song to his intended.

"Set me as a cover upon your heart, as a banner upon your arm.

For love is at the gate; do not hesitate nor deny my invitation to paradise.

Rejection is as cruel as the grave: The flashes thereof are streaks of fire,

A very flame of God! Oceans cannot quench love; Neither can the floods drown it:

If a man gave the substance of his house for love, He would be utterly despised.

But I would gladly give such treasure as a sacrifice on the altar of love's unconquerable passion.

I adore you, O, daughter of Geshur.

I have compared thee, my love, to a team of wild horses. Your cheeks are comely with rows of pearls. Your neck with chains of gold."

Dropping to one knee, David then declared, "My darling Maacah, will you marry me?"

Maacah was adrift in a whirlwind of emotions; her heart had melted. Her chest heaved with breaths short and shallow. David comforted the damsel, sensing her distress, "Please forgive my sudden and desperate amorous advances, especially in these most unusual circumstances. At the very least, it would be confusing and overwhelming. But my heart bleeds, and love demands this hasty attempt. So, take your time to reflect on my proposal and sleep soundly. For joy cometh in the morning. I am confident of your decision that our fates and destinies are intertwined, linked together as man and wife, creating a dynasty of royal and beautiful children." He then rose with his eyes fixed on Maacah, blotting out the gallery of shocked onlookers. Then, focusing solely on the love-hungry maiden, he pleaded, "My comely princess, until tomorrow with a wish and breath that your answer will be yes. Adieu and goodnight."

David withdrew. Every eye was on this brash foreign prince who had startled the entire gathering with his romantic advances. David quickly vanished down the darkened outer hallway, still clutching his crooning lyre.

Sensing Maacah's emotional distress, King Talmai hurriedly sought out his daughter to comfort her with the wisdom of fatherly advice. But, understandably, Maacah was visibly shaken—her mind's eye churning, unable to make sense of what had just happened. So, finally, Talmai soothingly began, "My dear child, your Hebrew suitor is bold and unpredictable, thus making him formidable in love and war. David has made his intentions unmistakable. He would have you. I am, for one, impressed with his focus and bravado. But of course, my daughter, you will be the one who must surrender to or reject this daring prince. I agree with your suitor, so let a good night's sleep clarify your decision. Tomorrow, you will both take time in the garden to speak privately and without an audience. But under the watchful eye of a trusted chaperone, of course."

"Yes, Father, I have much to ponder. I am so inclined as he is so handsome and manly. David's stature more than makes up for his lack of height. He takes my breath away. My knees feel feeble and unsure when I am in his presence. I must consider living among the Hebrews with their alien culture, language, and customs. But I would be 100 miles away from my people, gods, and especially you, my loving father."

"I am sure you will make the right decision for yourself and your people. Goodnight, Maacah, and may the sweetest dreams invade your sleep."

CHAPTER NINE

Eshet yefat to'ar

(The Inner Woman of Beautiful Form)

A daunting task lay before David. First, he had to woo a beautiful Gershurite princess, a former enemy giant, to salve his passion and secure a needed military alliance. Then, if that was not enough already, he had to convince Maacah to the Eshet yefat to'ar and, lastly, to resettle from Bethesda to Hebron, 100 miles south, and embrace an alien Hebrew God. No small feat, considering she was a descendant of the Nephilim and would tower over the common people.

The gentle morning breeze carried the delicate fragrance of sage and rock rose, which pleasantly awakened David from his restful slumber. A Geshurite servant assigned to the foreign king's comfort gently knocked for admittance. "What is wanted?" David inquired while hurriedly dressing.

"Excuse me, your lordship, but I will escort you to the royal breakfast. King Talamai and Princess Maacah await your presence in the private dining room."

David knew that these were the two people you never kept waiting for, a king for one, and worse than that, a lady you seek favor with. So, he hurried the best he could, splashing his face and combing his hair and beard.

Maacah looked radiant, and David noticed a blush as he walked through the door. Talmai stood tall and imposing, "Welcome, and thank you for your speedy response. But, before we partake, Maacah has an answer to your proposal; go on, my dear, before the meat grows cold and the porridge gets lumpy."

"Father, please, this is difficult enough."

She stood up and then directed her attention to David, her handsome and ardent pursuer. She began, "David king of Judah, a respected vassal of Prince Achish of the Philistine, and the prospective anointed king of Israel. I have thought long and hard about your proposal. I now feel compelled that it is my duty and obligation as a princess of Geshur to ensure the future safety and prosperity of the realm by securing your proposed alliance with family ties. So, I say yes, noble prince, to be your wife and, if the gods are willing, the future mother of your children."

David beamed, delighted by what he had just heard and feeling pleased with himself. The conqueror in him could do little else. He lovingly addressed Maacah, "Beguiling flower of Geshur, my happiness overflows, my heart leaps for joy at your acceptance. I can hardly wait to introduce your wit, wisdom, and beauty to my people."

David then turned his attention briefly to Talmai, "Exalted king and my future father-in-law, I beg your permission to take a private walk through your beautiful garden with your daughter. We have not had a moment to speak privately about my plans and designs. However, I must also know her wants, hopes, and desires so that I can be a dutiful husband."

Talmai was delighted at his daughter's decision and countered, "Yes, yes, of course, and by all means, you two need some private time to get acquainted, away from protocol and prying eyes."

Maacah eagerly agreed, "I would be so obliged as my stomach has butterflies, and I can't hold a thought for want of some fresh air. A refreshing stretch in the garden would be to my liking, for I have lost my appetite and would like to speak of needful things to my decided future partner."

David extended his arm to his lady love, and they were off through the garden gateway before any objection could delay their departure.

David took her hand and began, "From the moment I first saw you at the marketplace in Gath, a towering beauty overshadowing the bustling crowd. At that very instant, I knew that I was in love and would gladly move heaven and earth to find you. But now I have found you, and both you and your father have consented, there remains one last hurdle to overcome." David looked away, and in the silence, he dropped to one knee, unable to speak.

Maacah was curious but untroubled by the quiet and asked, "My dear David, you are a king, and I am a princess of two powerful kingdoms. By all the gods, who would dare to delay our blissful union?"

"My promise to wed you and be your provider and protector is heartfelt, sincere, and binding. But even I, a king, am under certain religious restraints concerning marrying a non-Hebrew woman. Consequently, specific requirements are needed to sanctify the agreement and enable our offspring to inherit certain rights, titles, and privileges. Furthermore, without these respected practices, you would be downgraded to the status of a concubine. Your father would rail against a lesser social distinction that would cause him to break our alliance and become my bitter enemy," revealed David.

"Pray, speak, my mysterious prince. What are these daunting obstacles perplexing to our future happiness?"

David sighed and thought perhaps this was a bridge too far. But with the gentlest tone he could muster, he uttered, "My dear lady, before I can marry you, you would be required to shave your head, pare your nails, and lament the loss of your father's house for thirty days. There, I said it."

Maacah's face flushed, and her back stiffened. Overhead, a crow screeched, and a brisk north wind ushered in a shuddering chill. Then, in a huff, she turned to walk away. David grabbed her hand and pleaded, "I understand, my beautiful lady. The sweep of your unbridled tresses was what first caught my attention. A glorious crown that frames your perfect loveliness and proclaims your noble heritage. I propose to you, my darling girl, that we marry here at Et-Tell with your friends and family in attendance under your laws, practices, and religious rituals. Then we will be man and wife in the eyes of your father and all Geshur. But then, as my wife, you will accompany me back to Hebron, where we can perform the Hebrew ceremony and be married according to our law in the sight of our God, Adonai. That is where you can shave your head, pare your nails, and lament the loss of your father's house for thirty days. Then, after we are legally married, you can go into seclusion and grow your hair and nails to their former glory, and none here in Bethesda would be any the wiser as to your humbling sacrifice. What say you, most gracious lady, to my plan?"

As she stared back at him in silence, David continued, "Do you have any questions, needs, or conditions to resolve this awkward challenge so I can reassure you that I only ask this of you for the prosperity and security of our future children?"

After what felt like an eternity to David, the princess finally spoke, "I can see that you have thought long and hard about marrying me, a foreign princess. But shaving my head and paring my nails here in Bethesda is out of the question. It would only stand to insult my father and diminish people's respect for me. So, yes, I have agreed to marry you and have received my father's blessing. I will stand by that arrangement. But two things I will require in return."

"Speak on, my strong-willed princess."

"First and foremost, our children will be allowed to grow their hair long, and no shears or scrapping blades will ever touch their heads. Secondly, I require a stable of she-mules, for I am fond of them, and they will act as a needed reminder to our children of their Geshurite heritage."

"I see, and I agree with your requests. Unfortunately, we cannot breed she-mules. In our law, two different kinds of livestock are forbidden to breed. We will have to purchase them elsewhere. Geshur would seem fitting, giving you a seasoned excuse to visit your family. I am most impressed with your wit, beauty, and self-sacrifice of obliging nobility. Still, remember that I am at war with Israel, and my long absence, if detected by my enemies, would put me and my kingdom in peril. Therefore, we must marry here as quickly as possible under the Geshurite ceremonial ritual and return hastily to Hebron. Once there, we will follow Hebrew law to the letter."

David, changing his tone and tack, softly spoke of romance, "Beautiful princess, I'm relieved by your acceptance of my Hebrew custom, more than you can imagine, for I have pined long and hard, imagining nestling in your arms. Yet I remain captivated by your willowy form and shapely slender legs that promise to reveal heaven's gate."

Then, reaching up, he pulled her down and commenced a long, sensual kiss. Maacah's eyes widened in surprise and slowly and dreamily closed in romantic delight. The passage of time seemed to have stood still as both were spinning in a whirlpool of heightened excitement. Finally, David's tender caresses and, in love's alluring whispers, he prodded Maacah to succumb.

The sensation of being swept away to some forbidden isle of pleasure. Looking to confirm that they were completely alone and away from spying eyes, David laid his mantle down upon the ground behind a blind shrubbery and under a sprawling oak canopy. He took Maacah by the hand and gently eased her down upon his cloak, shielding her body from the cool morning dew. Maacah raised in futile protest and then surrendered to her heated passions. Pressing her lips tightly, he deftly unfastened her stay, exposing the last barrier to his conquest. He then embraced her like a warm blanket; her breathing was heavy and deeply rhythmic. She whispered, "Be gentle, my prince, for I have never known a man before."

David whispered, "I have fantasized of your surrender both in night's dark hollows and in waking dreams at midday. This is the very moment when a girl becomes a woman. Together, we can relish the pleasures given to us in the act of creation by an all-knowing and loving God."

David's gentleness, affectionate touches, his soft, languishing kisses made their lovemaking awash in rivulets of sweat, dampening their hungry, fevered bodies. The spiritual bonding of a woman's first love ties her heartstrings into a knot of emotions, even greater than a threefold cord that is not easily broken.

"Princess Maacah! Princess Maacah!" A chorus of shouts rang out, echoing off the garden walls. Household servants fanned out, tasked with finding the missing couple.

Whispering so his voice would not carry and reveal their hiding place, David began, "Princess, we must right ourselves in some form of respectability and present ourselves to your father, the king, and belay all suspicions of our heated intimacy."

"I agree, my soon-to-be husband. Take the cone and brush my hair while reattaching my stays and stockings."

Then, the couple seemed to spring from the earth in full sight of their makeshift search party of guards and servants.

"There you are!" the head servant shouted out. "Your father has been anxiously awaiting your return, fearing incident or accident."

The young lovers were hastily escorted to the king's presence. Maacah clung tightly to David's arm, and her eyes were glassy and fixed on the man who had stolen her heart. Nevertheless, love was in the air, and King Talmai knew the world's ways and could sense that his daughter was enraptured with her future husband.

Attempting to hide his smile of satisfaction, David addressed his future father-in-law. "Most gracious king, your understanding daughter and I wish to be married as soon as possible, first here in Bethesda under Gershurite law, ritual, and ceremony and again in Hebron under Hebrew law, thus ensuring our posterity will be recognized as legitimate heirs in both kingdoms. But, unfortunately, as you know, great king, I am at war with Israel. Therefore, I had left Hebron under cover of night and disguised myself to make this difficult journey in the hope of uniting our two kingdoms and marrying your beautiful daughter. But, unfortunately, spies and liars abound, so please understand that I invite trouble and reprisal from an enemy bent on my destruction, especially when I am away from Hebron, my capital and stronghold."

Considering the urgency of David's petition and his daughter's dreamy-eyed condition, Talmai announced, "The royal wedding will take place tomorrow at sundown. We will prepare the high grove and the altar of Suen. The high priest of our moon god will preside as is our custom. The couple will now be separated and not look at each other until tomorrow's ceremony. The wedding feast will take place immediately afterward here in the great hall. The couple will then retire, spend their first night under the king's roof, and realize their marriage, making it fitting and proper under Geshurite law. The following morning, the newlyweds will leave for Hebron with a Geshurite escort and a pack of she-mules as my gift to the bride and groom."

Maacah's servant girl had to tug at her mistress's hand to release the tight grip on her gifted lover's outstretched arm.

Returning her affection, David uttered, "Until tomorrow, my precious darling, we will bind our hearts and lives together forever."

CHAPTER TEN

Lust and Alliances

David confidently strode into his guest quarters, eager to announce his coming Gershurite marriage to the princess and his return to Hebron and home the following day.

Shimeah spoke first, "I know that winning grin! So, speak up, little brother. What or who have you made trail this day?"

David beamed, "I have reconsidered the Hebrew marriage conditions. I had to think about Maacah debasing herself here at her home in Et-Tell by conforming to our awkward yet required ritual of shaving her head and paring her nails. That would not sit well with her family or subjects. So, first, the Gershurite wedding ceremony will take place atop their sacred grove. After which, a sumptuous wedding feast will be had. We will then spend our first night as husband and wife under her father's roof and realize our marriage vows as local custom requires. Then my new bride and I and our entire company will leave for Hebron the following morning. We have been gifted a pack of barren she-mules, and a company of Gershurite guardians will see us safely to Hebron and remain there as a token of our alliance. After reaching Hebron, Maacah will abide by the necessary customs in full view of the pious elders and commence her thirty days of lamenting about leaving her father's house. So, everything will be done according to the law of Moses. I will then be married again to Maacah, who has agreed to become a Hebrew bride, comply without reservation or objection, and meet me under the chuppah (wedding canopy), thus blessing our future posterity as legitimate heirs in both kingdoms." With their bottom lips stiffened and heads wagging in agreement, almost all were pleased with the news of returning to hearth and home.

Although Abiathar was not so pleased and scowled, "David, you are the king of Judah and the anointed king of Israel, anointed with the holy oil of separation. As I serve you, my lord king, you serve Adonai, the true God. Taking part in a heathen ritual is like putting a strange god before Him, the one true God. I cannot abide this farce and insult to Adonai."

Disquieted by the priest's response, David sighed, "My dear friend, I need you to bear this diplomatic necessity for the sake of our people. This alliance with giants could be the very factor that helps turn the tide against King Ish-bosheth and his Chief-Captain Abner's army, as well as to help realize my anointing as the future king of Israel, as proved by Samuel, the prophet when I was but a lowly shepherd boy."

"I can see your thinking, king of the Jews, and from the years of travels together, if I have learned but one thing, I will have a better chance of holding back the tide than changing your mind," Abiathar replied.

"Then let us hear no more of it, for it is God's will that I become the next king of Israel, and this alliance could ensure just that. Abiathar, you are more than my high priest; you have been a loyal and devoted friend. I depend on your advice and counsel; our secret affliction, the falling down disease, binds us more than brothers. Your presence is not required at the heathen ceremony. As luck would have it, the necessary full moon is tomorrow night. Ambassador Shimeah and no one else will accompany me. That way, there are no witnesses; it is better to deny the jaundiced eye and lessen the fuel of wagging tongues and gossip mongers," said David before adding, "Let us prepare for tomorrow's activities and our departure on the dawn of the following day."

The next day filled with preparation passed quickly as David addressed many details with his brother Shimeah, "I'm counting on you to make sure the men do not get drunk, pick fights with the Gershurite guardians, or disrupt our departure as rowdy vagabonds. I want you to get my future father-in-law King Talmai and his governing counselors to agree and acknowledge that the party of guardians will be stationed in Hebron until my war with Israel is over and, most importantly, that if called upon, the whole of the Gershurite army would come to my aid. Talmai has already agreed to these provisions, but it is good to cement good intentions with repetitions to avoid future misunderstandings."

Shimeah nodded his head in agreement, "I concur, as

some counselors and dignitaries were not present at the initial negotiations, many have made haste to be at the marriage ceremony. After all, nothing ensures attendance quite like a feast of delicacies, roasted beef, and all the wine you can drink at someone else's expense."

David smiled at his brother before laying out the plan, "Here at the castle and just before sundown, we will enter the courtyard and wait for the moon to reach its peak. The wedding party will be assembled, waiting for Maacah's entrance to start the ceremony. You, my brother, will stand to my left and Maacah to my right, next to her father, the king. Say nothing but look solemnly engaged. Their high priest binds our hands together three times and recites a heathen vow. Then, their priest slaughters a bull, ensuring the fertility of many offspring. Finally, the bride is taken away, and I do not see her again until we feast on the roasted beast and drink dark red wine. In the morning, and after partaking in my husbandly duties, I intend to arise early so that we can leave this place with as little or no fanfare, thus blinding the spying eyes of enemy liars. Let us rest and wear our best clean garments for tomorrow's wedding. That is to ensure an alliance of giants to help defeat Ish-bosheth and Abner, making the throne of Israel vacant and available."

Just before sunset, a brisk knock roused David from his nap. Gershurite escorts had come to collect the guest of honor. It was David's practice to get a midday rest, while Shimeah had been up and about since daybreak. He felt that late afternoon naps were the practice of night owls and shepherds needing to keep alert for wolves and lions on the prowl through the bewitching hours. He preferred to save the day to himself. Shimeah had prepared all the needful things in anticipation of the fast-approaching festivities.

The castle's imposing captain stepped into the room and began, "Gentlemen, I have been tasked by the king to guide the bridegroom and his party to the courtyard. All is ready, and the king awaits your pleasure. I have a troop of guardian protectors along with your entourage of escorts."

Shimeah responded, "Give us a moment to refresh and dress."

With a nod, the captain said, "Please, you must be in position before the moon reaches its zenith with all due haste. Timing is critical. If you are not in your place when the first shadow crosses the moon's face, if we miss the moment, the ceremony cannot be performed and must be postponed until the next full moon. The sky is angry tonight. This is a good sign, but there can be no delay, so make haste."

"I said a moment," snapped Shimeah as the captain quickly exited, not wishing to create an incident.

Dressed in their best, David and Shimeah joined their escort and made a regal entrance to the flower-adorned patio. A stone altar of an aroused bull had been erected for the ceremony. As David and Shimeah took their place, a procession of flower girls laid down a carpet of petals, followed by Maacah in all her finery. Her luxurious hair had been poled and oiled. The brushed gold flecks sparkled in the firelight. King Talmai and a pagan priest looked skyward, gauging the moon's ascent. Finally, there was a docile bull with its eyes half-closed and ready for slaughter.

Talmai's tight brow lines relaxed when he spied David and

his train entering the square and shouted, "Thank goodness my future ally and son-in-law has arrived without a moment to spare. As a seasoned politician, I can appreciate the heightened state of a well-timed entrance. Please come and stand next to your bride. The priest cuts the bull's throat as soon as the moon reaches its peak, and the first dark shadow passes over its face. Next, he will speak the words of the pledge, and finally, the beast's blood will be sprinkled on both your own and Maacah's hands, which have been fastened together with a ceremonial rope, signifying that you are bound to each other, and only death can release the bond. Do you have any questions or reservations? Speak to them now!"

David swallowed hard; was he not giving homage to a foreign god and going against the commandments of Adonai, the one true God? David's troubled spirit had come too far to back out now. Feigning confidence, hoping that God would forgive his heathen marriage for the good of his people Israel. He uttered, "No, your majesty, let us join our nations by blood and sacrifice."

There were priests and scantily clad priestesses forming a circle. Maacah and David stood before the joiner as a chorus of heathen drums beat a steady rhythm. Shimeah took his rightful place, supporting his king and younger brother over Abiathar's pious objection. Shimeah remained composed to the heathen display unfolding before him, knowing full well that politics make strange bedfellows, and this was but a small price to pay to ensure Israel's dominion under the anointed David.

After an endless wait, a clutching dark shadow passed

across the moon's face. The Pagan priest took his cue and slit the drugged animal's throat before catching a stream of needed blood to finalize the heathen ritual. He then addressed the royal couple, "Will you honor and respect one another and their wishes and seek never to break this covenant?" Each said "yes" separately. And so, the first binding is made. "Will you share each other's pain and seek to ease it? Will you share the burdens of each so that your spirits may grow in this union? Will you share in each other's laughter and look for the brightness in life by caring for each other?" In unison, both nodded and said, "We do." And so, with that, the final binding was made fast. Finally, the pagan priest sprinkled blood on the chords, thus sealing the couple forever by Gershurite law.

David pulled Maccah in and found her moist, full lips. He pressed long and hard, making the assembled guests uncomfortable.

All who had gathered then gave out a joy-filled cry. The drums beat a final chorus, and everyone pressed in to wish the newlyweds well-deserved congratulations. King Talmai kissed his daughter on the cheek, but Maacah could not look away from her new husband's face. Finally, Talmai dismissed the gathering by announcing, "The wedding feast awaits with wine in abundance and roasted flesh to sate the most ravenous of appetites."

Both great and small proceeded to fill the great hall.

Toast after toast was noisily hoisted until the room overflowed with merriment and laughter. Finally, Talmai nodded to David, signaling it was time to depart to the bridal chamber to consummate the union. He hoped in his heart that he would soon have a male heir. A grandson that could straddle three kingdoms like a Gershurite titan.

David took Maacah by the hand; the two quietly slipped unnoticed by the revelers and hurried down a dimly lit passageway. Maacah led the way, almost tugging at her new husband's arm. Guards and servants trailed behind should the couple require any food or wine. They then entered the chamber and quickly bolted the door behind them. The guards took their post, discouraging prying eyes and keyhole listeners. Maacah looked up and saw the lavish bedroom adorned with flowers in every corner. It was an exquisite sight. The sweet scent was intoxicating. David pressed her body hard against the bolted door, not wanting to squander a moment. Then, in a commanding voice, David began, "My eyes have been drinking in your beauty, and my only thought is to taste your lips and know you once more."

Held up only by the force of his hips, Maacah swooned. Reaching down, he hiked up her skirt, barring her long, shapely legs. She panted a timid protest, "But, my love, the bed is close at hand, and we have all night," yet her voice trailed off, succumbing to the moment's carnal frenzy. David claimed her red wine lips and consumed her hot honeycomb tongue. The scent of fresh jasmine in her hair beguiled his nostrils, raising passions to a fever pitch. The lust-filled couple, heightened from the day's rituals, exploded in unabashed love-making before collapsing to the floor in exhaustion. Their honeymoon night was whiled away in each other's endearing embrace.

CHAPTER ELEVEN
A Wedding Times Two

It was the darkest hour and the onset of vivid dreams when a rousing knock returned the spent couple to reality. Shimeah, long since awake, had thoroughly prepared for their hasty departure. He cleared his throat and whispered, "As you ordered, David, all is ready. The wagon has provisions, abundant cushions, your marriage canopy, wedding gifts, and sundries. Abiathar has consented to be your driver. The Gershurite she-mule mounted guardians, and all your Mighties stand ready at the outer courtyard gate. They await your arrival and are eager for a speedy departure for Hebron and home. Your father-in-law, the king, turns out to be a light sleeper and will be present to bid farewell to the happy couple. He is standing there still clad in his rumpled nightshirt, looking less imposing and more comical than regal."

Still groggy and feeling drained, David gently nudged his deep-sleeping bride and soothingly uttered, "My dear wife, our carriage awaits in the courtyard below, and your father will speak his fond goodbyes. Arise, my dearest, the night is our cover to lessen the view of enemy spies who could observe our travel plans and greatly increase the chances of a surprise attack."

Maacah rose, rubbing her eyes, trying to focus on David's silhouette in the flickering candlelight. "My dear husband," stifling a content giggle, "that was wonderful; now I know why the poets muse about lovemaking," she sighed. "But do we really have to leave right now? I prefer to while away the day in each other's embrace. Since we have only started getting to know each other properly as man and wife."

"I, too, would choose your caresses rather than our rutted road ahead. But the longer we tarry, the greater the risk of being discovered by my enemy Abner, chief captain of Israel, who hungers for my downfall," David replied.

"My dear husband, my father is sending his fiercest guardians for our protection. Even if our departure were discovered, it would take an entire army to overpower us, and besides, there would be no time for your enemies to organize a deadly ambush. They would need to determine our route and intercept us at an exposed location. But having said that, I will be a dutiful wife, concede to my master's wishes, and prepare for departure. Although will you promise me that we will continue to get better acquainted in the wagon's bed?"

"My thoughts exactly, my beautiful princess. I have had plenty of down-filled pillows to ensure ease and comfort on our journey to your new home. The transport wagon has also fitted a thick privacy curtain to avoid prying eyes. Besides, we have planned backroad travel with your father's help, lessening the chances of an enemy encounter."

"My dear husband, it seems that you have thought of everything."

Smiling, David then said, "I need you to collect some of your dearest keepsakes, dresses, jewelry, and the like—but no more than can fit into one travel trunk. You will visit your family and adoring subjects as often as is deemed safe and practical. You will oversee importing she-mules from Geshur back to Judah. I am confident that my victory over Israel is all but assured by my alliance with the Gershurite army of giants. Although, for now, please make all due haste, and I will meet you in the outer courtyard after speaking to your father. We depart upon your arrival."

The courtyard bustled with a collection of last-minute essentials. The she-mules replaced the wagon oxen to ensure fleetness of travel. All the beasts of burden had been fed and watered, and once harnessed, they brayed and snorted, anxious to depart. David's Mighties and the Gershurite guardians had formed an uneasy alliance to protect their precious cargo. The escort waited silently, avoiding bragging rights and chest pounding by honing and sharpening their weapons of war.

Entering the courtyard, David's Mighties let out a cheer. David signaled his mighty men by lowering and bouncing both hands so as not to arouse the sleeping populace. "There you are, my now official son-in-law. Where is Maacah? I wish to give her a father's blessing, as it may be sometime before I look upon her face again," said King Talmai.

"It might take a moment or two. She is gathering a few dearest mementos and saying some last goodbyes," answered David.

"Most women, when they are about to depart their childhood abode, search for a medley of keepsakes that might come in handy when their longing for home becomes an overpowering malady. I will miss my daughter; she is the joy and comfort in this old man's declining years. In times like these, I feel patience; however bitter it may be, this is the best ally, even for a king."

Torchlight and chatter pierced the gloom when Maacah finally approached the awaiting group of onlookers. She was followed by four stout servants carrying two overstuffed cedar chests. The torchbearers guided the entourage, casting sparks and shadows in the process. The princess was accompanied by two handmaiden traveling companions, befitting her royal station.

"My dear child," Talmai uttered as he cleared his throat. "I see the hint of rosy cheeks and a satisfied smile, revealing a woman in love. Before you leave our home for a foreign country, I wish to give you a father's blessing of comfort and protection."

Maacah embraced his neck and cheerfully agreed, "Yes, Father, I was hoping for your blessing and protection."

David stepped back, allowing this parting family drama to play out.

Talmai placed his hands on Maacah's head. He then took a deep breath as he paused for inspiration before uttering, "I, Talmai king of the Gershurite, call upon Hadad, the Moon-God who possesses the power of the bull to protect and comfort the royal Princess Maccha as she journeys far from home and loved ones to a distant country. Bless my child with marital bliss and that her marriage to David, king of the Jews, will bear the fruits of a royal posterity binding our two kingdoms forever as a family nation. Protect her over rocky roads and river rages. Keep her safe and unharmed and bring her back often to her father's loving arms. Do this for me, great god Hadad, and I will build you a temple on the high places to honor your glory."

Maccha turned and kissed her father on the cheek as she said, "I miss you already, and I will visit you often and bring your grandchildren, the true jewels in an old man's crown."

"I have one last gift to ease your mind: a large wagon fitted for travel. Now you have a second wagon allowing ample room for your maidservants and keepsakes," revealed the king.

"That is perfect, Father; this will ease my mind and give me the comfort of keepsakes and familiar companions cushioning my entrance into a foreign culture. Thank you, great king!"

David peeled in as he broke his silence, "The second wagon is a much-needed generosity; thank you, Your Majesty, for the kindness to your daughter and my wife. But we must depart, for soon the sun will give our intentions and route away, and all of our preparation would have been in vain."

With all mounted and hastily boarded, the honeymoon train moved quickly through the outer gate blanketed by silence and the cover of night.

Good weather and planning made the trip to Hebron almost as delightful as a picnic. First, the newly married couple took every opportunity to get to know each other better. But then, the couple knew they preferred to be alone. So, even during frequent rest stops, the couple hurried off to take advantage of any opportunity for an intimate picnic lunch.

The back road approach produced only a few sheep-herding onlookers. The lookout scouts reported no signs of enemy intrusion or local hostile intentions. There were only a hundred miles of wilderness and some small villages along the way. The clopping of braying mules and grumblings from the Gershurite guardians and the foot-weary Mighties helped to hide the couple's occasional giggling, heavy breathing, and playful banter. The second driver was deaf as a post; he never spoke and communicated with hand gestures, grunts, and groans.

The nights were glorious and clear. Once the caravan stopped for the night, David and Maacah hurriedly sought privacy away from prying eyes and well-tuned ears in search of whispers. They preferred to settle down away from the main encampment under an august moon and a star-studded sky.

On the fifth day of travel, the baggage train finally came into sight of Hebron.

David nuzzled Maacah and, in a reassuring tone, began explaining the cultural protocol necessary for her acceptance into Judean society, "My dear Maacah, as far as the elders are concerned, we are not married. Divulging that we were married by the priests of a heathen god would undermine my authority with speculation and backbiting. As I explained, the ritual of eshet yefat to'ar must be observed perfectly to ensure our offspring are legitimate heirs."

Maacah nodded in agreement as her husband continued, "Upon entering the compound, you will be taken to a royal barber where your hair will be cut off, your head shaved bald, and your nails paired down, hiding all trappings of privilege. Next, your ordeal will be scrutinized by the watchful eyes of ten pious elders. Then, finally, the most demanding require- ment: we must remain separated for thirty days while you lament the loss of your father's house wearing nothing more than sackcloth and ashes."

"Yes, my love, how often do you have to go over the same distasteful penance to become your rightful Hebrew wife?"

"I simply want to ensure you completely understand all the necessary details, for much depends upon your surrender. Not just to me but the Hebrew religion and culture."

Hebron welcomed the arrival of their king and his intended fourth wife, Maacah, a Geshurite princess of legendary beauty and size. She was exceptionally tall and stood head and shoul- ders above David. Some in the crowd discreetly whispered, "He is marrying a Canaanite giant; what will become of us?"

David's Mighties and the larger-than-life Geshurite Guardians riding atop stout she-mules finally made their entrance, turning the surreal scene into a spectacle. The wel- coming trumpets echoed off the city walls as the imposing escort crossed the threshold.

David stood on the wagon driver's seat, acknowledging the howls and cheers of the tumultuous crowd, who were jubilant to see their king unharmed and looking vibrant. Climbing down, he took Maacah by the hand and walked up to the elevated entrance together. At the top of the porch, being of one mind, they turned to face the boisterous mob. Still clutching the princess's hand, David raised his arms to a great uproar. When the thunder reduced to a murmur, David addressed the multitude. "My fellow Jews, thank you for your welcome. Allow me to introduce Maacah, a princess from the Geshurite kingdom. She has consented to be my wife and endure the ritual of eshet yefat to'ar to make our joining acceptable in the eyes of God. This will also permit our children to be royal heirs afforded all the rights and privileges of both our kingdoms. Our union will also bind our two domains in an alliance with family bonds. The Gershurites can now be relied upon to help us defeat King Ish-bosheth and the army of Israel." Another big cheer rang out that acknowledged David as their warrior king, cunning diplomat, and tactician.

David then announced, "The assigned witnesses will now escort Maacah to the place of shaving and paring. Once accomplished, she will be given a guarded place to live for thirty days according to our laws and customs. One month from now you are all invited to my wedding feast. Ahinoam, my second wife, and Abigail, my third wife, will attend if they agree. There will be a herd of bullocks and the fat of rams sacrificed on the altar of gratitude and thanksgiving. I invite all of Hebron to join in the festivities. Abiathar, my friend, and high priest were essential in our successful negotiations with King Talmai of the Geshurite; Abiathar will be honored by officiating at my wedding. He will perform the ceremony under the Chuppah, or wedding canopy, and the Sheva

B'rachot, or the seven blessings, will be recited. The feast will begin to celebrate my marriage that will bind our two great nations together." Yet another cheer rang out as the ten elders ascended the stairs and hurriedly whisked Maacah away to fulfill her commitment as a consort and Hebrew bride to David, king of the Jews.

CHAPTER TWELVE

A Recipe for Rape

Maacah went on to bear David two sons, Absalom and Jerimoth, as well as a daughter called Tamar. Jerimoth was named and circumcised but died before his thirty days of life; therefore, he was not valued, mourned, or counted as having ever lived.

The surviving brother and sister were undoubtedly David's most beautiful children. The siblings grew up together and were inseparable. The court often commented that the two children never parted and almost seemed one in disposition, form, and features.

One day, Tamar, a toddler, climbed the tower steps and dangerously sat on the edge of the uppermost balcony. Tamar called out in distress, "Absalom!" He immediately looked up, bounded the entire spire, and snatched her by the hair, saving her from certain death. Tamar paled with fright, and from that day forward, Absalom, her big brother, would be her protector and hero.

Tamar had a naturally occurring youthful beauty. She was as succulent as a date palm, laden with ripe fruit and sweet goodness. When walking, her gate had a modest, feminine come-hither swing that could entice all the virile young men to engage in erotic fantasy.

Tamar and Absalom had long virgin and luxurious hair, an inheritance from Maacah, their mother. She ensured that her children's hair was neatly trimmed and regularly poled but never shortened. She made that promise upon marriage to David when she submitted to having her lengthy defining locks shaved bald to sanctify her Hebrew marriage.

Most of David's offspring grew up eye to eye, meaning many at the same time. Some were born days apart, and some were within hours of each other. David returned home from another successful conquest as randy as a Nubian goat. First, he would delight his wives, whom he had set aside for the longest time, and then caress his many concubines until he was utterly spent in husbandly duties and relentless passions.

While most of his siblings had different mothers, David sired and loved each one individually.

Ahinoam, his second wife, often attempted to counsel her headstrong child with a motherly counsel, "My dear Amnon, we have spoiled you sorrowfully. We have indulged you with every wish, want, and desire. You are, by all rights, the next king of Israel. But only if your father, David, does not name another son. Or, God forbid, the kingdoms will fall upon your shoulders should he die suddenly. Accordingly, it would be best to hold your unbridled passions in check, for I fear they will be your undoing."

Amnon smiled and replied, "I am a man with special needs. Am I so unlike my father, with his many wives and countless concubines? I am afraid I have inherited my father's lust for life, and like any conqueror, I refuse to take no for an answer."

David made it known to Amnon that nothing would be beyond his reach if not his grasp if he set his mind to possess it. As a result, Amnon was overindulged and prideful.

Spring had sprung, and Amnon's half-sister Tamar had blossomed into full flower. He looked across the courtyard and saw her loveliness; it was like he was seeing her for the first time. He became instantly vexed and obsessed. When she approached, his heart skipped a beat, and his breath caught deep in his throat. Then, gathering his courage, he inquired, "My dear sister Tamar, it has been too long since we played sticks and stones together as children. I see you have grown into a beautiful daughter of Israel."

"Thank you, brother, you are most kind, and I adore flattery, even when coming from family."

Thinking quickly, Amnon asked, "Where are you going in such a rush, sister, and on such a beautiful day?"

"I am off to the scullery; I like cooking and find it satisfying. The head cook has complimented me on many occasions, saying that I 'bake and prepare with a love that seeps into the dough and sweetens the cake with the richness of healing.' He awaits further instruction. I must depart. Adieu, brother."

Unfortunately for Amnon, Tamar was a virgin, and being

of the same royal blood, she would be unattainable by the laws of Israel. But try as he might, he could not get her out of his mind. Weeks passed, and Amnon watched daily from afar, intent on knowing all her comings and goings. He would hope for just a glimpse of the elusive and unattainable damsel. Sadly, he became a pitifully obsessed, lovesick puppy, not eating and only sleeping in bouts and fits.

David's nephew Jonadab, also known as Jonathan, grew up with Amnon. They were first cousins and closer than brothers. Jonadab was the son of Shimeah. Jonadab was a clever fellow who kept a low profile. He had a ready wit and could navigate palace intrigue and, if necessary, sidestep the law through persuasion and cunning.

As best friends, Jonadab and Amnon spent much time together and had the confidence of conspiracy; no secret or fantasy would go unexamined or unexplored. However, Jonadab had noticed as of late that Amnon rarely ate; when he did, it was a sparse affair, mostly picking and pecking at his plate. Rightfully concerned about his best friend's loss of appetite, Jonadab inquired, "My dear friend, what has gotten into you, or better yet, what has not gotten into you? You are the king's son and have abundant food and delicacies presented daily, yet you get thinner with each passing day. Tell me, friend, is it an illness or ailment? Tell me so that I might find you a physician or a magician to conjure up a cure."

"I do not believe there is a remedy for what I have, a one-sided love affair. Tamar has enchanted me. I am off my feed, and I am sick with love. She is the most beautiful and unreachable woman in the world," Amnon revealed.

"Is that all? I thought it was something serious. This is only a passing malady; it will only last until you find another woman that strikes your fancy. She is your half-sister and, therefore, forbidden fruit. The more unattainable the fruit, the sweeter the nectar. But I must warn you; you can go insane if you linger on this emotional sinkhole longer than deemed sensible."

Amnon replied, sounding panicked, "But what am I to do? My heart feels like it is about to break, and I shall die for want of her. I am deeply and hopelessly smitten. I am in love with Absalom's natural-born sister and my half-sister Tamar, a princess in the house of David. She remains far out of reach, an impossible dream, and a dilemma without reprieve."

"Tell me, cousin, does Tamar have any interests or hobbies?"

"Well, yes, she had confided in me that she has a fondness for cooking and that her love for the art imparts healing in the preparation or some such thing."

"Cooking, you say. Give me a moment, and I might have the makings of a perfect solution."

Jonadab pondered and paced, muttering and giggling as his cunning plan formed. Finally, in a confident voice, he announced, "I have some bitter root liquid that will make you appear sick and pathetic. As thin as you are, convincing will not take much effort. Then you must lay down upon your bed, retching and pale, giving the potion ample time to work its magic. At this point, we will summon your father, and you tell him of your dire condition and that you wish him to minister unto you. As you are the heir apparent, he will be compelled to grant you any petition to help regain your health. Now comes your part in this charade, which will require some convincing acting. Say exactly as I coach you and vary not in the slightest. When the king comes, tell him, 'It has come to my understanding that my sister Tamar has been gifted with healing through the love she emits while preparing her delectable cakes with care. I pray thee, let my sister Tamar come and give me meat, and dress the meat in my sight, that I may see it, and know for a certainty that it is she that cooked it, and eat it at her hand.'

"Then, you must remain in bed when she enters your house. Greet her kindly and respectfully; tell her that her presence alone has inspired you to rise and escort her to the cooking hearth because you eagerly wish to watch her in the preparation of your super."

Amnon remained silent as Jonadab continued to explain his plan, "After a short time, and once she has cast her spell, she will present you with the sweet cakes. Do not partake when offered, but kindly refuse to eat at the fireside. Dismiss all your servants, ensuring intimate privacy. Tell Tamar that you need to return to your bed so you can lie back down and for her to bring the sweet cakes into your bed chamber so you can eat from her hand."

Amnon then interjected, "Well, this plan is clearly well thought out and undoubtedly intriguing and cunning. So let us say that all goes as planned, and I have the damsel in a secluded, private, and compromised position. Then what?"

Jonadab rolled his eyes, shook his head, and in a

high-pitched belittling tone asked, " Do you really need to ask me, 'then what'? By now, she should be eating out of your hand instead of you begging to eat out of hers. It is time to get to know her. What more is there to say?"

"But you forget she is one of the king's daughters and wears the virgin apparel of diverse colors, that is a sign of God and the king's favor?" Amnon replied.

"No, I do not forget, not at all; her virginity is the key to her heart and her need to be fulfilled as a woman. Tamar has never known another man; I can confidently say this. However, one can never be sure about anything regarding women. This means that if she does not surrender willingly, you have her in a compromising position, meaning you can dominate the object of your desire. Remember, once you have reaped the maiden's prize, her longing for you will be assured. There is an undeniable connection, for you will be in her thoughts for the rest of her life; for good or ill, the rest is up to you."

CHAPTER THIRTEEN

Incest's Folly and a Scoundrel's Rejection

The plan was hatched and ready to fly on the dark wings of deceit and deception.

The conspiracy to deflower Tamar was as brilliant as it was devious. All that was left was for everyone to play their part, enabling Amnon to pluck the petal of his lovesick obsession.

Jonadab was true to his word and gathered up the bitter herb, the essential ingredient of his strategy. He poured a sickness-inducing and pallor-graying venom into a small earthen vessel and then placed it into Amnon's eager outstretch hand.

"Here you are, cousin, as I promised, 'The I look sick unto death extract.' First and foremost, make sure everyone in question is available. It would be a pity to find out that your father, the king, or Tamar was not in residence after ingesting this potent elixir."

The day finally came, and all had been prepared with foresight and detail. A messenger was dispatched with dire and urgent words to stir sympathy and compassion. The practiced plea had the force of sincerity. It roused King David's soul to attend and minister to his eldest son, who lay stricken.

The messenger returned with the glad tidings, "The king was moved and will attend you tomorrow noon."

Downing the corrupt vial, Amnon swallowed hard and laid himself on his bed. By the time David arrived, Amnon did not need to pretend his sickness any longer. He looked deathly ill but even worse, he felt sick unto death.

David was deeply troubled by his son's ashen pallor. In a consoling tone, the king offered, "What ails you, my son, and what would you have of me to relieve your suffering?"

Struggling to rise on one elbow, Amnon choked out, "I pray thee let my sister Tamar come and make a couple of cakes in my sight that I may eat from her hand."

"I must say, my dear boy, this is a puzzling request. What is your reasoning for it?"

"Father, I inquired and have found that Tamar is a gifted cook. The care and love she releases pass through her hands as she kneads the dough with healing greater than medicine. I wish to witness when she does her loving labor to ensure she does not give the chore to a servant girl. I further trust that by eating out of her hand, the soothing in her fingertips will hasten my recovery."

"Very well, that is an unusual request, but if you think this will help you to regain your health, I will agree with your pleadings, my sick son. The greatest medicine is the love and kindness of others, so I support your reasoning. I will summon your sister

Tamar immediately before your condition worsens further."

Straight away and true to his word, David went to the palace apartments of his fourth wife, Maacah, and the home to Tamar, who wore the virgin garment of many colors.

David walked unannounced through the door and found Tamar brushing her long, lustrous hair. Then, with a sense of urgency, he compelled, "Ah, there you are, Tamar!" Startling the girl as if seemingly appearing out of thin air. "I have an urgent request that only you can fulfill."

"Oh, it is you, Father, of course; anything I can do. A request from a king is taken as a command; what would you have of me?"

"Go to your brother Amnon's house and dress levivot cakes, for he is ill and feels your cooking skills will help him heal because you cook from the heart. In other words, he needs food prepared with loving care and has asked for you."

"Yes, Father, I would be delighted to help. I shall go this moment and do whatever I can to relieve my brother Amnon's suffering."

Without a second thought, Tamar dutifully set out for Amnon's house. A burly servant greeted her at the door and ushered her immediately to his master's chamber. Amnon was lying in his bed when Tamar entered the room.

"My dear sister Tamar, so good of you to come; I feel better already just seeing you."

"I can see that you are ill, my dear brother; I will go to the cooking hearth and bake you levivot cakes using all my skill and with all the care that my heart can impart."

Sitting up, Amnon insisted, "I am feeling well enough to accompany you to the kitchen. I feel compelled to watch you perform your magic."

"As you wish, brother, if you feel strong enough, that is a good sign that you are getting your strength back," replied Tamar.

She was right at home at the measuring table and cooking hearth. Putting on a white cooking smock, she looked more like an angel than a baker. She took finely sifted flour, then slowly and carefully kneaded the dough before mixing the honey, eggs, and a cruse of olive oil to perfection.

When ready, the golden-brown treats were snatched from the fire. Tamar lovingly placed the cakes in a serving bowl and then put them in front of her ailing brother with a cruse of honey. The tantalizing aroma filled the kitchen, making everyone present salivate with hunger. To her surprise, Amnon shook his head, pushed back the plate, and refused to eat. He then stood up and, in a demanding voice, thundered, "Have out all men from me! I feel an onset of fatigue coming over me." Hearing the insistence in his voice, all of the servants took flight and scattered. "I need to return to my bed and lay my head down. Tamar, bring the treats into my chamber so that I may eat from your hand."

Concerned about her brother's decline, Tamar gently responded, "Certainly, my brother. I will gather up the cakes and come directly to your chamber so that you may eat and regain your health."

When Tamar entered the darkened room and viewed

Amnon lying on his bed, he abruptly ordered, "Shut the door behind you and place the cakes on the nightstand." He then took her by the hand and demanded, "Come lie with me, my sister."

Her face paled when it dawned on her that this was an elaborate scheme to put her in a vulnerable position. Tamar attempted to compose herself and knew she must use her wits to get free, knowing that she was physically no match for her brother's brutish demands.

"Nay, my brother, do not force me, for no such thing should be done in Israel. Do not play your part in this folly. What about my shame and disgrace? Where could I go to outrun the stain? And what about you? You will be counted as a wicked fool in Israel."

Tamar thought quickly and played for time, hoping her words would rouse a sense of shame and make him refrain, thus giving him hope for a different path to winning the object of his desire. She continued, "Please speak to the king; he will not keep me from you. As king, he can overrule the laws of Israel and sanctify our marriage."

Unfortunately, it had already gone too far, and there was no dissuading Amnon's lustful hunger. His strength increased like an aroused bull; he was far beyond reasoning. With unrelenting force, he knew her, reaping the flower of her innocence.

Amnon finally spent as he rolled off Tamar's ravaged and blood-stained body. Unexpectedly, Tamar's words of warning finally tingled her brother's ears, sending an embarrassed shiver down his spine. Tamar desperately mustered strength and grabbed any cover she could to shield her naked body in a futile attempt at modesty. Thoroughly bewildered, she stared at the ceiling and tried to make sense of it all; her instincts and emotions were in collision. She felt violated and dominated by a brute and had lost all control. Then again, as painful as it was going from childhood to womanhood, she had changed. Turning to look at her abuser, she stirred with a confusing longing and an unsettling connection. Tamar tried to convince herself that Amnon had a desperate love for her. She rationalized, had he not conspired and gone to great lengths by challenging every legal and religious convention to lie with me? I am the woman he most desired out of all the women in the world, and above all, he chose me.

His lust spent, Amnon felt shallow and empty inside, as if the spirit had departed and left him to kick against the pricks of shame and self-loathing. His love fixation had now turned into a greater weight of hate, while his very breath was an indictment of a crime against the laws of God and man that howled in his ears until he quaked. Then, unable to hold back a moment longer, he bellowed, "Arise and be gone. The sight of you troubles me. You must leave immediately!"

Amnon's offensive outburst startled Tamar into despair as if great darkness had swallowed her whole. She replied with dignity, "There is no cause for pressing upon me this evil in sending me away in disgust; this act is greater than the other you had done unto me."

However, Amnon would not listen. Seeing her now only gnawed his soul, and he wished with all his heart that he would never see her again. He lingered for but a moment, but even that was too long. Amnon called his bodyguard, "Put this woman out, do it now, for she vexes me, and bolt the door behind her."

Sad and dejected, Tamar managed a modest demand: "I still have pride enough so that my nakedness is not on full display of a hireling."

She angrily snatched her garment of many colors that signified the virginity of a king's daughter, laying at her feet, hastily pulled off and tossed to the floor, the last flimsy barrier to her violation. The servant appeared, and not a moment too soon, Tamar had just covered her nudity. Reluctant to put his hands on the woman after noticing the garment of a royal princess, the servant nodded in respect and said, "Madam, please follow me to the door and make it easy for the both of us."

Tamar thought, No longer a miss but a madam now that I have been ravaged. He brought her out as commanded, slamming the bolt home with a jolt and securing the door against re-entry.

As she left the room, Tamar looked down upon the hard and rocky ground, her heart melting with shame and embarrassment. She spied on a cold fire pit before scooping up a handful of ashes and placing them on her head. She no longer felt worthy and ripped her virgin garments of diverse colors. She put her hand on her head so the ashes would not fly or fall away, feeling that her shame would be everlasting. Torrents of bitter tears fell down her face, attempting to wash away her disgrace. Then, with a broken heart and contrite spirit, she called to heaven for her soul was rent in twain.

CHAPTER FOURTEEN

A Patient Reprisal the Foresight of Vengeance

After an endless trudge back to her apartment, Tamar opened the door only to face her brother Absalom. He knew her mission of mercy was to minister to Amnon with sweet cakes, care, and healing. Looking at her tattered and torn appearance and already suspecting the answer, he questioned, "Has Amnon, your brother, been with you forcefully?" Unable to speak, she hid her face in the shadows and nodded her confession. Absalom stood there in silence. He waited until the blood in his head returned to his feet. If there were retaliation, it would be deadly and calculated. Finally, after a long pause, he addressed his tattered and torn sister, "It would be best for you to hold your peace. For now, this is a delicate matter. He is your brother and of the royal household, and to make matters worse, he is the likely heir to the empire of Israel." Confused about what to do, Tamar remained in Absalom's house, desolate and unable to find solace.

The only thing that travels faster than bad news is good gossip. David had in his employ a legion of informants and spies. He was told about the assault on his daughter Tamar, committed by his favorite son Amnon. He was furious, but he, too, held his peace; no punishment or even scolding was forthcoming. David had decided that the family's dirty laundry should remain a best-kept secret. Therefore, it looked like Amnon would not be held accountable for his actions. It was surmised that since Tamar and Absalom's mother, Maacah was a Gershurite and a heathen Canaanite, they were of mixed heritage and not fully Hebrews. Therefore, Absalom could never be king, and Tamar would never be admitted to the inner circle. Absalom was now more keenly aware of the jibes and slights of his purebred Hebrew brother princes. The lesser positions seemed to be permanently assigned to him and Tamar at parades as well as at the banquet table.

Anytime Amnon and Absalom found themselves in a position to speak, Absalom showed no hostility, neither good nor bad, and was cunningly neutral both in speech and manner; observing the two men in polite conversation, you would conclude the politeness of strangers. Of course, the truth is that Absalom hated his brother Amnon for forcing his sister, and he would have his revenge. But he waited until the incident was gone from recent memory, and vengeance and punishment had long passed from recollection.

Considering his next move, Absalom heard a rumor that the wisest man in Israel had a seasoned bitterness against David. His name was Ahithophel. In the past, he was one of the king's most valued counselors, a noted sage and seer without equal, and a long-standing next-door neighbor. It was later said that he sold his house over hard feelings, thus enabling David to enlarge the king's compound. He then retired and moved to a villa five miles south of Jerusalem.

Absalom thought this might be the man who could advise him on addressing his hot, bitter ash of vengeance that had gone too long unanswered.

Absalom saddled his Gershurite she-mule and set out for the house of Ahithophel. Coming upon a well-manicured villa at a lightly traveled crossroad, it retained a rustic charm and was exactly as described. Tying his mule to a hitching post, the beast gave a rousing bray when a distinguished-looking fellow popped up and through the hedgerow. The man had a hoary head, thick and gray, proclaiming wisdom and practical knowledge. Absalom knew at once that this was the man he came to question. He called out, "You must be Ahithophel, the oracle!"

Walking up to the young man, Ahithophel answered, "You do me honor, young sir, but my claim to wisdom is that I don't know what I don't know, and the rest is a mystery to me; that is all I know."

Both men laughed at the sage's clever remark. Finally, Ahithophel inquired, "Who are you, sir? You have the markings of a prince of Israel on your saddle. If you seek reconciliation with me and your father, David, you have wasted your trip and my time."

"No, not at all. It is just the opposite that brings me to

your door. My name is Absalom, a prince of Israel and Geshur. But, sir, can we speak in private confines? My matter speaks of vengeance and betrayal at the highest level."

"In that case, of course, come in. I have a private study that is perfect for the express reason of ensuring confidential conversations."

Settling into some comfortable chairs, both prepared themselves for a long talk.

Absalom began, "I have come to you because of the rumor that you have a long-standing hatred against my father. But, before I confide in you about my grievous insults and plans for revenge, I would first like to hear about your falling out with David and what made you so resentful and unyielding in your hatred. In this way, we can develop the intimacy of strangers and agree to a common objective with confidence and purpose."

"Very well, and as you wish. I once owned a large home and a sizable parcel of land inside the walls of Jebus, Jerusalem's ancient name before we changed it, through force and a flourishing population. Your father was already the ruler of Judah and had just become king of Israel. He wished to have his main capital in Jerusalem. The Jebusites challenged him to conquer the Blind and the Lame guardians, or brazen idols of Isaac and Jacob, symbolizing Abraham's oath of non-violence against the city's capture by his posterity. Abraham, in return, was granted an eternal deed to the cave of Machpelah, his and Sarah's burial place, and all the other Patriarchs and their wives. It is also known as the Cave of the Double Tombs. David offered that anyone who would go up the gutter and destroy the guardians of the Blind and the Lame would become his chief captain. Joab, his middle nephew, agreed and climbed up through the muck and mire of the gutter runoff on the right side of the eastern outer gate. It was night, and all the gates were closed, locked, and guarded. He destroyed the idols and their guardians and broke Father Abraham's promise and covenant. Consequently, by doing so, David's heart was full of hatred, but he had captured Jerusalem with the least amount of bloodshed."

As the man continued to speak, Absalom remained silent. "I must admit that David was gracious in his leadership in that all Jebusite property, bidding deeds, contracts, and agreements remained enforced under Israeli law. He wanted his mansion or seat of power made from cedar. I had met your father years before, and we became fast friends. He was always delighted with my sage advice. When he heard that I had available land, he approached me to purchase it. One, because the price was right, and secondly, he wanted me nearby to help him steer his course of empire. Everything went well, and we both profited from the friendship," the sage paused before continuing.

"The falling-out occurred when my granddaughter Bathsheba, a married woman, was found to be with David's child, the forbidden fruit of an adulterous affair. It is almost impossible to hide such a clandestine affair from a neighbor, especially when it is that close to home. An open wound ensued with the conspiracy to eliminate Bathsheba's husband, Uriah, a converted Jew formerly known as Horite the

Hittite. He was a soldier battling in David's army when the affair occurred. A contrived slaying by the sword of Ammon enabled David to marry Bathsheba to hide the shame and squelch the scandal. God's judgment was swift and sure. The baby died seven days after his birth, and I privately grieved the death of my great-grandchild. Unfortunately, he was neither named nor circumcised. He breathed for less than thirty days, considered not to have lived, and so not openly mourned, as is common in our traditions. The prophet Nathan became aware of David's murderous affair, and he troubled David by saying, 'Now, therefore, the sword shall never depart from thine house.'" The sage paused before looking the boy in the eyes and concluding, "I believe you might be that very sword, Absalom."

CHAPTER FIFTEEN

The Surest Course Is Massacre

Legend tells that Abimelech, the blended son and love child of Gideon and his concubine Drumah, the daughter of the house of Milo, or the people of the tower, slaughtered his seventy brothers to become the first but short-lived king of Israel and a king of Canaan.

Ahithophel set forth his many grievances and hardened enmity towards David safe in his private quarters. He confided, "Once I heard the news of Uriah the Hittite's death coupled with the heart-wrenching loss of my nameless great-grandson, whom David fathered in an adulterous affair with my granddaughter Bathsheba, an enmity followed that I could not reconcile. I once was David's most trusted advisor. I sold my adjacent mansion to David, allowing him to expand his compound. Having no choice, I retired to my country house, avoiding David, and attempted to restrain my seething hatred for my one-time friend and current sovereign."

Ahithophel then questioned Absalom, "All right, young prince, I have said my piece. Now tell me why you have sought my counsel. I take it that you wish to right some wrong; you feel slighted or belittled at the highest level and seek revenge masquerading as justice?"

"You are closer than I would have supposed with your offhanded estimate of my dilemma, wise sage. I have a dear sister, Tamar, and we are the children of Maacah, princess of Geshur, and David, king of Israel."

"Yes, I am quite aware of your partial Canaanite heritage. Please go on."

"Ignoring the consequence of his folly, my oldest half-brother Amnon and heir apparent, through trickery and deceit, lured my sweet virgin sister into his clutches and raped her repeatedly. Then, after the dirty deed, the scoundrel cast her out like so much refuge, adding even greater insult to her injury. Whispered gossip, but never officially acknowledged, has reduced her to a fool in Israel, ashamed even to show her face in polite society."

"Tell me, what was your father's reaction to this offense, the forceful violation and loss of dignity of one of his precious virgin daughters?" Ahithophel asked.

"Privately, he was furious at the disgrace. But publicly, he remained silent and guarded. As far as I know, Amnon was even spared the customary wrist slap and tongue-lashing for his outrageous misconduct. It has been two years since the deplorable incident. It took my best not to confront or stir the pot and signal my true intentions. I have even chatted with the knave on several occasions. We speak about simple everyday things, the weather, the newest vintage, and the cost of barley and corn. I have not shown any emotions, one way or the other, and no scornful words have passed my lips, nary a hint of my revengeful intent. The matter has been forgotten and dismissed for all intents and purposes as the careless plowing and seeding of a young man's wild oats."

Ahithophel pondered Absalom's confession with the utmost interest and compassion. Finally, after a long pause, he again questioned, "Does this poisoned dart fester in your heart? I wish to know what lengths you will go to satisfy this insult and get revenge on your sister's behalf in avenging her lost honor."

Without a pause or hesitation, Absalom yelled, "I would murder the lot of them. My father David and all my half-brothers if I must, but Amnon, whom I despise most of all, must die, even at the risk of my own life. If one good thing has come from this many years of barbs and jabs based on my Canaanite heritage cloaked in good fun, my eyes have now been open to the cruel insults." The young man then fell silent.

"Speak on, young Absalom," nudged Ahithophel.

"My mother is a Canaanite, making my sister and me of mixed heritage. We will never be fully accepted as pure-blood Hebrews. I will never be king while David and my half-brothers live. My sister will neither be completely recognized as a princess of Israel. Now I realize the slights and barbs my siblings expressed that I thought to be mere playful jests but were, in fact, said in harmful and hurtful earnestness.

Therefore, Amnon was not held in contempt or suffered the king's ire," Absalom concluded with hurt in his eyes.

"I feel your pain and outrage, slandered prince. The rape of your sister Tamar has uncovered a festering wound of ridicule. You now realize that you and your sister have been belittled in the eyes of the royal family and all your brothers. But then, on the other hand, I applaud your lengthy restraint of word and deed. You have blinded all suspicious eyes; they have no thought or fear of a deadly and calculated reprisal. Terror and shock are the handmaidens of revenge. Now, the question is, what can be done to elevate you to the highest level of power?"

At this moment, Ahithophel's eyes rolled back as if inspired by the divine. A kernel of a scheme took root and spouted blood-soaked vines of treason. He had decided on a life-and-death plan that would leave no loose ends.

"The objective here would be to gather the king and all the princes in one unprotected location. Does a particular place or time come to mind, Absalom?"

The younger man took a few moments to think before answering, "It is soon the time of sheep shearing at my Baal-Hazor property. It is located beside Ephraim's border and about eight miles south of Jerusalem. An accompanying festival with overflowing wine and unbridled merriment going long into the night."

"That sounds ideal, if not perfect. First, you must invite all the king's sons. It would be best to press the unabashed revelry and relief from mind-numbing boredom. Stress that gaiety is the welcomed reprieve from the everyday privileged palace monotony. Once your brothers have committed to attend, then and only then approach your father, the king, with an invitation to attend the festivities. Stress the importance of freedom from the rigid protocol of royalty. David must be present at the sheep-shearing festival. When the king and all the princes are in one place, you can take revenge on Amnon, the king, and all his would-be successors. With one fell swoop, my dear friend, you can become the next king of Israel by right of conquest."

"I have no words. My tongue is stuck to its roof. Your plan is daring; better yet, such a move would be completely unexpected, a murderous massacre of the king and all his sons. Nothing like this has been done in Israel since Abimelech killed his seventy half-brothers. As of the last count, I only have eighteen half-brothers."

Ahithophel nodded. "Our strategy depends on David being at hand. You will have to invite all your brothers, but remember to save Amnon for last, avoiding the slightest hint of suspicion by making his invitation an afterthought. If David is not inclined to come, press him as hard as you might, but even then, he may not consent. He has keen instincts and evades many a well-laid trap to the bewilderment of many an overconfident adversary. If David agrees, I will gather a band of seasoned killers with a long-standing hatred for the king. If David declines, I will not take part in the assassination of the princes; David's vengeance would be unrelenting. He would find me out no matter where I hid or how long it took. Do not forget to ask David to permit you to allow Amnon to attend as a consolation if he refuses to participate. You alone will have to see his slaughter. David is sure to ask why you want Amnon to go. Tell him, 'You wish to show your brother that you harbor no ill will or hurt feelings for his past youthful lapse of judgment.' It is now time for you to depart, young prince who would be king, and invite your brothers and father. Remember, when asking them to the sheep shearing, portray a cheerful mood so as to help encourage their attendance at our carnival of carnage."

CHAPTER SIXTEEN
A Royal Slaughter

R oyal protocol demanded a personal invitation and a sincere commitment to attend the sheep-shearing festival at Baal-Hazor, which is on the border of Ephraim. Each of the eighteen sons of David had varied appetites, but Absalom promised fulfillment of such unique pleasures to entice ready agreements. For instance, Solomon was fond of wine and women, while Adonijah always fancied himself as being the one in charge. One thing they all had in common was that they reveled in any excuse to escape from the boredom of the palace routine. In time, each brother agreed and pledged to attend, which continued to build momentum as everyone wanted to be acknowledged. It wasn't easy, though, taking weeks of coaxing and flattery along with the promise of a she-mule, a generous gift for their attendance from Absalom, their host, and Gershurite half-brother.

The critical invitation to David, king of Judah and Israel,

his father, had to be well prepared if he were to become the only living heir to the thrones of three kingdoms.

David was alone in his study, pondering his next move, for he had run out of worlds to conquer. He was now the master of all he surveyed. A guardian at the entrance announced Absalom's request for admittance. Granting his permission with a nod, David was glad to see his tall and beautiful son, and he inquired, "What good fortune brings you to my door this glorious day that the Lord God has made my beloved Absalom?" Showing his humility, Absalom bowed and began, "Lord king, it is time for the sheep shearing and the accompanying festivities. My section is well stocked with food and a delicious vintage of new wine. The shearers, wives, and young daughters gather with the local townspeople for revelry, music, and dancing. I pray thee that you join me with your household servants in attendance."

The king paused in thought for a moment before saying, "Nay, my son, the cost would be burdensome for me to go down to Baal-Hazor with my extended staff of servants, and you, my dear Absalom, will be chargeable personally as a matter of course. But in any event, I am not so inclined."

Absalom pressed, "Father, I sincerely wish you would reconsider. I will gladly pay all the necessary expenses to encourage your participation. I look forward to your esteemed company and wondrous tales of conquest."

"No, do not press my good favor and instead accept my decision. I will, however, give you a father's blessing that your travels will be in the safety of the sun's warm light and that your festivities will fulfill all the needs, wants, and desires of your innermost heart."

"I thank you, Father, but to ease my disappointment in your absence, will you allow my brother Amnon to attend the shearing as my guest?"

"Why do you wish the company of Amnon?"

"To show that no ill feelings or unresolved disputes exist between us. If it pleases the king, grant me leave that all my brothers may attend to partake in my hospitality of brotherhood and friendship, enjoining the gaiety of lighthearted comradery."

"You have my consent to invite all my sons to the sheep shearing in Baal-Hazor. Now be off with you; I have ambassadors clamoring for favors, lands, and titles."

Without further ado, Absalom left for Giloh, a short three-mile trek south of Jerusalem to counsel with his mentor, Ahithophel.

Approaching the old oracles' rustic home, Absalom tied off his she-mule and drank his fill of sweet county water. Meanwhile, hearing the bray, Ahithophel put away his puttering and planting in his garden oasis. He then hurriedly strode to his guest, with his crown of long gray hair full of the wisdom and knowledge of God rustled in the rising wind. He was extremely anxious to get the news as to whether David consented to attend the sheep-shearing festival with his entire male heirs or not, thus putting his plan for a royal massacre into motion.

Absalom bowed in deference and began, "Hail, master oracle, I come bearing vital news that we need to discuss at length."

"Let us retire to my study where I can catch my breath and take the world's weight off my legs."

Upon entering the room, a familiar-looking fellow named Nigel addressed Ahithophel, "Is there anything required, master?"

"Yes, two brown nut bowls and a cool wineskin of our newest vintage to refresh our royal guest."

Absalom looked puzzled and thought he recognized the servant, so he called out, "Nigel, is that you?"

Without missing a step, Nigel replied, "Yes, Prince Absalom, it is I. The king gifted me to serve Lord Ahithophel upon his retirement. Will there be anything else?" Ahithophel shook his head, and Nigel nodded and set out for the wine cellar.

Once alone, Ahithophel began, "Please tell me, young prince, what have you put forth? Please do not overlook any detail you consider unnecessary or immaterial, no matter how trivial."

"As you suggested, I cordially invited all my brothers except for Amnon and patiently waited for their pledges to attend. Amnon was lastly sought. As you know, Amnon takes what he wants by force or guile and will not be denied. He is spoiled and unbridled and does not take rejection in stride. I heard he felt disheartened and sullen, believing he had been left behind. But when I invited him, he cheerfully agreed as if given a reprieve from the monotony and boredom of palace life. I used this ploy to remove any suspicion or fear of reprisal, as he was nothing more than an afterthought."

As Ahithophel watched on, Absalom continued, "I asked

David to attend, but his seasoned excuse was the sizeable expense and a chargeable amount to transport and maintain his needed entourage. I pressed as much as I dared and said, 'I would gladly reimburse his treasury, for it was a small price to pay for the pleasure and honor of his company.' But he would not budge, and he was steadfast in his refusal. So, as a consolation, I was granted royal permission to invite Amnon and all the king's sons to Baal-Hazor. Oh, yes, he did ask why I wished for Amnon's presence. I replied, 'To prove that no ill feelings or unresolved disputes exist between us.' So, I first invited all my brothers, thus putting our plan into motion, and then sought David's approval later. I would rather ask for forgiveness than permission that could cause suspicion and then suffer denial of my petition."

Sighing in frustration, Ahithophel whispered, "Either by dumb luck, fate, or God's will, David always makes the right move and, in this case, a deadly dodge. Therefore, I too will show restraint and not attempt any murderous action against the house of David."

Absalom roared in response, "I would still love to kill all my backstabbing siblings. What better place as they will be gathered in one place, the sheep-shearing festival, and all by my calculated invitation? Amnon's death would be a bonus and deliciously sweet revenge."

At that moment, a nut-brown bowl hit the floor and clattered behind the slightly opened hallway door.

"Is that you, Nigel?" Ahithophel questioned.

"Yes, lord, it is I. Apologies, I tripped and clumsily lost my footing. A thousand pardons for the interruption."

Ahithophel, leery of being exposed, questioned, "It would disturb me to think you overheard our delicate and private conversation. The consequences could be easily misunderstood as treasonous at the highest level, and retribution would be swift and deadly. In other words, you could jeopardize me and your position here, and any slip of the tongue could forfeit lives."

"No, lord, not a word. I slipped just as I approached the door; I heard nothing, nothing at all."

Nigel lied to ensure his living. He had been shaken to the core upon hearing Absalom's outburst and his damming words about executing a royal massacre.

Ahithophel stressed, "Keep in mind my warning of having a loose tongue and busy lips just in case your hearing and recollection become uncertain about what was spoken. Now go and leave us."

"Yes, my lord."

Forced to withdraw his support, with a heavy heart, Ahithophel admitted, "I cannot and will not take part in this scheme for you to become king. It was solely conditional on the king's attendance. Slaying all the sons of David without a full complement of mercenaries would be foolhardy, and even if you succeeded, David's wrath would be unrelenting. You would have accomplished nothing besides presenting yourself as a bloodthirsty murderer forever looking over your shoulder."

Ahithophel took a deep breath before continuing, "On the other hand, killing Amnon is a delicate matter. He raped your sweet virgin sister Tamar and, worse yet, left her to suffer the scorn of abandonment. Your father was furious, but he took no action. I am sure he thought it best to keep this shameful incident wrapped up as a private family mishap so as to avoid a public scandal. The lack of punishment gives you a license for retribution, even a killing could be considered justifiable. With ample time all could be forgiven once wounds heal and the dust settles. How the deed is done also needs careful consideration to ensure your survival. Now this is important… do not inflict the killing stroke with your own hands. Your brothers could rise and slaughter you without a second thought or a moment's notice. Instead, order your servants to strike when Amnon is drunk and take aim for his heart.

"It would be best to assure your novice assassins that there will be no punishments because they dutifully followed your orders. Your brothers will kill them on the spot, giving you time to slip away unnoticed. Then, the lot of them will hurriedly depart, not knowing who or what is lurking in the darkness, perhaps ready to spring and kill the rest of them. Make sure you have enough supplies to make it safely to Geshur and stop for nothing or no one. You will be afforded protection from David's initial reaction to seek vengeance by fleeing to your grandfather, King Talmai's domain. Still, you will not be out of danger until you cross the Gershurite border."

CHAPTER SEVENTEEN

Murder Overheard and Overdone

"Nigel, where are you?" Ahithophel barked.

"Coming, my lord, I will be there in less than a moment," Nigel's voice forecasted from far down the hall corridor. Slightly panting, he entered the seer's study. "Yes, my lord, what would you have of me?"

"I need you to go to Jerusalem and pick up some writing tools, ink, and reed pens. Also, purchase an epha each of oats, barley, and figs. As well as a cruse of olive oil and a homer of oats. Here is a shekel, negotiate well and be back by eventide. The difference in time and money is yours to enjoy. Now be off with you, my good and faithful servant."

With the promise of pocket change and some time to spend it, Nigel rushed to hitch up the she-mule to the rickety farm cart and was off in a trot to the bustling metropolis of Jerusalem.

The grease that ensures rapid completion is the incentive of pleasure and pocket money.

Nigel crossed over Zion's gate in record time. First things first, the finest squid ink and the sharpest reed pens. Then to the farmer's bazaar for barley, oats, and figs. He negotiated to half a perutah and squeezed his master's shekel, thus increasing its face value. He would not let go until each merchant began to perspire and threw their hands up in a near-profitless transaction.

With all his supplies loaded and time to spare, Nigel slaked his thirst at a once familiar haunt—the Red Heifer, a shady oasis where the wine cups overflowed for a fair price.

Entering the windowless hut, Nigel was met with the familiar smell of musty urine and fresh sweat. The den was dim, and it took a moment to adjust to the light of flickering candles. Then, homing in on a familiar voice, the face of an old comrade came into focus. Nigel cried with glad recognition, "Milo! I suspected you would be here. Are you still telling anyone who will listen to your tales of our younger days in the army of David?"

"Nigel, I haven't seen you since you left the king's mansion three months ago. You just seemed to disappear. Rumor was you were gifted to the old seer Ahithophel when he left Jerusalem for his county home."

"That is all true and correct, as the old sage keeps me busy. I was sent here to purchase some sundries and was given some free time and the spare change from the fruits of my steely negotiations."

"Excellent news. Let us have a wineskin to celebrate your fleeting reprieve from bondage."

Milo called out to a stout fellow wearing a red-stained

apron and standing before a cadre of wine barrels, "My good man, we thirst and need some of your finest ambrosia to wash away sadness and celebrate merriment and gladness. A wineskin, please, my good man! And be quick about it; our time is short, and we must be back in our places before sundown."

A plump bota bag was carefully offered, waiting for payment before letting go of the liquid ambrosia. Nigel emptied his pockets and gladly paid for the wistful nectar of the gods with his entire day's profits.

Two brown nut bowls were wiped clean with the end of the server's apron and placed on a splintered tabletop.

"Drink up," Milo smiled and poured another round to the delight of the thirsty Nigel.

Nigel inquired, "What are your duties in and about the king's mansion?"

"I have a great job; I deliver meals to the men in the watch tower. I service the needs of the night guards. I carry their food up and their slop bucket down. The stairs are tiring, but nobody bothers me late in the day, and I get all I can eat. I often watch the evening sky give up its light and witness the bustling city bed down for the night."

Milo soon became boisterous, getting louder with each joy-filled gulp. But, on the other hand, Nigel said nothing as if possessing a great secret.

"What ails you, man? You sit there like a ghost without a tongue or voice?" Milo curiously questioned his sullen drinking companion.

If the truth is known, wine loosens the tongue inside the

bowl, and heads could roll.

Nigel sighed heavily and began, "I have something haunting me, but I am afraid to give my thoughts wings. If voiced in the wrong ears, it could cause untold turmoil. So, I will unburden myself, but only if you give me your word that you will keep my confession confidential and nothing I say will ever pass your lips, so swear to me by Adonai your silence is a covenant between us."

"I so swear, now speak on; you can rely on my discretion," Milo replied.

"Do you know who Absalom is?"

"Certainty, King David's larger-than-life, half-Canaanite son. He is known for importing Gershurite she-mules and his poled long hair that hangs below his knees. But what about him?"

"Well, he is a regular visitor to Ahithophel's country house. One day, he came alone and, as usual, sought counsel with the seer."

Milo lamented, "I can tell you will make a long story endless. So let me pour another bowl to ease the wait and loosen your tongue; speak on."

Nigel nodded and then continued, "The master summoned me to fetch some new wine, and I promptly returned to the study with fresh vintage and two brown nut bowls as requested. I approached the partially opened study door, and that is when I heard Absalom's blood-curdling outburst, 'I would still love to kill all my backstabbing siblings. What better place, as they will be gathered in one place, the sheep-shearing festival and all by my subtle invitation? Amnon's death would be a bonus and long-awaited revenge.' There I said it; it has been gnawing at me since I overheard the plans for a royal massacre. I feel like a weight has been lifted from my shoulders."

Suddenly less boisterous, Milo pondered what he heard carefully before saying, "Is it not best to tell the king of a pending slaughter of all his sons? There is probably a hefty reward and reams of gratitude. Moreover, it would put you in good stead with the king and undying devotion from a father."

"That might be very well true, but I was immediately questioned. I swore I heard nothing and that nothing I did not hear would give voice to my lips. Besides, there is no certainty that any of this could happen. I then would be made the fool and summarily executed for making such charges against a prince and his co-conspirator, my master Ahithophel, a former king's minister. But I had to tell someone to ease my conscience."

"A wise decision, Nigel. Your jeopardy is deadlier than any fleeting reward of gold and gratitude, especially when your life is forfeited for repeating a rash utterance that was said in anger and misunderstood. My friend, sundown approaches, and the wine is all but gone. I need to get back to the tower, and you back home and deliver your cargo while daylight permits. Fair thee well, my old comrade, and thanks for the wine and good company."

"Shalom, Milo, thanks again for your patient and wise counsel."

CHAPTER EIGHTEEN

Revenge Tis the Cold Relish That
Seasons Two Graves

All was made ready for the sheep-shearing festival: wine, food, music, and an abundance of young serving wenches in attendance. After delivering Absalom's generous party bribe, the gifting of eighteen stout Gershurite she-mules ensured participation.

It was late afternoon before eighteen of David's sons were saddled up in the mansion courtyard, and each prince sat anxiously upon their she-mule transport. The boys were excitedly anticipating several days of merrymaking and self-indulgence. It was a rarity that all the brothers were together in one place because rancor, politics, and mean-spirited competition were often the order of the day.

The siblings waited uneasily for their father's blessing. The restless mules strained at the bit, kicked and hawed, eager to stretch their legs on the open road.

David appeared on an upper balcony and began, "It does my heart good to see the princes of Israel together in harmony without bickering or fighting in unrelenting brotherly rivalry. Now go, my royal posterity, and sow your wild oats, and return rested and refreshed, ready to do a man's work for God and Israel."

A cheer echoed off the parapet walls, and the gathering was off in a trot that quickly turned into a race for Zion's gate. Absalom had left earlier with his needed servants in tow to the sheep-shearing stalls and the garland-laden main hall in preparation for his night of death and destruction.

The race to the gate was soon reduced to a trot; both animal and rider needed a breather from the headlong sprint to be the leader. Many of the princes were not comfortable in the saddle. Some spun unseated and nearly tumbled to the ground. Many passing hours were filled with small talk and complaints of sore bottoms, cramping legs, and pounded crotches. Finally, the pack of princes approached Absalom's compound at Baal-Hazor. The main house was surrounded by sheepcotes and shown to be as bright and full of light as the sun. Absalom greeted his weary brothers with a blazing torch that snapped and popped with the sparks of menacing hatred. Then, wearing an inflated smile to hide his murderous intent, and in the most cheerful tone, he declared, "Welcome to my home away from home. All has been made ready for your comfort and pleasure. I have just tapped a barrel of my special red wine. I have been saving this full vintage for just such an occasion. A feast of lamb, leaven bread, figs, and sweet date cakes will be served once you have slaked your thirst, so please eat and drink to your heart's content."

Solomon was first to dash for the flowing river of dark red wine and its promise of ease and comfort from the first swallow. He was fond of wine; some would say a little too fond. In fact, his mother, Bathsheba, often scolded him for his reckless drinking. Amnon followed close behind; he, too, had an excessive taste for the grapes that gave way to laxity and grandiosity and often unbridled his darkest passions.

The feast was delivered as promised. The wine was excellent, and the meat was succulent. The serving wenches winked and flirted with the rowdy crowd, and some hinted at an after-hours rendezvous. A curious addition was that candles had been generously strewn about, lighting dark corners and brightening shadowy alcoves.

The time was ripe, and the stage was set to pluck vengeance's low-lying fruit.

Absalom called his trusting servants, "I command you to watch for when Amnon's heart is merry with wine. Then, I will signal from the shadows to smite Amnon. Strike deep and kill him without thought or hesitation!"

One servant, concerned about committing such a heinous act, protested, "But, lord, will we not be liable by the king's judgment?"

Absalom convinced his amateur assassins, "Fear not, for I have commanded you; I alone will be held responsible on the day of reckoning. You are but an instrument that wields my long-overdue need for justice. Be courageous and valiant in the execution of my will."

Soon, the moment arrived, and Absalom, in a hushed

whisper from the shadows, said, "Strike, strike now!"

Stinging blades were raised high above the slayers' heads. One from the right and one to the left, piercing Amnon's heart with such force and speed that it exploded. His death rattle caught in his throat, leaving him gurgling blood and exhaling a whimper of shock and surprise.

The sobering effect of witnessing such a horrific display spurred the princes to draw their swords and dispatch Absalom's bewildered servants before they could utter a word in their defense. Meanwhile, Absalom was nowhere to be found. He had slipped out of the back to his waiting and well-provisioned she-mule before anyone could make sense of just what happened. Absalom had upended several candles in his hasty flight to get away, adding to the confusion with smoke and fire. The cracking blaze stampeded the lambs, and they started to bleat, baa, and cry in a panicked frenzy. They then proceeded to batter the walls of the wooden sheepcote pens in a desperate attempt to escape the threatening holocaust.

Solomon took charge by counting heads and warning, "We must leave this place at once as this could very well be a prelude to a massacre!"

Heeding their brother's warning of an impending bloodbath, all the king's sons arose and fled back to Jerusalem, spurring their she-mules into action. They galloped for their lives without wasting a moment in idle chatter.

Back in Jerusalem, Milo was climbing the tower steps with food for the night watch. A guard called out after hearing the echo of footfalls approaching the uppermost landing. "Is that you, Milo?"

"Yes, tis I, the night cook, with a portion of cold mutton to ease your hunger."

"Milo, you have perfect timing; set your eyes eight miles south, and just below the horizon, there is evidence of a fiery commotion at Absalom's country holdings. It was the destination of all the king's sons who had departed, one and all, late this very afternoon."

Riveted, Milo watched the growing blaze and rising smoke with nervous anticipation. He immediately recalled Nigel's story about hearing Absalom's boastful wish to kill all his siblings.

Unnerved by the unfolding turmoil, even viewed from such a great distance, Milo was convinced that Absalom had accomplished his vicious goal and that the king must be immediately told so action could be taken to arrest the wrongdoers.

Milo flew down the tower steps and went to the king's balcony. David often stayed up late into the night. It was his favorite time when he could be alone and speak to God directly, like one man talking to another without constant interruptions. He also loved the majesty of stars and the wonders of all creation found solely in the night sky.

David's personal guards challenged the anxious intruder, "Who goes there, and who dares disturb the king during his private time of prayer and meditation?"

"My name is Milo, a servant to the king and a former soldier in the army of God who served under King David's command in many a fearsome battle. I have an urgent and personal message for the king's ears only."

One of the guards took his leave and approached the king,

"Your majesty, please excuse the interruption, but a fellow is at the door requesting an audience. His name is Milo, a former soldier under your command. He insists on delivering a personal and urgent message for only you to hear."

"Milo? I have not seen this man since the siege of Rabbah; by all means, let him join me. I crave his company," the king replied.

"Great warrior king," Milo bowed in respect as he entered the room, "I know how much you detest small talk, so that I will get to the unsettling and criminal matter directly. I was up in the watching tower and witnessed a blazing hold and sheepfold near Ephraim's border, where Absalom invited all your sons to the sheep-shearing festival. I believe from hearing a rumor of gossip that I dismissed as fanciful at the time that it might be very well true and correct."

"What? Speak, man, of this trouble, and be done with it once and for all!"

Milo took a deep breath before answering, "Absalom had plans to gather all your sons in one place and murder everyone, leaving no one alive. I believe, great king, that Amnon has accomplished this heinous feat, evidenced by the fire on the horizon in the course to Baal-Hazor."

David's face turned ashen, and he began reflecting on all that had happened. An exceptional amount of effort and forethought went into Absalom's plan to massacre the house of David. The only thing that spared David was his refusal to participate in this now obvious assassination plot, not once but twice. If there was a saving grace, something did not feel right, so he refused to attend, and that decision could have saved his life and dynasty.

David retired to the garden and, in the act of Kriah, tore his garments in grief and anger and laid upon the earth lamenting the loss of so many loved ones. All in attendance stood by and tore their garments in solidarity with the king.

The ugly news of the slaughter of sons whipped through the crevices, cracks, and corridors until everyone awoke and lamented such a grievous act.

Jonadab approached David, saying, "Uncle, let not my Lord suppose that Absalom has slain all the young men, the beloved sons of the king. I pray that you believe me when I say only Amnon is dead. I was Amnon's best friend and counseled him that it was only a matter of time before Absalom took revenge on him. I could sense that Absalom was determined from the very day of the rape to seek justice from when Amnon forced his sister Tamar to lay beside him, and he knew her. Unfortunately, my dear uncle, it is well known in the family that you had declined to inflict punishment or consequence on Amnon. Your complete lack of action forced Absalom's hand to seek honor for the violation of his beloved sister, an unaddressed insult that festered and turned deadly."

Just as Jonadab made an end to speaking, the young man who kept the high tower watch looked out and witnessed the princes galloping over the hillside directly behind him and peeled the excellent news that echoed in the ears of the king. Jonadab was pleased with himself and said to the king, "Behold, the king's sons are here, just like I predicted!"

Seventeen of the king's sons passed over the threshold and

announced the loss of Amnon and their continued well-being to their father, the king. They all wept sore, as did David and all his servants, both for gladness and sorrow.

The initial shock lessened, and Adonijah found himself counting his blessings. With Amnon eliminated, he had moved up in the line of succession and was now a viable contender for the throne of Israel.

"Who witnessed the murder? Was it Absalom's hand that struck the fatal blow?" David demanded.

Speaking up from the back of the hall, Solomon recounted the killing, "I did not see Absalom directly, but I caught a glimpse of him running from the aftermath. Two of his servants hid in the dark, waiting until Amnon was merry with wine before stepping out of the shadows and striking with vengeance. Those of us close by, and after we collected our senses, drew our swords and dispatched the felons before they could speak or run into the night. Unfortunately, in the distraction, Absalom escaped, leaving three corpses and a trail of fire. He was last seen mounting his well-provisioned she-mule and disappearing into the night."

David listened carefully to every word, thinking hard before speaking, "I know where the young man went. It is the only place I cannot follow him unless I declare war on my father-in-law and longtime ally. Absalom went to seek sanctuary with his grandfather, King Talmai of the Geshurite. I long to go forth and seek Absalom and balance the scales of justice. But I will not be consoled or comforted until Absalom forfeits his life."

CHAPTER NINETEEN
Beyond Et-Tell, A Coup Unattended

Towering over his beast of burden, Absalom made a striking silhouette against the setting sun. His distinctive long hair was now tangled and gritty from the gusty winds and clumping mud. He skirted the well-traveled roadways and stayed to the unmarked hills and valleys. He rested at night without the comfort of a warming campfire or dining on the roasted fat of a succulent rabbit. The chances of pirates and brigands were lessened by keeping to the goat paths, but the main threat came from the fear of David's far-reaching and unrelenting need to balance the scales of justice.

After cresting the last steep hill, he viewed the tall towers of Et-Tell. Finally, Absalom could take a deep breath and release the tension in his neck from constantly looking over his shoulder and straining to see if David's minions were gaining on him. Absalom began to heal both his body and soul once he saw his mother's ancestral home.

The gate guardian recognized the weather-worn prince and alerted the king that his grandson approached alone, covered in dust and mud. Talmai received the disturbing news and hurriedly appeared at the opening gate to welcome his grandson with a familiar, friendly face.

"Grandfather, it is I, Absalom."

"I can see that; your presence gladdens my eyes and enlarges my heart, but your wretched state disturbs me. Why is a prince of Israel and Geshur traveling alone through the wilderness without servants, guards, or companions?" Impulsive in his compassion, Talmai hugged his bedraggled grandson and commented, "You have slept on the ground, evidenced by the burrs and beggars' ticks in your hair and tattered clothing. Before we have a searching and fearless account of your exploits, you must go up, eat a hot meal, drink your fill, and rest. Know that you are now safe and secure in the bosom of your family. I have informed your sister Tamar that you are joining us here at Et-Tell, and for all intents and purposes, this was a planned extended stay. A surprise, if you will. There is no sense in disturbing the girl with sordid details.

"Until we speak at length, I can only guess that some powerful force beyond these borders is seeking your destruction. Tamar would be heartbroken to see you in such a wretched state. Therefore, let us delay the reunion with your sister until you recover and regain some likeness of your former beautiful self."

Absalom nodded in agreement as his grandfather continued, "In the meantime, I will provide you with fitting royal attire, and we will burn your filthy rags. Now go, Absalom, my exhausted grandson. We will meet in private, but only once you fully recover. You can then tell me of the trials and mishaps that have brought you to my door in this wretched condition."

Absalom was escorted to the reserved family apartments, where he washed the grit and grime from his sorrow. He savored the ease and comfort of the first gulp of potent red wine. Feeling fresh and relaxed, he hungrily ate his fill of sweet fatted calf before laying in a soft duck-down feathered bed. He slept nonstop for a day and a half, so unmoving and still that his breathing was often checked to confirm that he was still quick and not dead.

After finally rising from his death-defying slumber, Absalom felt stiff and groggy. His hunger was ravenous, while his need to tell all he had endured was just as pressing.

A standing order from the king, when Absalom stirred, he was to be informed and brought forthwith to the dining hall.

The king was the first to arrive, followed by Tamar, anxious and delighted to see her brother's face in the safe confines of their grandfather's domain. Knowing the ravenous appetite of this virile young man, Talmai had ordered enough breakfast to feed half a dozen men.

A short time later, Absalom arrived outfitted with his customary royal trappings. His luxurious hair was polled with oil and powdered with gold, not waiting for his yearly grooming ritual to feel beautiful and powerful again.

Tamar excitedly ran over with a generous hug for Absalom's ongoing loving support and on the whispers that he had avenged her honor.

"Brother, you look well and completely healed, even regal, considering your ordeal of solo travel through the wilderness."

Sitting at the breakfast table and wolfing down a steaming bowl of porridge, a round of cheese, and a mountain of bread, Absalom blurted out between his gulps and chews, "I feel even better seeing my dear sister here in a safe place. I am glad you are here to hear my tale of a long overdue reckoning against Amnon, your defiler. But let me first enjoy my family's long-sought-after company. Allow me to eat my fill before explaining my attempted coup and the satisfaction one gets from vengeance well accomplished."

After a sigh of satisfaction from a full belly, Absalom addressed Tamar, "In our brief time together, your sorrow set my sure course of justice. Your retreat from the world because of Amnon's folly made me angry, while your pain was unrelenting. His cruelty to you troubled my every waking moment. Your misery and refusal to join polite society weighed heavily on my mind and increased my need for retribution. I was waiting for our father to acknowledge Amnon's crime. Privately, I know the king was furious, but publicly, he left the incident to the biting tongues of gossipmongers. He waited patiently until it all blew over as an unproven rumor. Father never admitted the incident openly. He preferred to keep it as a family matter so as to avoid a public scandal. I spoke to our mother about the incident, but she was in denial and defended David's every action. However, she did advise you, my gentle sister, to relocate to Et-Tell until everything settled down and short memories give way to more pressing matters."

Tamar looked down, hiding a tear and reliving the ordeal.

"Mother Maacah knew that eventually Amnon would be king. He could make all our lives a living hell if we attempted any criticism that would make him suffer public humiliation and social ridicule. I knew I had to bide my time because everyone expected an outburst of fury. So, I never spoke of my outrage and insult to my sister's dignity. When I could not avoid talking to Amnon on the rare social occasion, it was always pale, neither good nor bad. I took great lengths to disguise my seething hatred. Overhearing us, you would have supposed there was no lurking enmity or hidden agenda. For this, I required wise counsel from someone offended by David's excesses, the wisest seer in all of Jerusalem and David's former prime minister Ahithophel. He was Lady Bathsheba's grandfather, who resented his granddaughter's adulterous affair with David. The killing of her husband, Uriah the Hittite, and the grievous loss sustained seven days after the birth of his unnamed great-grandson."

Talmai agreed, saying, "All this is true and correct. The old sage has cause to lament and will make a fitting ally."

Absalom continued, "I contacted a go-between to arrange a meeting with the old sage at his country home three miles south of Jerusalem. My request for an audience piqued Ahithophel's curiosity, and he agreed to meet with me.

"We had an immediate rapport from a mutual dislike of David, our powerful and cunning adversary. We discussed in detail how to avenge my sister's honor and for me to become the next king of Israel in one calculated masterstroke. The oracle told me that being half-Canaanite and half-Hebrew, the throne room would never be mine to rule. At that moment, I realized the brotherly backbiting ridicule I had endured for these many years, which I had perceived as a playful jest, was masking the sting of prejudice. The insight clarified why Father did not punish Amnon for his rape because Tamar was a Canaanite of the Geshurite clan. She was looked down upon as lacking the essential pure-blood Hebrew heritage.

"The sage then advised me that time was my best ally, and I needed to prove that the hot burn of passion had grown cold and no longer recounted and fallen well below the everyday horizon.

"Ahithophel proposed festive gathering miles from Jerusalem, making a far-away location an ideal killing ground. It had been three years since Amnon's crime, and it was the time of my sheep-shearing celebration. I was to invite all my brothers, but Amnon lastly as if he was no more than an afterthought. Ahithophel counseled, 'That this sequence of events will belay any suspicion about your real intent. The key element to this political intrigue will be the attendance of your father, David. If we can get them all in one place, we can tidily dispatch them to the afterlife, leaving no monarch or claimants to the crown alive in the bloody aftermath. You will be the rightful master of Israel by default. Once we have accomplished this massacre, the elders will have no choice but to proclaim you their new sovereign and king.'

"Everything was going as planned. My half-brothers took a little coaxing, but with a gift of sturdy she-mules and the promise of a good time, I quickly gained their pledge to attend. But David refused, claiming the undue expense of his necessary staff and that he would have to pass that burden on to me. I cheerfully agreed to absorb the cost for the pleasure of his company, but he was steadfast in his refusal. I pressed him as much as I dared without tipping my hand. After the fact, and as a consolation, I obtained David's permission and blessing to invite Amnon and the rest of his sons to the sheep-shearing festival. Once hearing of David's refusal, Ahithophel backed out, saying, 'If David is alive and hears that all his sons were slaughtered, his fury would know no bounds and would hunt you and me down no matter how long it took, even to the ends of the earth. I would strongly urge ending Amnon's life and his alone. Fortunately, your retribution is justifiable in the eyes of many. In time, you could be reconciled with your father, that is, if he does not track you down and kill you to ease his suffering and salve the loss of his firstborn son and heir apparent.'

"The seer advised me not to employ the killing stroke by my hand but to have my servants deliver the death blow. I protested because it seemed cowardly, and I longed to pierce Amnon's black heart and gain a measure of satisfaction. But Ahithophel insisted that I remain discreet and direct the slaying from the shadows. He thought my brothers would immediately rise and kill the assassin without a second thought or question. During the ensuing confusion, it would give me the needed seconds to escape before my half-drunk brothers turned their vengeance on me for luring them into harm's way. I had my she-mule loaded and packed for the many miles to

Geshur. I stayed on the goat paths and spent fireless nights, shivering and shaking in an uneasy sleep. I was constantly warding off snakes and scorpions, seeking my body heat. Finally, the God of the Hebrews and the Geshurite gods led me here alive to your sanctuary doorstep and the haven of a loving family. The rest, now you know."

Overwhelmed with emotions, Tamar choked out, "Brother, you have restored my standing, but I am both relieved and saddened by the death of Amnon. He was the first and the only man I have ever known. A bond, emotional, spiritual, and physical, laments his passing. Yet, there is something in me that regrets his downfall. I am sure time will heal this unsettling sense of abandonment."

Spellbound by Absalom's incredible story, King Talmai rose and said, "I have much to ponder. We will have much to discuss reinstating you in David's good graces. But in the meantime, rest easy, as he will not dare to invade or make you afraid. I am David's ally and father-in-law. My borders are secure, and your safety here is assured."

CHAPTER TWENTY
Banishment and Redemption

Maacah pleaded with David for permission to visit her missing children, Tamar and Absalom. The siblings were together, settled in Bethesda at Et-Tell, the secure Gershurite castle. They remained guarded and protected by their maternal grandfather, King Talmai, son of Ammihud, a direct descendant of Rephaim and heir to the Nephilim race of giants.

Maacah approached David with a mother's plea for restraint, "My unsettled and impatient husband, I know your soul longs to go forth to set right a wrong in the murder of your firstborn Amnon, the rightful future claimant to the throne of Israel. But sadly, the slaying of our son Absalom will not bring back Amnon and will only serve to ignite a second burial pyre. When a pot boils over, and the froth attempts to drown its fire, it is time to remove the seething cauldron before it damages everything and everyone with its overwhelming scalding fury. It is for you, my dear husband and sovereign, to calm the nation's troubled waters and not to cause a wake of conflict."

The king remained silent as his wife continued her plea, "Tamar is soulful and heartbroken and has been made the fool in Israel. She now has her loving brother to comfort her stress and disgrace. Banish Absalom, deservedly so, for if he is out of sight, there will be no fuel to inflame your mind bent on justice for your dead son's folly. I can go forth as their loving mother and as your deputy to inform Absalom that his banishment is fixed and he dare not approach Jerusalem. If the king should behold his face, he will be executed without hesitation for insulting your righteous judgment."

Considering all that was imparted, David pondered his fourth wife's sage advice and praised her insights, "I have always admired you for more than just your stately beauty but also your fine-tuned mind. You can see far beyond the ordinary and are correct in your approach. Therefore, I cannot and will not embroil Israel in a war against my father-in-law and my Geshurite ally. Doing this only satisfies my need for justice for my oldest son, Amnon, by ending the life of another son, Absalom. So instead, I will do as you wisely suggest and enforce his death-defying banishment until cooler heads prevail or as God-conscious and good sense once again direct my thinking."

"With your permission, my lord king, I will take my leave and go to comfort Tamar and inform Absalom of his father's decree of absence or death. Fair thee well, my wise and merciful husband."

Sparing no expense, David gifted Maacah with all the necessary trappings of royalty on her journey.

A personal entourage of bodyguards, cooks, and maid-servants ensured her comfort while traveling through the wilderness. Finally, the train approached the Et-Tell gate with sounding horns and waving banners announcing the unexpected arrival of Princess Maacah of the Gershurite, consort to the king of Judah and Israel. The caravan master petitioned for entrance to the castle. King Talmai, her father, her two children, Tamar and Absalom, and cousins and courtly dignitaries were immediately alerted to form a welcoming party. Entering her former playground, Maacah jumped down from her well-appointed wagon onto the courtyard lawn and scurried to embrace her castaway children. Tears of joy ran down her cheeks as she choked back the news of Absalom's death sentence reprieve.

Onlookers held their distance, affording space for the family reunion. They witnessed a mother's sacred love for her banished offspring. Maacah dutifully recognized her father, the king. She nodded in respect and immediately clung to his neck, giddy with tears of joy. She whispered, "Father, much news must be imparted, but not here. It is a private family matter that is best discussed behind closed doors."

"Indeed, my dear child, assure me that no Israeli army was hot on your heels and headed for my gate in the act of war and that your only purpose was not that of a decoy so that I would relax and let down my guard."

"Father, dismiss your worries about a hostile invasion. My

spouse, the king of Israel, has no such intentions. Calmer heads have prevailed, at least for the time being. I have been deputized as an emissary to speak my husband's mind regarding his decree and disposition. To say any further in the open could put us all in jeopardy. Knowing David as I do, we must talk behind closed doors, even the trees have ears. His network of spies and informants is numerous and well-organized."

"I am pleased to witness that my daughter has grown up and has become wise in the ways of the world. Let us go to the castle-keep, far away from prying eyes and grounded ears. You can rest from your journey and reacquaint yourself with friends and family once you have revealed David's decree and the nature of Absalom's punishment."

King Talmai gave the order at once and explained to the waiting throng that their need for privacy was paramount because of a critical dispatch that needed to be discussed at once. The trusted palace guardians led the immediate family members to the inner sanctum. Talmai ordered some freshly cooked meat, a round of cheese, and a skin of vintage wine and remarked, "I always hunger after travel, and wine is especially needed to wash down the choking dust." Once the meal was delivered, to ensure that even his trusted servants were not in earshot, he commanded, "Stand alert on the far side of the passageway and let no one approach more than ten paces."

He then slammed home the inner bolt to seal the thick wooden door tightly shut, thus shielding all uttered words with oak.

The king began, "Maacah, drink some wine to relax your

tongue and speak of your urgent matter. Then, tingle our ear with King David's decree. Speak up, madam, as we are held in life and death suspense."

The princess was parched and took a generous gulp from the wine skin to wet her lips, ease her mind, and comfort her senses. She looked around the table and then locked eyes with her son Absalom.

"Absalom, my beautiful son. Prince of Israel and rightful heir to Geshur. I agree that you have avenged your sister's honor with deadly accuracy. Your half-brother Amnon is no more. You were patient with your revenge, a sure mark of nobility. Your father took no action, punishment, or public acknowledgment of this grievous act against his house. He was furious privately but wanted to avoid widespread scandal, undermining the future king of Israel's ability to rule. But you have found grace in his eyes; if not justifiable, at the very least, your act was understandable. The good news, my dear son, is that your death sentence has been reduced to a lifetime banishment. David has made it abundantly clear that you will be put to death without hesitation if he sees your face. All is not lost; your patience will be tested. For time blunts anger. He has seventeen other sons who are all vying for his favor to be named the next king. Bide your time here in Geshur. I cannot think of a better mentor than your grandfather. He will advise your best action to recapture the king's good graces, but not until the moment presents itself."

Maacah then turned her gaze and thoughts to her daughter, "As for you, my beautiful Tamar, your father, the king, conceded that 'Tamar can come and go as she pleases and will be afforded all the rights and privileges of a princess of Israel. She can return to Absalom's lodgings and make them her own if desired.'

"However, I urge my deflowered daughter to stay in Geshur, where scandal and gossip cannot bite or belittle your sense of belonging. Why enflame a still smoldering reputation? Also, I believe your presence in Jerusalem will keep Amnon's murder at the forefront of David's mind. So, remain here, my dear, where you are loved and cherished, for you and Absalom's ultimate benefit."

Absalom accepted his mother's warning, saying, "It is either life or death then, and I choose life. I am confident in my mother, who skillfully guided David's change of heart and mind. Therefore, I will stay here under the protection and guidance of my grandfather until the time is right to make my bid for power."

Tamar then confessed, "I prefer to stay here. I feel like a great weight has been lifted off me. My sisters are all catty prima donnas. They take every chance to demean and disparage me and quickly remind me that I am of a blended heritage, not pure in the house of Israel and not a sanctified princess in the eyes of many. However, God works in mysterious ways with His wonders to perform. I am now free from that torment, but I must admit that the price of my peace of mind was to escape to my mother's culture."

Clasping her father's hand, Maacah solicited his vast experience, "Great king, do you have some wise insights into our dilemma?"

"My dear daughter, I could not be any prouder. You are indeed the future mother of kings and queens. Grandchildren are a gift from the gods to ease an old man's passing. So, I welcome Absalom and Tamar to make Et-Tell their permanent home. Tamar is a delight; she always sees my comfort and needs, and I look forward to teaching Absalom about human nature and, more importantly, political intrigue. From his birth, I had envisioned him wearing three crowns. So let us look to that future."

CHAPTER
TWENTY-ONE
The Trade Value of Goodwill and a Barley Field

For many years, Talmai was grounded in the teaching of warfare and civil conspiracy. Absalom was learning from a master, his grandfather, the king of Geshur, who was a wizard in both strategy on the battlefield and in the back corridors of political intrigue.

Princess Maacah had permission to visit her home whenever she wished and exported a ready supply of she-mules to princes and nobles. This ensured that the two kingdoms remained cordial trading partners and strengthened their military alliance.

On one such trip about three years after the killing of Amnon, Maacah cheerfully announced to her father and children, "It seems David has put away his anger and his need for revenge and never speaks of Amnon or Absalom and acts as if both were dead. I dare not approach him about Absalom's banishment as this might be the spark that rekindles his desire for justice for his dead son and leaves a question in the line of succession."

Talmai replied, "Interesting. The time might be ripe to go forward with our plans to overturn Absalom's banishment and to get him close to the seat of power. The least you know, the better, my dear Maacah; it is best for your safety and peace of mind. If questioned, you can honestly answer that you knew nothing about any plans or designs."

King Talmai turned to his grandson with excitement in his voice. "Absalom, please accompany me. Let us walk long, for we have much to discuss."

Entering the garden gate, Talmai signaled his ever-present bodyguards to hang back well beyond earshot.

After a long period of silence that allowed Talmai time to collect his thoughts, he turned to his grandson. "What a beautiful day, a cooling breeze and the warm sun on my cheek. It is one of the simple pleasures only appreciated when your journey is nearing its end." Talmai heightened his tone, causing Absalom to pay closer attention. "Now, young man. Listen carefully to what I am about to tell you. Your three-year wait was not in vain, although you often thought it a bitter trial of patience. It took that much time to cool your father's searing anger that has now turned into acceptance. We need a disinterested third party with access to David's ear, and that is adept in crafty manipulation. Someone whom David might owe a favor and would be sympathetic to your plight in promoting your father's forgiveness and recall to his court. Does anyone in David's circle of influence come to mind?"

"Well, grandfather, now that you mention it, someone might fit that description: my cousin, Chief Captain Joab, David's middle nephew. We are neighbors and have always enjoyed a cordial and even likable relationship. Lord Ahithophel and I have become very close, and as you know, he had planned my near-successful coup attempt and the slaughter of Amnon. He also aided in my narrow escape from the sure vengeance of my brothers. Ahithophel had disclosed to me that Joab had devised the killing of Uriah the Hittite by the sword of Amon under the direction of David. That would mean David is obliged to him. Joab always seeks wealth and power and holds a grudge once crossed. He has a mean streak and a killer's instinct, so we must be cautious."

He paused before continuing, "Joab has eyed my adjacent barley field and offered to purchase it several times. Because it is so productive, I have been reluctant to part with that section. Yet, I am confident that, if I offered that choice land in exchange for his assistance, he would find a way to get me back into Jerusalem with the king's blessing."

The boy's grandfather looked thoughtful as he responded, "I believe your cousin Joab is the very man we seek. However, we are too great a distance to meet in person without raising suspicions. We will first solicit his help by citing his goodwill and the exchange of the coveted parcel. If he agrees, we can count on his greed and a creative conspiracy to complete your restoration of privileges. We will write to him with your proposal. First, the banishment from Jerusalem must be lifted, but that does not ensure the king's good graces or the invitation back into his presence. We must stress that these two conditions must be met to secure the barley field. The second obstacle is getting you back into David's presence, which might be more challenging than overcoming your exile. Seeing the king's face will be a significant hurdle, requiring time for David to get used to the idea and remorseful humility on your part. Your contrition must appear genuine and sincere, as your life could depend on a convincing performance. Let us adjourn to my study and compose that letter that is your first step to gaining the throne of David."

Joab, chief captain of Israel, and Judah

My good neighbor and esteemed cousin. I hope this letter finds you well and in good health.

I am sure you know of my banishment for our cousin Amnon's death. This regretful circumstance, amongst other things, was only taken to restore my sister Tamar's honor. The poor girl was raped and cruelly cast out with unkind words and barred doors. I waited years for justice from your uncle, the king, and so David, my father, to take some punitive action but no punishment was forthcoming with the family scandal instead of being neatly swept under the carpet.

I now live here in Geshur under the protection of my grandfather, King Talmai. I was born in Hebron and grew up in Jerusalem with access to the Tabernacle of the congregation where the Holy Ark of the covenant resides. Although I am afforded every luxury, I feel like a stranger in the land of my giant forbearers. My sister Tamar is here of her own choice and is a daily comfort and reminder of my home in Judah. But I long to be back amongst familiar faces and, more importantly, to be reconciled with my father, the king. Cousin, you are known as a fearless warrior for your cunning and creativity in overcoming seemingly impossible barriers. I know my father always valued your opinion, and in this manner, I wish to implore and employ you to plead for my return to Jerusalem. By accomplishing this feat, I will assign a provisional deed to my adjacent barley field that you have so long sought after, and when the time comes that I can behold my father's face, I will make it a permanent transfer of ownership.

I pray you will agree with my proposal and that you will keep our communication secret and private. I look forward to restoring my rights, titles, and privileges with your assistance.

Your cousin, Absalom, prince of Israel, and Geshur.

Absalom inquired, "What do you think, grandfather? Will he take the bait?"

"I do, as you have covered all the factors that could lure him into our service. I especially like the 'valiant assistance' as it gives Joab a sense of the moral high ground instead of being a cheap opportunist trying to gain more ground. I have a trusted messenger who knows where to find Joab's residence. We must be patient; it will take Joab some time to devise and execute a plan. That is only if he agrees to take on the mission at all. Unfortunately, if he botches his approach, he can lose favor with David, put his chief captaincy in peril, and make your expulsion permanent. I have come away with the impression that David views Joab's talents and ambitions as a necessary evil. Joab's timing is also critical, as you must approach David when he is in the right frame of mind. If he is in a foul mood, heads will roll. We will probably not know the outcome until Joab is at our door to join you in exile or escort you back to Jerusalem and receive his provisional deed for services rendered.

On the other hand, we may have to resign ourselves to a prolonged silence. A direct assault on David would be fool-hardy. In time, he could mount a vast army consisting of his Philistine allies and men from all his conquered lands, from Edom in the south to Syria in the north. No, the only way to defeat David is from his family inside his house. It is our time to wait and to do nothing that might cause suspicion. Until then, we will continue to strategize our next move."

CHAPTER
TWENTY-TWO
Hatching the Scheme

A dust cloud appeared on the well-worn dirt road and entrance to the stately villa of Joab, son of Suri, the middle nephew of King David and the chief captain of Israel.

A giant of a man approached, astride a she-mule with a messenger bag hanging from his saddle. A guard at the compound entrance challenged the intruder, "Who goes there, and what is wanted?"

"I am a messenger from Geshur with a private and personal message for Lord Joab."

"Give it here; I will deliver it."

"No, I am tasked by my master to put it into his hands personally and without exception."

"All right, I will notify the chief captain as you wish. You wait here!"

Entering the villa, the guard found Joab and his older brother Abishai eating supper. The guard explained, "Please excuse my interruption, lord, but a messenger from Geshur has a private and personal message and claims he is tasked to give it to you and only you."

"All right, bring him in, but take his weapon. You cannot be too careful with strangers."

The messenger was swiftly disarmed and brought into Joab's presence.

"Lord Joab?" the messenger asked.

"Yes, it is. Now let me see what you have brought me that is so private and important as to disturb my supper."

After breaking the royal seal on the dispatch bag, Joab reached down, lifted it out, and began reading the letter. Joab shook his head and reread it before passing it to his brother Abishai.

Joab then turned to the Geshurite messenger, "I will have a response to take back to your master in the morning."

Joab addressed his guard, "Take this man to the kitchen to be fed. Stable his mule and show him to his quarters. Fetch him up and ready to ride at the end of the fourth watch."

"Yes, my lord."

The two men turned about and set off to the cookhouse.

Turning to Abishai, Joab inquired, "Well, what do you think of Absalom's proposal?"

"I think you must weigh in the balance of two factors. Are the gratitude of Absalom the forsaken and obtaining the desired barley field worth the chance of suffering David's ire?"

"All right, let us explore those two proposals. First, Absalom remains a prince of Israel and Geshur. Kileab, the innocent, David's second son, died fourteen years before he knew a woman's charms. That makes Absalom next in the line to be king of Israel. He is also the next king of Geshur. His favor could prove essential in maintaining our grip on power. Remember, David has accumulated enemies like down on a duck. This act of service could very well ensure I keep my chief captaincy long into the future. But in the end, our loyalties must remain with our uncle, the king. Besides, on a practical matter, Absalom's adjacent barley field is extremely productive and increases my holdings by twofold."

"It sounds to me that you have already decided to assist in Absalom's restoration. Brother, remember that Absalom is half-Gershurite, and for him to be accepted by the elders as the next king of Israel is unlikely. Although David will first adhere to tradition and nominate the eldest, in the end, he will choose whomever he favors to succeed him to the throne, over-ruling any challenge to his authority. In practice, I believe our best action is to plumb the depths of David's emotions. I no longer hear our uncle cursing Absalom or grieving for Amnon. Perhaps he is in a place of acceptance, and a direct approach would be agreeable and best serve our purpose."

"But how do you suggest we explore his complicated mind?" Joab inquired.

"Subtly, of course, and at supper. During some small talk, I will ask if he knows how Absalom is faring. After all, we are his cousins; therefore, inquiring about family matters should not be a great surprise. David's reaction should tell us all we need to know unless he visits one of his eight wives or ten concubines. He eats early, then takes a nap, rises at sundown, and retreats to his balcony for prayer and meditation under the stars. As a shepherd boy, he acquired the skill of guarding his sheep against lions, wolves, and jackals honed from his youth. Let us plan a visit tomorrow late afternoon. We will say that we happened to be close by and considered visiting our favorite uncle and checking on his well-being."

"My brilliant brother, indirect, yet telling. That will give us a starting point on how to make our approach or not at all. I will compose a short note to Absalom. To ease his mind and give him hope."

Absalom, prince of Israel, and Geshur

Dear Cousin,

At this very moment, I am considering how best to approach your father. Be assured, my esteemed cousin and good neighbor, I would gladly do you a good turn. The barley field is a gracious gesture. I gladly accept your generous offer if my twofold efforts are fruitful on your behalf, securing your return to Jerusalem and reaffirming King David's good graces. Please be patient, as this might take some time to accomplish your restoration. I cannot promise the outcome you desire, only that I will do my utmost to make it favorable to your need to be reunited with your father, the king.

Your favored cousin Joab ben Suri, chief captain.

Abishai nodded his approval of the wording and sentiment. Joab then folded the note, placed it in the dispatch pouch, and added his seal to the flap. He was making it ready to go at first light.

The morning broke fair and bright, and the dispatch to Absalom was now in flight. Sitting at the breakfast table, the brothers were hatching their plans and schemes of clever conspiracy. Chocking down bread and cheese, then washing it down with a cup of new wine, Abishai gave a satisfying burp and addressed Joab, deep in thought, "Daydreaming, brother?" With a scolding look, Joab answered, "Perhaps a bit. I was picturing Absalom and me entering Zion's Gate. I believe it's always wise to see a successful ending even before the task begins. Since we are going into the big city, let us make our travel and time useful. We always need tools, seeds, and delicacies only available in the capital. We can make a list and take a wagon with enough servants to do the heavy lifting. This way, when we barge in on Uncle David, our story of doing business in the vicinity will ring true, evidenced by a cart full of goods."

"You are always thinking, my cunning brother, let us get to it. The day awaits!"

The Jerusalem Bazar was a place of wonders. Jerusalem was now the central way station on the trading route known as the King's Highway. The road stretched from the Euphrates in the north to Egypt in the south. The bazaar was a mecca of merchants and traders from all over the empire. African ivory to silks from Egypt, iron, bronze, brass, copper tools, and weapons. Exotic perfumes, foods, and spices. A chorus of competing voices could be heard from sellers and buyers arguing over the value of a shekel. While the sizzle of succulent meats on dripping grills, flutes, drums, and dancing girls created a gay and festive atmosphere—anything you could imagine eating or wearing was there to be seen. There were even gem-encrusted killing swords and stabbing knives. Everything was negotiable; bargaining was encouraged and considered disrespectful if you paid the asking price without an argument.

Abishai shouted over the din, pointing to the sky, "Well, brother, our wagon is overfilled. I believe we negotiated some great bargains. But look, the sun is dropping. The time has come to test our uncle's hospitality."

The king's mansion was a fair distance from the bazaar but raised high to get a view of all of Jerusalem. The guards recognized the two brothers, uncrossed their stays, and let them enter. David was informed of their presence. He hurriedly met them at the portico entrance. David beamed, letting his brothers know he was genuinely glad to see them, "My two favorite co-captains and esteemed nephews." The brothers bowed in response, respecting the king as fitting and proper.

"I see you have a wagon full of goods. Both of you have been to the bazaar, have you not?" David inquired.

Joab answered, "Yes, uncle, some needful things and some not so much. During our shopping expedition, Abishai asked me, 'When was the last time we had beheld the king's face?' To which I replied, 'I do not remember when.'"

Abishai then countered, 'Well, that's much too long, and since we are so close by, let us take a chance and see if the king is in residence.'"

Joab continued as the king smiled, "We will stay but a moment. We know you have affairs of state and are busy administering to the nation's needs."

David cheerfully announced, "No, I will not hear of it. I hope you two brought your appetite. You are staying for supper, and that is the end of it. Come inside, we will have wine and speak of friends, family, and both past and present adventures. I am glad for the company."

The brothers looked at each other, slightly confounded; neither could recollect their uncle being so upbeat and inviting. David was not known for his cordiality; it was so unlike him. They supposed someone must have recently filled his coffers or perhaps a new concubine.

The king spread a fine table with roasted meats, aged cheese, and flagons of vintage wine. The meal was sumptuous. With full bellies and a glut of wine, the conversation turned to the warrior's tales of harrowing battles. Rabbah and Joab's brilliant escape from a Syrian chariot trap and the final assault on the impregnable citadel of the royal city. David chaffed at the mention, for it was where the sword of Ammon devoured Uriah the Hittite. Seeing David and Joab both stiffening up, Abishai smartly changed the subject. "Tell me, uncle, how are our cousins Adonijah and Solomon maturing as potential successors to the crown?"

At this moment, David's demeanor changed; he was back

to his old self, distant and pensive.

David candidly responded, "Adonijah is a competent administrator who weighs, considers, and contemplates. However, he is not adventuresome or a warrior, certainly not a risk taker. He takes after his mother, Haggith, in that regard, and he is not at all festive in any respect, always cautious and thoughtful. Solomon, on the other hand, is the exact opposite. He is gifted and possesses natural wisdom spurred by an insatiable curiosity. He is both festive and adventuresome. But, unfortunately, he is too fond of wine and women, which I believe will be his undoing. But adoringly, his mother, Bathsheba, dotes on the boy and has even written a song about him. He is her pride and joy; she spoils, never scolds, and holds him above reproach."

Abishai replied, "Thank you, my lord, for those insights; that knowledge might come in handy one day when maneuvering the halls of power. I am confident you will be among us for many years by God's grace. Oh, by the way, how is Cousin Absalom? It has been three years or so since I beheld his face."

It was the very opening that Joab was waiting for, and he swiftly interrupted, "I, for one, miss the company of my cousin Absalom. It is much too long to hold a grudge. What Absalom did was unforgivable, even though he was avenging his sister's honor. I believe that nobility is obliged to have compassion and mercy. Does not God Himself devise a means that his banished are not expelled from him forever?"

David's pent-up anger suddenly erupted. He stood up and locked eyes with Joab and Abishai, "How dare you bring up that murderer's name at my table? I banished him instead of hanging him for treason, as he deserved worse. He had my oldest son and heir slaughtered on his orders. He is as good as dead to me. Never mention his name again in my presence unless you want to feel the sting of my vengeance. You have also spoiled my digestion. Enough has been said; not another word if you know what is good for you both. It is time for my nap; perhaps that will help to calm me down. It is said that 'Sleep soothes the troubled mind.' Think again when you two feel like visiting me without an invitation. Gentlemen, I leave it to you to see yourselves out." The brothers raised and bowed, acknowledging the warning and not saying a word in the hopes of quelling David's ire.

It was about two hours till sundown as the brothers reached the outside compound. Their servants were catnapping and in need of some rest. Abishai yelled, "Turn the ox cart; we must make our way home before nightfall." A whip cracked; the ox shuttered, and with that bag and baggage were on the move. Joab turned to Abishai, "You misspoke, brother; retelling the battle for the city of Rabbah put David on edge. Perhaps a reminder of the prophet Nathan's words, 'That the sword would never leave his house.' I did not expect such an outburst of emotion. I thought more of a chilly reception and, at worse, a dressing down. If anything could be wrenched from that scolding, the good news is that we now know exactly where we stand. A direct approach is out of the question. I shall have to think further before dismissing our efforts completely. I will need several days to explore options and possibilities."

Abishai replied, "You are a better man than I, brother. To me, it looks hopeless. But I have learned over the years that your creativity and tenacity are legendary when needed in dire straits. I will wait patiently to see what ingenious plot you concoct."

CHAPTER
TWENTY-THREE
A Telling Story

Distracted in thought, Joab was irritable by the lack of a viable solution for Absalom's dilemma. How does one convey a personal message without being present that is informative, spiritually directed, and, most importantly, compelling?

After several days, a trusted servant approached Joab with a petition, "Lord, a serving wench has asked me to speak for her if you permit me."

Gruff, at the interruption, Joab shook his head in annoyance and said, "Speak on and speak up. Make it quick."

"The woman in question was notified that her father had died and wished to go home and attend the funeral. However, she needs a week of leave because of the distance and the time necessary to comfort her mother from her grievous loss. Lord, these are the words she asked me to impart to you."

"What do you say? Can we manage that long without her help?" Joab asked.

"I already took the liberty and inquired of the staff; they are willing to shoulder the extra burden. She is well-liked and a hard worker. They are glad to help."

"Very well, tell her she has my leave for a week as long as she makes up the difference in missed chores upon her return."

Joab's eyes widened as he nodded to himself and smiled, "Of course, it was right in front of me all this time."

"Sorry, lord, I do not understand,"

"Never mind about that. Tell me, what is her name?"

"It is Naomi, lord."

"Now go and tell Naomi she will be given two extra shekels, one for her journey and one to help with her father's funeral. Next, I need you to find and fetch my brother Lord Abishai; tell him I have been inspired and have the seed to solve our daunting problem. Be quick about you before my joy turns into displeasure."

Joab was beaming when Abishai walked into the room. "There you are, my dear brother, the calculated thinker."

"What is this all about? Your manservant presented me with a riddle. I do not believe a letter will have the needed impact; it would be a waste of time."

"No, it is better than a letter and even more powerful than me making my plea in person."

"All right, let us dispense with the drama and tell me how you intend to overcome our seemingly impossible predicament

of delivering a convincing speech while not being present?"
Abishai inquired.

"There is a wise woman named Haṣoṣrah, meaning trumpet,
a performer, and a storyteller. She lives in Tekoah. I have had
dealings with her in the past. But first, I must find her, and if
she is agreeable, we can weave a compelling story by putting
my words in her mouth. Perhaps even a fitting parable she
can deliver with conviction. She will present herself as a long-
grieving mother whose son has killed his brother, still aptly
dressed in torn black mourning clothes. I can fill her with my
words to beguile the king's sympathetic agreement. Then, I
can deliver her to the king's hearing with cunning coaching.
I have seen men put away the everyday and mundane when
young women have important things to say. I believe this is so
because, in a woman's heart, they have the spark of the home
and the spark of creation in their womb. This might be our
only chance to soften David's hard-hearted stiff opposition to
the reversal of Absalom's exile."

"Brilliant brother, from you, I would expect no less. I
know the outcome is not chiseled in stone, but the effort and
creativity are still worthy of applause."

"Thank you, brother, for the acclaim and confidence.
Tekoah is about twelve miles from here. Since she knows me,
I must be the one to go; we must secure her hire before composing the compelling dialogue. I will bring enough shekels
to persuade her to audition for the king's forgiveness. Half
now and the balance upon completion, with a hefty bonus if
David succumbs to her performance and invites me to escort

Absalom back home to Jerusalem."

His brother nodded in agreement, and Joab continued, "Since that is settled, I will leave tomorrow morning at dawn. I will ride my she-mule to Tekoah so as to reduce travel time. I will then locate the storyteller and propose my strategy. If she so agrees, I will make Haṣoṣrah a generous offer for her participation in our staged deception."

In the shadowy gray morning mist, Joab was off in a trot. A mild day was in the offing as the sun peaked over the horizon. The miles slipped away until, and just up ahead on the crest of a hill, Tekoah finally came into view.

Stopping at the town well for some needed cool water for himself and his lathered mule, a matron from the village walked up to the rim of the water well and started filling her bucket. Joab inquired, "Madam, I seek Haṣoṣrah, the story-teller. Do you know her, and can you direct me to her home?"

"I do, and I can, and she is quickly known for her wit and wisdom."

The woman pointed to a shelter under an ancient oak, shielding the dwelling from the glaring sun and desert heat.

"It is your lucky day, my lord. Haṣoṣrah just entered the commons area."

Now refreshed, both rider and beast approached the per-former. Recognizing Joab instantly, Haṣoṣrah acknowledged the reunion, "Lord Joab, this is an unexpected pleasure. What brings you to Tekoah? Are you lost, or is this a way station on a long journey?"

"No, I am here for you. I remember you telling me this was

the village of your birth and where you would most likely be until your death. So, I have come all this way from Jerusalem to offer you a commission for what you do best: mouth the words born from someone else's thoughts."

"Pray to tell me, my lord, your handmaiden was about to search for work, my purse is empty, and my belly growls. A shekel right now is more valuable than life itself."

"Very well, madam, keeping your mind on business is hard when your belly demands attention. So let us go to a nearby inn, and you can eat your fill. Then we can go to your home to discuss my hire in more private confines."

"Thank you, kind sir, I starve."

Joab ordered a princely feast, and Haṣoṣrah ate her fill until she was unable to swallow another mouthful. Joab also hungered and joined her in dining but would not publicly disclose his agenda, instead filling the silence with small talk. Haṣoṣrah, finally satisfied, sighed her contentment. Joab took the opportunity and was eager to start crafting the perfect dialog, "Let us walk to your house and help aid in our digestion, and there I can explain what is required of your acting abilities."

Before entering the dark shack, Joab unpacked some writing instruments from his rested mule.

Haṣoṣrah opened the shutters, brightening the hovel and making it almost cheerful. She then cleared the table for Joab and his writing scroll.

Locking eyes with Haṣoṣrah, Joab questioned, "Are you familiar with the killing of Amnon, King David's oldest son, by his half-brother Absalom?"

"Yes, lord, I know the names; both are princes of standing and power," Haṣoṣrah replied.

"But did you know Prince Absalom is exiled from his father's presence, Jerusalem, and all of Israel? He is forever left to wonder if the revengers of blood will find their mark behind the secure walls of Geshur, his maternal grandfather's domain. It is where Absalom finds refuge from his father's longing for justice."

"Yes, my lord, even in this small town, rumor, gossip, and criers fill us with the news from the walled cities and outer territories."

"Well then, allow me to explain why I am here. My brother Abishai and I had recently engaged my uncle King David in a casual dinner conversation. Abishai innocently inquired about Absalom's well-being. The king abruptly scolded us in the harshest terms for breaking a seemingly long-standing protocol just by uttering the name of Absalom in his presence. We were then asked to leave and not return unless formally invited.

I feel obliged to try to reinstate Absalom, my cousin and to secure his father's forgiveness. But since the king does not welcome my attendance, I considered your unique talents and how you could transmit my request in my absence. I propose that I put my words in your mouth. You, in turn, express my thoughts with sincerity and compassion and inspire the king to repent of Absalom's banishment by employing emotion, reason, and understanding. If you agree to undertake this deceit, I will pay you handsomely for your efforts. Half now and the balance upon completion, whether our ploy succeeds or fails miserably. If our ruse has its intended effect and David is remorseful, a substantial bonus will be forthcoming upon a successful outcome. Do you agree to these terms, madam? If so, we can get started."

Haṣoṣrah took a moment to digest the final words before responding, "I agree and look forward to providing a stellar performance in reuniting a murderous son with his like-minded father."

Joab then covered his mouth, barely subduing a snort and a chuckle at her whimsy.

"A word of warning, Haṣoṣrah… no matter what is said or how it all takes place, if the king questions you, the most grievous blunder is lying to him. Be forewarned; the one thing he cannot abide is a liar. Do you have mourning attire?"

"Yes, lord, but it is old, tear-stained, and torn with grief."

"Perfect, that should do nicely, and remember, refrain from applying anointing oil. It must appear that you have grieved for your dead son for a season and that your heart still breaks from the unkindness of fate."

"When you are ushered into the king's presence, it is expected to put your face to the ground, showing humility and homage."

"I am prepared to accomplish the task set before me."

And with that, Joab unfolded his writing scroll and spoke the words out loud. Next, he began to plant the seeds of deception and doubt, filling Haṣoṣrah's eager mouth with empathy, compassion, and the gentle dew of understanding.

CHAPTER
TWENTY-FOUR
The Practiced Seduction of Cold Feet

With compelling words learned and correctly rehearsed, Joab and Haṣoṣrah engaged in some practiced role-play. Joab tried to predict David's responses with questions and answers so that Haṣoṣrah could be confident in her performance. Once he was satisfied with their preparation, Joab disclosed how and when she was to stage her fate-filled plea for mercy.

"Listen closely. The following series of events are critical to our success. First, David will grant any citizen an audience the day before the Shabbat," Joab announced.

"You must appear in the receiving line early on Chamishi or Thursday morning. There is always a rash of people seeking royal favors, jobs, and long-sought-after property settlements. You must be in Jerusalem the day before on Revi'I or Wednesday and obtain lodging. Being the first visitor is ideal, and before an endless line of competing petitioners dulls David's interest. It would be best if you approached the mansion well before daybreak. I will provide you with the needed funds for both transport and boarding. I will remain close by but out of sight of my uncle's all-seeing eye."

Fatigued from the intense charade, Joab observed, "It is getting late, although our time has been well spent. I prefer not to travel the twelve miles in the dark, making myself easy prey for bandits and liars."

Haṣoṣrah offered lodgings to the tired Joab with a come hither lilt, "Lord, I have a suitable pallet up in my loft. You are welcome to stay the night, and I would be honored for your company."

Joab considered his options. Night travel was too risky, and the village inn was unappealing while refusing Haṣoṣrah's hospitality could dampen the passions of the well-coached actress.

"I would be delighted, madam," Joab graciously accepted Haṣoṣrah's timely offer.

"I will see to a light supper," Haṣoṣrah said as she stoked the dying embers to resurrect a cooking fire. She then set a simple table, and like an old married couple they ate in silence, neither having the energy nor inclination for idle chatter.

"It seems, madam, that I have worn out this day," Joab said, inhaling with a snort, then stifling a telltale yawn.

"Yes, my lord, where are my manners?" Lighting two oil lamps, she beckoned, "If you, please follow me and watch your step. Some of the boards are loose and notched with age."

They proceeded up the rickety staircase creaking and

snapping with every footfall as if it was about to give way. Topping the landing, the flickering lamps revealed a tidy made-up pallet.

"Here you are, my lord, the hospitality of the house. I know it's not what you are accustomed to, but as a marshal in the army of God who has spent many cold nights under the stars, I think these lodgings would be acceptable. If you would, my lord, put your lamp on the stand. The wool blanket should ward off the night chill, and the privy bucket is convenient and close at hand. Suppose you have any other needs or desires, any at all, that your handmaiden can provide. In that case, you only need to inquire."

After an awkward silence, Joab mulled over his options of having a warm body to pass the night in comfort but was too weary and preferred an uninterrupted night's sleep. "Thank you, madam. This will be quite satisfactory. Goodnight."

Ḥaṣoṣrah felt a slight sting of rejection and answered, "As you wish, my lord, good night." Then, holding her single flickering flame high, she navigated the stairs to her dark, empty chamber.

God's creatures were fast asleep when a melancholy owl hooted his single-note love song question to the moon. The distant echo broke the silence and roused Ḥaṣoṣrah from her uneasy sleep. She noticed that the cold had a deeper bite this chilling night and was concerned for the comfort of her esteemed guest. He was, after all, a far distance from the hearth that was now down to its dying embers. Lighting her lamp and returning up the steep steps, she found Joab fast asleep, buried in his blanket. Haṣoṣrah felt a deeper chill of loneliness and recalled the comfort of a warm body, especially on such a frigid night as this. She pondered momentarily and slowly pulled back the blanket, uncovering Joab's feet. In a short while, Joab awoke chilled to the bone and glimpsed Haṣoṣrah with her lamp at the foot of his bed.

Haṣoṣrah whispered, "Lord, please excuse my intrusion; the night has turned unseasonably chilly, and I was concerned for your comfort. Therefore, I am here to offer my warm body so the lord can get a good night's rest without ill effects."

Joab lifted the blanket with one hand, grasped Haṣoṣrah's hand, and pulled her down next to him.

The morning began to fade when they finally rose to meet the day. They lingered longer than expected. Giggling, Haṣoṣrah cheerfully commented, "Lord, your body is like a furnace. I slept warm and toasty."

Now amply satisfied, Joab replied, "Yes, madam, it was just what was needed, and by the way, under the circumstances, I think you should call me Joab."

Again, Haṣoṣrah giggled, "Lord, I mean Joab, let me make you breakfast. It will only take a moment."

"If only I might. We remained entwined for a long time, and the morning slipped away. I must be on my way and dare not delay another moment. Here is the purse I promised with the needed cost of transport and lodging. Oh, yes, and a little extra for your extended hospitality." Changing to a business tone, Joab completed their interaction, "The next time we meet will be in Jerusalem. I will be at the king's gate waiting for the results of our storytelling conspiracy. Until then, comely madam, thanks again for your hospitality, and remember to practice your lines to perfection, as much depends on your convincing David. He must be compelled to end Absalom's exile. Adieu until then."

Saddling his mule, Joab rushed his departure as if leaving a crime scene. It was nearly sundown before he approached the long, winding road that led to his hearth and home.

Abishai rushed out to greet him, delighted to behold his brother kicking up dust in the distance.

"I was concerned when you did not return as planned yesterday and all this day with no sign on the horizon. Tomorrow morning, I would have formed a search party and scoured the road to Tekoah for signs of foul play. You look fit enough, in any case. I take it that all went well, brother?"

"It did, and much better than expected. The rehearsal was demanding. I wrote the dialogue on the spot. I believe our plot will play out better than expected. At times, Haṣoṣrah will have to rely on her quick wit to gain David's confidence, but she fully understands the spirit of mercy and reconciliation she needs to convey. We will see her next as she waits dutifully in line at the crack of dawn at the petitioner's gate this coming Chamishi morning.

"I need a meal, for I starve. I long to stretch out on my feather bed. I slept very little last night for want of unexpected company, making a cold makeshift pallet exceptionally cozy."

CHAPTER
TWENTY-FIVE
The Word of God, The Second Time

Early on Revi'I morning, Haṣoṣrah arranged for a ride to the big city at the local market. There was an obliging vegetable farmer with room in his ox cart.

It was late in the day when she arrived at Zion's gate. Paying her alms to an old and wise-looking beggar, she asked, "Sir, can you direct me to an inn close to the king's mansion where I might spend the night safely and comfortably?"

"Yes, madam, I do, and I can take you there. It is just a stone's throw from the king's mansion. One thing I would ask in return, tell the innkeeper that Elisha, the beggar, recommended you. I am afforded some table scraps and a lean-to in the back."

Entering the well-appointed inn, Hasosrah proceeded to engage the landlord, "I require a room, and I need to be awakened before the cock's crow; oh, yes, I was recommended by Elisha, the beggar."

"Excellent, madame. Well, you are in luck, as we have a room available, and your timely awakening will be managed for an extra penny. Where do you hail, and what is your business, if you do not mind me asking?"

"Tekoah, I am here to petition the king." Feeling a pinch of an intrusion, she nipped, "As if it is any concern of yours. Now show me to my room, I have a long day tomorrow and wish to start early."

There was a rap followed in short order by an insistent knock. The night was black as coal when Haṣoṣrah responded to the intrusion of dreams. "I am awake!" She tried vainly to clear the frog in her throat as it came out garbled. Then, a familiar voice came from the other side of the door. "Are you all right, madam? This is Elisha, the beggar. I was given a half penny to rouse you from your slumber. The innkeeper told me you are here to petition the king. If you hurry, madam, I know a shortcut, and I can guide you to the petitioner's entrance before the line coils around the mansion like a hungry snake."

"Very well, Elisha. I will rush for much depends on my timely appearance."

Haṣoṣrah wore her mourner's costume; she was ready with just the right tear of grief and telltale stain of dried anointing oil, proving she had been grieving for a long time.

The shortcut proved to be valuable. Haṣoṣrah was first in line and she gave a penny for the service. Elisha bowed with gratitude as if it was a king's ransom.

The line filled with the high and low born seeking favors and pardons. It was hours after the cocked crowed before the doors opened, and the guards escorted Haṣoṣrah to the King's judgment seat.

David was crowned and regaled in his royal attire. When Haṣoṣrah first laid eyes on the monarch, she beheld an unmistakable aura surrounding him. She immediately fell on her face to the ground displaying humility and homage.

"O king, help me!"

David curiously inquired, "What is your problem that only the king can resolve?"

"I am a lone widow long grieving for my dead husband. I was comforted by my two sons, who were equally loved. One day they struggled in an argument in a secluded field as brothers often do, but it heightened, and there was no one to part them. One fell on the other and, in a rage, killed him. My dead husband's family and my own family have revolted against me and demanded that I deliver up my remaining son that killed his brother so that they may do the like unto him and seek justice for the blood of the slain. The death of my only son and heir will quench my coal, erase my husband's name, and leave no remainder of his seed upon the earth in memory."

The widow's heartfelt plight visibly moved David. Then, reassuringly, he attempted to console her anguish, "Go to your house knowing that you go with the king's protection for you and your son."

Moved by the king's compassion, if but only attesting to the convincing acting of Haṣoṣrah, she took responsibility for her words, "My lord, my king, the iniquity be on me and my father's house, and the king and his throne be guiltless."

David wielded the power of life and death and replied, "Whosoever says different and goes against my wishes, you bring him to me, and if he touches you or causes distress, he will suffer the king's wrath."

"Oh, great and noble prince, I implore you, let the king remember the Lord your God. That you will not allow the revengers of blood, who live in the shadows, to destroy anymore, lest they destroy my son without restraint."

David, moved by compassion, reassured the widow once more, "As the Lord lives, not one hair of your son shall fall to the ground."

Haşoşrah, emboldened by David's kindness, continued to press her real intent, "Please find favor with your faithful maidservant and allow me to speak one more word and not kindle the king's anger for the need of revealing my innermost unsettled thoughts."

"Speak on, madam."

"You are the king; whatever you do is a beacon and a standard that all of Israel will follow. So why have you done something that brings so much harm to God's people? When you judge permanent exile, you convict yourself and brand a pretense against God's will and teachings. Sire, your thinking is faulty in refusing the son you drove away and not allowing him to return to a forgiving and loving father. God has taught, 'For we must need to die, and are as water spilled on the ground, which cannot be gathered up again; neither doth

God respects any person: yet he does devise a means, that his banished be not expelled from Him forever, but makes way for all to return to his presence.'

"I have now come to speak with my lord the King about this matter because the people have made me fearful. But your maidservant said to the people, 'I will speak to the king! Perhaps the king will do what his maidservant asks. Yes! The king may listen and deliver his maidservant from the hand of the avenger of blood who seeks to remove my son and me from the inheritance God has given us.'"

David's ears perked up and his attention focused; he leaned in. He knew only the King could shield against the avenger of blood when balancing the scales of justice.

Haṣoṣrah continued, "May the word of my lord the king be my security, for my lord the king is like an angel of God when deciding between right and wrong! May the Lord our God be with you!"

David weighed and pondered everything said and sensed some mischief was afoot.

"Indulge me, madam, for my curiosity is aroused. Hide not from me my inquiry that I may know with certainty whether I have been made the fool in this elaborate charade."

"Let my lord ask, and as God is my witness, I will not hold anything back," Haṣoṣrah replied.

Confident in his appraisal, David questioned, "Is not the hand of Joab with you in all that was said?"

Haṣoṣrah looked down, unable to look David in the eye, and answered, "As surely as you live, my lord, my king, one cannot turn to the right hand or left, hiding anything that my lord the king cannot recognize through the grace of God. It was your nephew Joab who commanded me. It was he who put all these fine words in my mouth. He used this means to change the course of your thinking. He wished to bring order back to Israel and reconcile a father with his son. But my lord has wisdom like an angel of God to know all things on the earth."

Realizing Joab's intentions were sincere, although his methods were devious and suspect, David inquired, "Where is Lord Joab? Knowing my nephew, he is nearby, waiting in the shadows. His ear to the ground and eager to know if your performance was successful or kindled my ire?"

Haṣoṣrah confided, "He told me he would wait outside the compound gate for my report before he dared an approach to the king."

"Go now, Haṣoṣrah, and summon Joab and tell him the king has words of his own for him to bear. Answer no questions and sidestep inquiries; let us keep him in wonder and suspense."

David sent two burly guards to ensure Joab's return to the king's presence to hear the verdict firsthand.

When back outside, Haṣoṣrah called out over the din of the milling throng, "Lord Joab!" Almost instantly, Joab and Abishai eagerly stepped out from behind a dark shadow. The two brothers promptly walked over to the woman of Tekoah, flanked by the king's guards stationed at the portico entrance. With nervous curiosity, Joab could not stop questioning,

"Please tell me madam, how was your performance received? Was the king moved to compassion, or did it evoke his anger?"

Haṣoṣrah relayed the king's wishes, "The king wants to tell you personally and only you of his judgment." Joab singled Abishai to wait outside while he faced the lion of Judah in his den. Haṣoṣrah insisted, "Let us not keep the king waiting." The two guards fell in line, and the four proceeded to the king's chamber.

Seeing Joab, David raised. Joab was prepared for the worse when David, in a remorseful tone, uttered, "Behold, I have done this thing, as your words have made plain to my understanding. I have banished my son and have made no way to reclaim him from exile. Now go with the king's charge and bring the young man Absalom back home to Jerusalem."

Relieved and gratified, Joab fell to the ground on his face, humbled himself, and thanked the king. "Today, your servant knows that I have found grace in your sight, my lord, my king, for the king has fulfilled the request of his servant."

"Before you scurry off to Geshur, Joab, a warning to convey to the young man. Not enough time has passed since I longed for retribution for the slain Amnon. You can bring your neighbor back to his own house, but he must not see my face without my invitation or permission, for on that day, he will suffer the king's longing for vengeance that still calls to me from out of the grave."

Not wanting to overplay his hand and seeing David still wrestle with his decision, Joab grabbed Haṣoṣrah by the hand and departed, bowing and scraping as if the room was on fire.

They found Abishai anxiously waiting when they reached the outer compound; he began, "I see your head is still in place. Pray, tell me, what was the king's verdict?"

Joab smiled, "All went well, brother. I am tasked to bring Absalom back to his house but not to David's sight. He is still haunted by the specter of Amnon's ghost that cries for justice from the dust. The total reconciliation of father and son will take time to mend."

He then turned to the woman, "As for you, Haṣoṣrah, your performance must have been a plea to the angels; well done, madam. There is a hefty bonus with my best wishes and gratitude. We should not be seen together, reminding David of our ploy, even to a good end, as nobody likes being made the fool by subterfuge," concluded Joab as Haṣoṣrah nodded in agreement.

"Let us retire, brother, before David has a change of heart and mind. Then, let us prepare for an early departure to Geshur."

CHAPTER
TWENTY-SIX

Plots, Plans, and the Advice of Sages

"I am coming with you, brother, and give me no argument," insisted Abishai. "I know you prefer to travel alone, but it is nearly 100 miles to Et-Tell. Moreover, the route is teeming with liars, brigands, and pirates, not to mention jackals, wolves, and lions. So, for security, we will take a wagon of supplies for our needs and a company of armed guards for protection."

"I agree, brother, with its practical necessity. But only a force small enough not to pose a threat but large enough to ward off ill intent. The gain of Absalom's adjacent barley field will more than offset the cost of trouble and travel," Joab replied.

The four-day trip passed as predicted without incident or accident.

The tall gates of Et-Tell opened without the typical

challenge as if Joab had been expected well before his arrival. Instead, Absalom was first on the scene, eager to hear glad tidings from Jerusalem.

"My two favorite cousins, esteemed neighbors, and my sole advocate to the king's conscious."

Absalom was beside himself. His long-awaited expectation was about to be disclosed with seemingly good news.

"Hello and salutations, my former exiled cousin." Joab could not contain himself, "Let us retire to private confines and invite your grandfather to the conversation. I am sure he has more than a passing interest in your future well-being."

The three men passed through to a secluded alcove only to rise again when King Talmai entered the room. The king began, "It is always good to see familiar faces of extended family. Lord Abishai, our ambassador and Chief Captain Joab of Israel and Judah, we are honored by your presence." Talmai then turned and addressed a waiting servant, "Fetch us vintage wine, cheese, and bread for our guests, and be quick about it. I fear a long talk is about to commence." A needed chuckle broke the tension. Talmai quipped, "Let us get on with it; I refuse to remain hostage to expectations."

In a bid to reassure the king, Joab said, "It is good news, excellent news indeed. David has relented and released Absalom's banishment without forfeiting titles, rights, and privileges. But one demand remains that is more of an inconvenience than a punishment." This was a feeble attempt by Joab to minimize the consequences of Absalom's defiance.

"Speak on," Talmai insisted.

"Absalom can return to his home but cannot see the king's face or be in his father's presence. David forewarned that the blood of Amnon still called to him from the dust for justice and that not enough time had passed to allow the ghost of his conscience to reconcile his grief with acceptance. If you agree to that one condition, I will bring you home, Prince Absalom."

Absalom was ready to agree, but Talmai then spoke up. "Gentlemen, thank you so much for your efforts on behalf of my beloved grandson Absalom, not to mention the long journey you suffered to deliver these good tidings. However, before Absalom commits to your condition, we must speak privately about his options and how best to address this turn of events. So, if you will excuse us, we have much to discuss. Please take every advantage of your stay here."

"Certainly, great king, your wisdom to impart is as precious as gems," Abishai replied.

Talmai shook his head and mused, "Always the skilled statesman, Ambassador Abishai."

Joab nodded in respect and added, "We shall wait for your answer, Absalom, when you feel confident in adhering to the king's conditions." The brothers found the door, hastily departed, and were ushered to the guest apartments.

Talmai turned to his grandson and praised his foresight, "It would seem, young man, that your offer of property and favor spurred Joab to find a promising intervention. Although being shunned by royal authority is an obstacle, it makes you appear out of favor and weak. It would be best to bide your time, no matter how bitter. When the time is right, or you cannot bear another moment, solicit your cousin Joab, the near miracle worker. He has earned a provisional deed to your adjacent barley field, giving him farming rights but not total ownership. Not until you are allowed back into David's presence. Once this is accomplished, Joab will get full possession as promised. Once you have access to the seat of power, you will be taken more seriously. Then you can win over the people's love and respect away from David's long shadow. The people see him as aloof and distant. He is only visited by a handful of petitioners once a week. He never travels to towns, villages, or the outlining provinces. He seems reasonably content to live in his ivory tower with no more worlds to conquer and basks in his former glory. David relegates affairs of state to judges and low-level administrators. He entertains himself by communing with his eight wives and ten concubines regularly.

"Once you are back in Jerusalem, it is time for you to marry and start producing offspring. People feel more assured when they see virility in their leaders, which gives them confidence in ongoing governing continuity."

"Grandfather, you are an impressive man and a wise king. Your advice is weightier than gold, lo even greater than the ransom of kingdoms. Please continue with your sage words, for they are a roadmap to empire."

"Very well, I am pleased that you recognize their depth and weight. After your father relents, and because of his stubborn reluctance, you must demonstrate patience for knowing David as I do; it will take some time for him to release his grief fully. Now, once you are accepted back into the king's household, that is when, and only then, you can begin your political scheming. First, in Hebron, you and your father's birthplace. Gain favor with the elders who resent David for favoring Israel over Judah. It is the perfect place to gather strength to launch an insurrection.

"When you make a public entrance, make your arrival a grand affair, chariots, and footmen proclaiming that someone of consequence has arrived. Continually station yourself early at the gate to offer the downtrodden a caring and personable leader intent on their well-being. You provide a consoling ear, a steady hand, and an outstretched arm. A holy kiss will proclaim you as a friend to nobility and the commoner—a man for all seasons in Jerusalem. Your greatest ally, proven by word and deed, is Lord Ahithophel, the seer. He will be the key to your strategy for a sudden, decisive show of strength with a much smaller force. Ahithophel represents your best chance at violently overthrowing your father's regime. But first things first, and before we get carried away with ourselves. It is crucial that you do not divulge your plans to anyone, especially Joab and Abishai. They are captains in David's army and men of rank and privilege. They would not hesitate to see to your ending if a question of loyalty jeopardized their positions and power.

"Be wise as a serpent, keep a low profile, and let the dust settle around you. No matter how hopeless a problem or how grand the victory is, things will change, often suddenly and without warning."

After a pause for reflection, the king continued, "When

you were born, I envisioned you wearing three crowns: Geshur, Judah, and Israel. Now go and make your grandfather proud."

The caravan was well-provisioned and heavily guarded for the journey back to Jerusalem.

Saying his farewells, Absalom took the opportunity to make one last plea for Tamar to join him back home to Israel. "Dear sister, my home will not feel complete without your peaceful spirit."

"No, brother, I feel settled and appreciated here. Mother Maacah visits regularly, and Grandfather and I have grown inseparable."

"As long as you are happy, sister, I can abide by your decision. Grandfather has advised me to start a family, and if I have a daughter, I will name her Tamar and hope she has your beauty and gentle manner. Adieu."

The journey back to Israel was uneventful, and Absalom kept his counsel.

CHAPTER TWENTY-SEVEN
A Bittersweet Homecoming

The sight of his home after a three-year absence was pleasing to Absalom. It looked inviting, even though a little overgrown and untidy. The lack of the master's touch was evident, but it soon would be remedied with some elbow grease and visible weeding.

The barley field promised to Joab was now weeping with grain and ready to harvest. Absalom got down to business in a cheerful mood, "As I had promised you, cousin, a provisional deed to that adjacent section awaits my signature with my undying gratitude. As a reminder, you have access, with a limited title but not ownership, not until I am allowed back in the king's presence."

"Yes, Absalom, I am fully aware of the particulars, but it will take longer than I imagined. Last I spoke to your father, he was still anxious at the thought of your presence. I think it best to avoid Jerusalem; coming face-to-face with your father is a line not to cross. Time is necessary to close this wound, and nothing else will do.

"I will have a dinner party with neighbors and friends sympathetic to your cause. It will be next Rishon or Sunday after the Shabbat. It would be best if you reentered society, relaying to your father that you are obeying his dictates by not seeking the comfort of his face. It is the one intrusion he will not sustain. Unfortunately for you, he will not hesitate to inflict a deadly punishment. He will deem your uninvited presence to challenge his authority and will not abide the insult, so be forewarned."

"Yes, cousin, I fully understand the danger of an untimely approach."

Absalom then added, "On a better note, you said the king promised to restore my prince's pension, so no luxury is out of reach except for my father's good graces. I look forward to your dinner party. Thank you again for your successful efforts on my behalf."

Joab's villa was lavishly decorated for the dinner party, adding to the festive occasion. A succulent fatted calf spun slowly on the spit until the meat fell off the bones, and wine goblets and loud chatter overflowed with merriment. Many nobles disliked Amnon, dreading the day he would be king, and secretly felt a sense of relief at his timely demise, while many nobles felt Absalom's reckoning was justified in revenging his sister Tamar's honor. Well-wishers were in abundance pledging their loyalty in the hopes that someday Absalom would ascend to the throne of David. Even a few of Absalom's half-brothers attended, risking the wrath of their kingly father.

The seating arrangements were calculated for effect. Absalom was seated next to a beautiful and unusually tall Hebrew woman. Their eyes locked in a soulful familiarity as if they had met before in a long, forgotten age.

Absalom was instantly and hopelessly smitten. He dared not look away at this vision of loveliness sitting next to him because she might vanish as mysteriously as she appeared. He clumsily reached for his goblet just so his fingers could barely brush against her hand, confirming that she was flesh and blood and not a wishful angel of his imagination. Seeing the intense connection, Joab whisked over to do the honors, interrupting the touching moment. "Please excuse my intrusion, but it seems that the two most beautiful people at my dinner party were destined to meet, be it luck or fate's smiling face. As your host, a formal introduction is required by polite society. This is my honored guest, Absalom ben David, prince of Israel and Judah and heir to the crown of Geshur. I am pleased to introduce Lady Shifrah, meaning beautiful, and the granddaughter of Ahithophel the oracle."

With a genuine glow of reverence, Absalom confirmed, "Ahithophel, the seer, my beloved teacher and advisor, an indispensable guide. He is a beacon of light in these troubled times. I could not be more pleased and impressed. I am sure wit and wisdom are a family tradition."

Shifrah questioned, "In what subjects has my great-grandfather taught you?"

"I have many interests in a variety of subjects." Absalom slyly slid in a term of endearment, hoping to pique her interest. "Shifrah, that is a beautiful name, I might add, for such a beautiful woman, and it falls gently on one's lips." Absalom was rewarded with a slight blush and a modest smile as he continued, "I have the greatest respect for your great-grandfather Ahithophel. He has mentored me in politics, husbandry, commerce, and philosophy."

Shifrah quipped, "That is a welcomed relief, a handsome and well-tutored prince. I am confident we have much to discuss."

Once the proper etiquette was addressed, the closeness between the two new friends took on a life of its own. Joab fell uncomfortably silent, feeling like an intrusive eavesdropper. Both were so engrossed that neither one could look away, not even for a moment. Finally, Joab hurriedly departed, mumbling something or other and allowing the enraptured couple to continue their captivating conversation without interruption late into the night.

Weeks passed, and Absalom was caught up in a whirlwind romance, threatening his undoing. He was in love, heart and soul, tears and sweat. His appetite was gone, and his sleep was fitful and shallow. Shifrah's needed presence became obsessive, and he wished to make her his queen and loving wife. After all, he had been advised by King Talmai, his grandfather, to get married and start a family so his name could continue and not be erased from the memory of men.

Absalom was bewildered, anxious, and perplexed, as a man of love can often attest to such a multitude of conflicting emotions. He sought the advice of his cousin and neighbor Joab, his advocate with his father, King David.

"Cousin, I am in love and wish to marry. However, as hard as I try to concentrate on something or anything else, I cannot. All my waking thoughts betray me to her loving charms."

"Who is the lucky girl? Allow me a guess. Shifrah, is it not?"

"It is. I have already asked Lord Ahithophel, her only living male relative, for permission, and he has consented and will help me achieve all that I ask of him."

"Have you proposed to Shifrah?"

"I have, and she has agreed to be my wife. Is that not wonderful, cousin?"

"Congratulations are in order then! So why are you here, surely not just to tell me the good news?"

"It is my father, the king," Absalom admitted. "Do I need his permission to marry, and how do I accomplish that without being in his presence to ask? If you go cousin, and he is in a vindictive mood and says no, I will be beside myself in grief. What are your thoughts? You know him better than most."

"I believe it is always better to ask for forgiveness than permission. Regarding women, your father was never one to stand on formalities. He never gave required practices a second thought unless he had no choice but to accomplish his desired result. So, in the end, he took the woman and the kingdoms he wanted and later dealt with the resulting aftermath. I am confident David will pay no heed to your marriage, especially since you are wedding the great-granddaughter of Ahithophel. He always feared and applauded Ahithophel's wisdom and knowledge as being inspired by God. Therefore, your best course of action is to marry with all due haste and become legally bound in the eyes of God and Israel. In this way, when it comes to David's notice, there is nothing he can do or say to annul what God has joined together. Suppose you are blessed with children; so much the better. It will go a long way in soothing your father's fury. After all, grandchildren are the jewels in an old man's crown, which would go a long way in ensuring his dynasty."

All were agreed and prepared for a simple ceremony that was hastily organized.

The day had arrived, and it was bright and sunny. The needed minion was recruited from ten local righteous men to witness the ceremony as a sacred tradition and established ritual. Vows and rings were exchanged as prescribed underneath the Chuppah canopy. Ahithophel gave Shifrah and Absalom a handsome dowry to begin their new life together as man and wife.

The young, newlywed couple settled down in Absalom's villa. Joab, their immediate neighbor, passed along all of David's reactions or more like his ignoring disinterest, which was taken as passive acceptance.

Soon, Shifrah was aglow with new life in her belly. God had blessed their union with the fruit of the womb. The pregnancy went full term without incident, and it was time for the midwives to prepare for the birthing. Absalom was beside himself with anxiety and kept popping in on the delivery room until a wise old midwife scolded, "You need to boil a kettle of water and soak clean rags in it and keep them coming until I tell you to stop."

A novice asked the matron, "Why is that errand needed?"

To which she replied, "It's to keep the meddling husband busy and out of our way so we can go on with the delivery without constant interruptions. Besides, some men have fainted when the baby passes through the matrix."

After what felt like an age to Absalom, the matron finally called out, "It's a girl, healthy and plump!" Absalom burst in, grinning from ear to ear. Looking up, sweaty and pale from her ordeal, Shifrah said, "I know you were hoping for a son to carry on your name, but we are still young, and besides, little girls are like a song full of wonderous melodies. I know she will grow up to be a woman of fair countenance and a comfort to her father. So, what shall we name our little angel?" Absalom knew immediately, "We shall name her Tamar after my sister. I believe it is only fitting."

Shifrah agreed, "And so it shall be, baby Tamar."

Time passed, and Shifrah was once again with child despite not being entirely rested and not fully expected. Unfortunately, there were problems right from the beginning this time. She was ill and sick with nausea, headaches, and bleeding. The midwives were at a loss as they had seen this event before, which never turned out well. The head matron pleaded, "A healer is needed; the mistress requires lots of rest and herbal medicine." There were good days and bad days, and Shifrah's belly continued to grow. There were signs of life and hope.

The time was ripe, and without warning, everyone rushed Shifrah into the birthing chamber. Her breath was catching. The midwives cried, "Push harder!" Shifrah cried out in agony, her bottom wrenched with pain. Unrelentingly, the midwives demanded, "Push, push harder!" Finally, the baby's head emerged. Then, the shoulders and the rest of the torso slid through the opening; a boy screamed from the sting, and the breath of life filled his lungs. But behold, there was another child in the canal. A second head shone full of hair, peaking through the matrix. All were elated at the good fortune of yet another son. But yet another head appeared in the channel, ready to come forth to the earth. Miraculously, there were three sons: what a gift from God. Shifrah was depleted from the ordeal and was left pale and barely breathing. With the strain and the loss of so much blood, she gave up the ghost in childbirth. So often, the price of a new life is a mother's loving last dying breath.

Besides himself in grief, Absalom blamed fate. The woman he truly loved died, giving birth to new lives. His consolation was that now he had three sons who could carry on his name, a name that would not disappear from the earth. This was his sole satisfaction, and he would have to make the best of it.

Naturally, the infants needed their mother's milk for life and nourishment, so wet nurses had to be recruited to fill their crying hunger. Try as Absalom might, even venturing into Jerusalem proved to be difficult for him. The word was out that the king did not favor him, and any who would help him could feel the wrath of David. Moreover, goats' milk and cows' milk made the infants wretch. They could not digest it, and it would sour in their bellies. A woman was finally found, but it was too late; the baby boys died from complications seven days hence, so they were never named, circumcised, or mourned.

In sackcloth and ashes, Absalom carried the news like a sack of rocks to Ahithophel's door.

Absalom sought solace in the old sage's wisdom with his heart all but broken.

Absalom choked out, "My lord, I have some crushing news. Shifrah died giving birth to my three sons, who died shortly after from the delivery stress and lack of proper nourishment. My father's shadow covered me, and I am still viewed as an outcast, so help was not forthcoming. As a result, I now have no sons to carry on my name; I shall quickly fade from memory and be unknown after I die."

Pondering momentarily, Ahithophel said, "Yes, my prince, your tragedy is profound, but this is the time to salvage your life and make a name for yourself. But first, let us build a monument so that whatever happens, your name will be remembered to the end of time. Experience has taught me that a distraction from a creative and redirected undertaking is the best remedy when struggling with great emotional loss. I know the ideal place, Shaveh Valley, where the Kidron River flows. It is also known as the king's dale. It is where Abraham was tempted to compromise his faith and violate his oath. Was it either to receive the spoils of war from the king of Sodom or a blessing of God from Melchizedek? Abraham chose God and tithed. So, your pillar will have two meanings in the plain of compromise. First, having no sons is a way to keep your name alive. Second, David will soon hear of your loss; this news might move him to compassion. But in the meantime, it will attest that you are getting on with your life. So, let us get busy with our construction and plans to raise you to the throne of David."

CHAPTER
TWENTY-EIGHT
Slash and Burn Until You Are Heard

I n all of Israel, there was none so praised for his beauty as Absalom, even surpassing the glory of David, his sire. He had no scars, pockmarks, blemishes, or wounds. He reflected bodily perfection from the soles of his feet to the crown of his head. Absalom was topped with a long and lustrous head of hair, a promised inheritance from his mother, Maacah. Because she married a Hebrew, she had to shave off her luxurious locsz, pare her nails, and lament the loss of her father's home for thirty days to satisfy the ritual of eshet yefat to'ar. She swore that her children would have extended tresses as a reminder of her sacrifice. Absalom's practice was to have his hair polled at the end of every year. His magnificent mane was oiled and powdered with gold, which weighed 200 shekels by the king's measure.

Two years passed, and Absalom's pillar of remembrance was finally completed in the king's dale. He tried to make do with country living but felt he was missing his higher calling. He was still banished from court and treated like an outsider. No one wanted to show respect to a prince unseated and denied from the inner circle of power. With his options limited, Absalom once again considered his cousin Joab. After all, he had performed once before in securing his reprieve from exile. Besides, the agreement for the barley field hinged on returning him to David's good graces. Absalom warmly invited Joab, but he would not come. Absalom beckoned a second time, but again, he was shunned. He was being avoided without courtesy or explanation by his own cousin. More drastic methods would be needed to capture Joab's reluctant attention. Felling the sting of insult, Absalom called his most obedient servants and resorted to desperate measures, "See Joab's field of barley that is close by and ready to harvest. Set torches hot with my frustration and scorch the earth, leaving no stalk standing. If nothing else, that should get his attention to my unanswered invite."

A natural fire break contained the blaze as it lit up the night sky, rousing Joab to confront the inferno. Rounding up the amateur torchers, Joab questioned, "Why has this been done? Are you not the servants of Absalom?"

The fear-struck servants confessed, "Yes, my Lord, we were ordered by our master Absalom, for he was at wit's end trying to get the respect of your attention."

With the arsonists in tow, Joab took them all to Absalom's door.

Fitfully perturbed by the scorch and scorn, he confronted Absalom on his portico. "Why have you done this?"

Absalom answered in a business-like tone, "It is not your field until our agreement is fulfilled. Remember, legally, you have farming rights, but it is still my property. I had asked you twice if you would go to the king and ask him for me, and you have ignored my pleas. For all intents and purposes, I am under house arrest. I was better off in Geshur, where I had freedom of movement. So let me see the king's face, and if there is any iniquity in me, let him rise and kill me and be done with it, for it is better than living in this dark place, neither free nor confined and suffering disrespect from all sides.'

Joab then replied, "All right, cousin, your point is well taken. However, your father warned me before about taking your part that I weary him with the bother. But I will plead your case, hoping it does not seal both our fates."

Daring not to barge in and hoping to catch David in an agreeable disposition, Joab proceeded to make the proper appointment.

David, not angry or distressed, addressed Joab, "Nephew, I heard of your barley field fire adjacent to Absalom's holdings."

"Yes, uncle, it was an unfortunate bolt out of the blue. However, everything has been handled and restored as it was before. It was more of a mishap than a tragedy but thank you for your concern. Before I express my plea, I beg the king's pardon. I am relentlessly pressed to present a plea for reinstatement from your third son Absalom. He longs to see the king's face and yearns to be welcomed back into the family. He feels that his situation is worse here and that he might have stayed in Geshur where he was honored. Absalom pleads that, if the king finds any iniquity in him, he will gladly forfeit his life to the king's justice."

Surprisingly to Joab, David was not cross at his petition for Absalom's restoration. But in a sympathetic tone, David expressed his heartfelt sorrow, "I was made aware of Absalom's horrific loss of his wife and three sons. The loss of a child goes far beyond the pale, as it ushers in exquisite pain that few are cursed to endure. I have lost one son, but eighteen remain to guarantee my dynasty and secure my name through the ages. On the other hand, Absalom has lost three sons and has none to carry on his posterity.

"Consequently, he was compelled to build a memorial pillar, so his exploits would not vanish from the memory of men. The scales of justice have been so balanced. So, tell my son Absalom that his father has put away his vengeance, and he is invited back into his presence."

Joab was surprised at the king's leniency and was instantly excited to reveal the outcome to his cousin. He bowed, face to the ground, saying, "I have found favor in the king's sight. Therefore, I will go immediately to Absalom's house and tell him of your gracious decision and that all is forgiven."

Reaching Absalom's front gate with all due haste, Joab announced even before the door fully opened, "You have been reinstated, cousin!"

Absalom, hearing the commotion, rushed into the hallway. "What is this I hear? I have been restored? Do you affirm that my father has allowed me back into the fold?"

"Yes, cousin, your father, the king, has taken pity on you for losing three sons, and in his own words, he believes that 'The scales of justice have been balanced.' So, if I were you, I would immediately present myself while David's contrition is still fresh and before he has a change of mind that overrides his heart."

Overjoyed, Absalom signed off on the barley field deed and, with thanks and gratitude, placed it in Joab's hands.

Nervously Absalom entered the king's gate. The last time he beheld David's face was the day he tried in vain to invite him to the sheep-shearing massacre. The very place where he had Amnon slaughtered by his order. Entering the king's presence, he bowed his face to the ground in humility and respect. David was moved and glad to see his son, "I have lost a son, and you have lost three sons. Let us put the past behind us and go forward from here with the comfort of family grief. Let us never speak of these tragedies again and forever."

The king stepped down from his throne and gave Absalom a holy kiss of forgiveness.

CHAPTER TWENTY-NINE

The First Coup failed.
The Second Coup Will Prevail

Absalom was ready to take the next step. He had regained free rein, and it was time to formulate a strategy, even an armed insurrection if necessary. King Talmai, his grandfather, had whispered cunning plans in his ear for three years, and for the past two years, he and Ahithophel, the seer, had counseled about the intrigue of power politics. The sage advised that, before a successful coup could be accomplished, the people's hearts and minds must follow in support before engaging in any armed conflict. Having regained his princely status and freedom of movement, Absalom realized it was time to put into motion his plan to take over the house of David.

A grand entrance became Absalom's hallmark, proclaiming him a man of power and reckoning. He prepared himself with chariots, horses, and fifty men to run before him.

Absalom rose early, often before the cock crowed. He stood beside the way of the king's gate; it was the best possible place to engage anyone seeking relief from the king's judgment. Being personable and charming, butter would melt in his mouth, and sweet honey of concern for injustices or plight would drip from his consoling lips. Moreover, Absalom was adept at the friendly familiarity of strangers and would engage every inquirer in a personable manner. He would regularly inquire, "What city do you come from?" Often the response was, "I am from one of the tribes of Israel."

Absalom would offer solace and reassurance, "I am sure your matters are good and right, but the king deputizes no one to hear such things. Some have come a long way, but only to be turned away for practicality's sake, for the king is often overwhelmed with petitioners. If I were made judge in the land, every man with a suit or a cause could come to me, and I would do him justice."

When any man, no matter high or low rank, came to Absalom and gave him his due respect, Absalom would extend his hand in friendship, pulling him close and giving him a holy kiss. He did this to any man of Israel who came to the king and sought justice; in this way, Absalom stole the hearts of the men of Israel.

Unaware of the sword in his house, David did his business as usual. Absalom pressed his father for an audience; it was promptly granted to him without a second thought or hesitation. Absalom put his face to the ground in homage. David asked, "What is so important that you have come to share a meal with your father?"

Absalom responded, "I do have a hunger to fulfill a vow I swore to God to uphold."

"Speak on."

"While I was banished to Geshur, King Talmai, my grandfather, encouraged me to worship Hadid, the chief moon god of rain, rivers, and water. Instead, I worshiped Adonai and vowed, when I was pardoned from my exile and could return to Jerusalem, that I would return to the place of my birth and make a sacrifice to the highest and only one true God of the Hebrews. For this, I ask your permission to make my pilgrimage with some noted and pious friends to honor my sacrifice with a host of like-minded people."

Impressed with Absalom's piety and his wish to honor God by granting his plead for amnesty, David agreed, saying, "Go in peace."

Three things were needed to travel to Hebron: a valid reason, permission from the king, and a small army of dignitaries. Policymakers and pious men of substantial authority were duly invited to make Absalom's pilgrimage to Hebron, the resting place of Abraham and David's first seat of power.

Absalom gathered his two hundred men of standing to gain credibility and show the steadfast backing of powerful men. The goal was to sway the undecided to his cause for him to be the next king of Israel and Judah. Unfortunately, none of the two hundred were aware of Absalom's deception. All believed they were on a holy pilgrimage supporting the prince's heartfelt promise to God for His favor and mercy.

The needed years of preparation were deemed fruitful. The centers of power were bargained away to benefit Prince Absalom, courtesy of his grandfather, King Talmai of the Gershurite. All the necessary payoffs, bribes, and political promises of wealth and position to ignore Absalom fermenting a civil war in Judah against his father, King David, was not only ignored but encouraged.

Absalom sent spies, chroniclers, and secret envoys throughout all the tribes of Israel, saying, 'David has had his day and is too far removed from the people, and his son Absalom will be the new king bringing equal justice to the realm. Listen for the sound of the trumpet; then, you can rightfully say Absalom reigns in Hebron.'

Absalom sacrificed the bullocks and rams in Hebron as promised. Still, the plot to support Absalom's rousing speeches grew strong, with many flocking to his banner.

Absalom realized it was time to summon Ahithophel from Giloh, his childhood home. He was the paternal grandfather to David's eighth wife, Bathsheba. Ahithophel was once David's wisest counselor and the man David feared above all others. Ahithophel possessed the wisdom of a sage and, like an oracle, could see beyond the veil. He was the very man who could overcome David's glory and supernatural cunning.

After covering fifteen miles, he arrived just in time to advise Absalom on his best course of action, "Very well done, prince, you have captured the hearts and minds of your followers and have amassed a sizable army. It is time to march double quick to Jerusalem. We might catch David unawares and flat-footed if we are fast enough. We have enough men to put the city to the sword. If David flees before us, we will be relentless, never giving him a chance to organize a defense. The element of surprise is on our side. Let us march lighting torches if we must at nightfall."

Unfortunately for Absalom, the insurrection had grown too large to keep secret. A messenger warned David, "The hearts of the men of Israel and Judah are after Absalom and would have him made king once you and your sons have been eliminated. Absalom's army is only steps away and is coming for your head."

David was in a predicament as the timing of the invasion could not have been worse. Ahithophel's spies had alerted Absalom that the army of Israel and their Chief Captain Joab were miles away, busy chasing down Amalekite pirates raiding trade caravans that plied the King's Highway, leaving Jerusalem undefended.

David called all his servants, men at arms, and household guards, "We must flee immediately, or we shall not escape the onslaught of Absalom for fear that he overtakes us and does us evil, and attack Jerusalem with the sword."

All of David's servants then said in one voice, "We are ready to go wherever you lead us, great king!"

Taking only the essentials for the time was of the essence, David departed with his household. He left his ten concubines to keep the house, implying that this remained the king's house and any violation of that refuge would be a trespass against the king's honor and would be held accountable on the day of reckoning.

David crossed Zion's gate and traveled far away, where he could reassure the people who followed him. So, the Cherethites, all the Pelethities or the congregation of God, and all the Gittites, the original six-hundred that recently came from Gath.

Then said King David to Ittai, the Gittite chief captain, "You came only yesterday, so return back to your home in Jerusalem, and accept who now has the power of a king, even my rebellious son Absalom, for you are a stranger and an exile. You do not have much concern about our recent affairs, so you should not be involved in our troubles. Fortunately, as a stranger, you can hope Absalom will treat you respectfully because of your recent arrival. How could I, in good conscious this day, make you go up and down with us? Should I unsettle you again so soon after your recent arrival? Especially since I do not know where I am going, where to lay my head, or even if I will return. Take back your brethren, your countrymen, the Gittites. Mercy and truth be with all of you. Regrettably, I cannot now reward your kindness and fidelity shown to me. My hearty prayer to God is that He would offer you His mercy in blessings and benefits for all your faithfulness and making good on all the promises He has made, not just to Israelites but to all the newly converted to the faith, such as you are. May mercy and truth go before you."

Ittai answered the king, "As the Lord lives and as my lord the king lives, surely in what place my lord the true king of

Israel shall be, whether in life or even in death, it is there your servant will also be."

Honored by loyalty, David said to Ittai, "Go and pass over," and he and all the Gittites, their wives, and the little ones with them. But sadly, the king and all the people wept as they passed over the brook Kidron towards the way of the wilderness.

CHAPTER THIRTY

Restraint is the Handmaiden of Valor

Zadok and all the Levites were with him, bearing The Ark of the Covenant of God, setting it down on the near shore. So Abiathar, the priest, went up until all the people were done passing out of the city. David was not pleased with the removal of the Ark from the Tabernacle of the Congregation and scolded Zadok, the priest, "Carry back the Ark of God into the city. If I shall find favor in the eyes of the Lord, He will bring me back again and show me both the Ark and His dwelling place. But if He has no delight in me, behold I say here am I, let Him do whatever He judges as proper with me, and I will accept and abide His judgment. Are you not a seer and have been gifted to see beyond the pale? Therefore, please return to the city in peace with your two sons, Ahimaaz, your son, and Jonathan, the son of Abiathar. I will wait in the plain of the wilderness until you can inform me what the intentions of the army of Absalom are before I make a decisive move." So Zadok, Abiathar, Jonathan, and Ahimaaz carried the Ark of God back to Jerusalem and tarried there, with eyes wide open and ears to the ground seeking the much needed information.

In the meantime, David went up the ascent of Mount Olivet and wept as he climbed. He had his head covered and went barefoot. All the people with him covered their heads, and they too went up weeping. David went up to the holy place, the rocks bruising his feet, his head covered in submission to God's will. David was hoping that this act of contrition would be enough for offending God and that God would intervene and provide an escape from the power of his enemies.

Abiathar sent a man to warn David that Ahithophel was among the conspirators with Absalom. Hearing this, David's blood ran cold, knowing the counsel of Ahithophel would be correct and perfect and would confound his strategy. So, David called on God, saying, "O Lord. I pray thee, turn the counsel of Ahithophel into foolishness."

From the top of Mount Olivet, David worshipped God, and suddenly as if an answer to a prayer, Hushai the Archite came to meet him with his coat rent and dirt upon his head. In his darkest hour, David sensed a glimmer of light. He excitedly began, "Hushai, my friend, and counselor. The man renowned for cunning and insight appears before me like a phantom, a sign from God. Indeed, a shield and protection against the wisdom of Ahithophel."

David could see that his prayer was answered and told Hushai as much, "If you go with me, you will be a burden to me; instead, return to the city and pledge to Absalom that you will be his servant and acknowledge him as king. Tell him that, as a servant to David, his father, you would be a servant to Absalom, his son and the new and rightful king of Israel. In this way, you will have the opportunity to defeat the counsel of Ahithophel, whose perfect guidance can undo my kingdom. In Jerusalem you will find Zadok and Abiathar, the priests. So, whatever you see or hear, no matter how trivial, coming out of Absalom's mouth or the counsel of Ahithophel, immediately bring it to the priests. They will give these whispered secrets to their sons, Jonathan and Ahimaaz. Then they will carry them to me, waiting in the Plain of the Wilderness so that I might remain one step ahead of Absalom, my treacherous son."

Coming down from the crown of Olivet and unto the roadway below, David was greeted by an unlikely benefactor. Ziba, the servant of Mephibosheth, was hurriedly driving a caravan of saddled asses. Upon these beasts of burden were two hundred loaves of bread, a hundred bunches of raisins, and baskets full of summer fruit for the young men to eat. Proud at the timeliness of his well-regarded gift, Ziba bragged, "I have also brought vintage wine for any faint in the wilderness, so they may partake and restore their strength and continue to serve the king."

David was compelled to inquire, "Where is your former master Saul's grandson Mephibosheth?"

"He is staying in Jerusalem because he thinks, and said as much, 'Today the Israelites will restore to me my grandfather's kingdom.' He believes the house of David is in turmoil, even in a civil war, and that he would be the legitimate heir and that this violent division will open up enough room for him to claim his proper place as king and, by doing so reinstalling the house of Saul."

The king then told Ziba, "For this treachery, all that had belonged to Mephibosheth is now yours."

Ziba bowed and said, "May I find favor in your eyes, my lord the king."

In their flight from Absalom, David and his people came to Bahurim, or Nob, a place in the territory of Benjamin, which lay on an old road from Jerusalem to Jericho. It ran over the Mount of Olives and down the slopes to the East. It was the home of Shimei, a man of the house of Saul and the eldest son of Gera. Catching sight of the hated David, he ran along the ridge of the hill, cursing and throwing stones at the fugitive king. Finally, he came into the open and swore at David loudly as he approached. Outrage turned to rage, and Shimei continued casting stones at David, his servants, and even the mighty men who were the king's bodyguards that protected his left hand and his right. Frustrated, Shimei bellowed, "Come out, come out, you bloody man, you are a man of Belial or the Devil. The Lord has returned upon you all the blood of the house of Saul, in whose stead you have illegally reigned. The Lord has delivered the kingdom into the hand of Absalom, your half-Canaanite son. Witness that you have been taken in your mischief because you are a bloody man, and the scales of justice seek balance."

The king's oldest nephew Abishai, the son of Zeruiah,

David's sister, was angered by the charge and said unto the king, "Why should this dead dog curse my lord the king? Let me go over with sword in hand; I implore you to allow me to remove his head."

David replied, "This has nothing to do with you, my thin-skinned nephew. So let him curse me and say what he will. Perhaps the Lord has encouraged him to trouble me. Who can say with certainty?" David lamented to Abishai and all his servants within hearing, "Witness, is it not so that my son, which is my flesh and blood, has sought my life and my crown even a second time. How much more now can this Benjaminite cause me greater distress? Let him alone and allow him to vent, for the Lord compels him. It may be that the Lord will look at my affliction, and He will return me good for not revenging Shimei's evil intent."

Continuing along their route David and his men pressed on to the Jordan. Shimei, undeterred, went along on the opposite hillside, stalking and taunting David while remaining just out of reach. As his ire intensified and contempt with vile cursing, he continued throwing stones of scorn and casting clouds of hatred's dirt.

The sun was setting as David and all the weary people refreshed themselves on the crossover banks of the river.

Meanwhile with Jerusalem now an unprotected open city, Absalom and all the people, the men of Israel, and Ahithophel, the mastermind, took possession.

The time was right for Hushai the Archite, David's friend and accomplice in deception, to begin his plea to Absalom, assuring the new king of his turnabout loyalty. Bowing low with his face to the ground, Hushai cried out, "God save the king! God save the king!"

Uneasily puzzled, Absalom asked, "Is this how you show kindness to your friend David? Why did you not flee with your friend giving him comfort and support?"

"No, I only recognize with whom the Lord, and these people, all the men of Israel, choose; this is where I belong and with whom I will abide. Besides, whom should I serve? Should I not serve when in the presence of his son? Then, I shall be under your authority and in your service as I had performed in your father's presence."

"So be it, your wisdom and knowledge proceed you, Minister Hushai. You will make a fitting addition of valued opinions, assuring a victorious stratagem in securing my kingdom."

CHAPTER THIRTY-ONE
A Lustful Change of Guard

Absalom required an act to elevate and inspire the men of Israel, confirming that he had the makings of a king. He needed to exhibit the strength and power of will to step out of his father's legendary shadow.

Absalom appealed to Ahithophel, "Give me your counsel of what I need to do to garner the awe and respect of the men of Israel."

To which Ahithophel wisely advised, "Go unto your father's concubines and ravage them at your leisure. Know all the women fully that David had left behind to keep his house. Then watch them melt with lust from competing with one another to find a place of honor in the new king's carnal heart. Then, when you do this thing openly in the light of the sun and by his son, all of Israel shall hear that your father despises you for the insult of uncovering his nakedness. Only then will all the hands with you be strong enough to overturn

David's impotent and lackluster regime in favor of your more powerful and virile leadership."

The spectacle of his prowess satisfied Absalom, and he gave the order to spread an open-air tent high atop David's abandoned habitation. He had the curtains pulled back to provide all the men of Israel an unobstructed view and to witness for themselves a more powerful pretender. With this wanton performance, Absalom would diminish his father's reputation. He was uncovering the king's most private pleasures and exhibiting them bare for a mob of ogling onlookers. Ahithophel knew that this very act would confirm the foretelling of Nathan the prophet when he said, "Thus says the LORD: 'Behold, I will raise an adversary against you from your own house; and I will take your wives before your eyes and give them to your neighbor, and he shall lie with your wives in the sight of this sun. You did it secretly, but I will do this before all Israel, before the sun.'"

All was made ready when Absalom emerged onto the tent-covered rooftop patio. His beauty was legendary, and he had no scars or blemishes. Absalom's hair, poled with flecks of gold, shimmered in the sunlight. His elegant mane partially covered his nakedness until a rogue gust of wind revealed his masculinity to the "oohhs" and "aahhs" of the waiting concubines. He possessed a stallion's stamina by engaging with a bevy of striving women. A tableau that had never been previously conceived or even imagined was now being witnessed by the gawking eyes of Israel. Absalom's unabashed and brazen performance became legendary, thanks to the retelling by washwomen and gossip mongers throughout all the provinces, from the Euphrates to the gateway of the Nile. Late in the day, the king's concubines lay still and unmoving, overcome by repeatedly experiencing extended bouts of pleasure, hours passed until Absalom, completely spent and covered in sweat, finally rose. The prince bowed to the spellbound crowd, who then applauded the shameless spectacle and the legendary endurance of the man that would be king.

At that very moment, the tower guard blew the shofar horn, warning that the army of Israel led by Chief Captain Joab was returning from a campaign against Amalekite pirates. He was completely unaware of David's hasty flight and the sudden change of leadership, and he was now within striking distance of the Jerusalem citadel.

Dressing quickly into tight-fitting royal attire from his father's discarded wardrobe and sporting a makeshift crown, Absalom called upon Ahithophel for the sage's advice, "What say you of the approaching army captained by Joab, David's nephew?"

"Let them enter the city, as they are unaware of David's sudden departure. This is good news, as David does not have his host present with him. Therefore, in the army's presence, and as their new king, you must replace Joab with your man Amasa as the new chief captain. Thus, giving us control of a twelve-thousand-man militia."

"But what about Joab?" Absalom pressed.

"If it were my choice, I would have him executed, as he will never abandon David to follow you and could very well, in time, spell trouble. But life and death is a kingly privilege. This alone is your decision."

"I owe Joab a great deal and a promised favor. As king, I am obliged to honor that pledge. Therefore, I will speak to him before the transfer of power. If he agrees to concede and informs the army that Amasa is the new commander and that I am the rightful king, he will live and be released to meet whatever fate awaits him. But, on the other hand, if he refuses to acknowledge me as sovereign, his head will find itself in want of a body."

The army stood at attention in front of the king's portico. Joab was escorted into the throne room, thinking he had been brought forward to report on his mission. Instead, to his utter surprise, he found Absalom wearing a lopsided crown and ill-fitting royal attire sitting on the throne of David. Joab shook his head in amazement and said, "Is this a joke? Where is your father, the king?"

Absalom attempted to assure him, "This is no joke, cousin. I am the new regent. Your uncle bolted when I approached with my armed militia. I have won the hearts and minds of the men of Israel. They are with me to a man and follow me without question."

"So, what do you want from me, Absalom?"

"I am dismissing you as chief captain in favor of Amasa, son of Ithra. I need you to assure the army that this change is lawful, and this is because I am the legitimate monarch by consent of the presiding elders. Know this, cousin; I have been advised to have you executed because your loyalty to David is unswerving. However, I owe you a debt for your painstaking service on my behalf. If it were not for you, I would still be in Geshur. Rest assured that, if you participate in acknowledging me as sovereign and Amasa as the new chief captain, you will be free to find your uncle, who is, no doubt, in a pit somewhere, and has now become my mortal enemy. David will realize that your part in planning my reprieve and setting me free caused all this turmoil. I am sure he will take punishing action against you. Our scales are balanced once you leave my sight, with your head still on your shoulders. If I see you across the field in combat, I will kill you without mercy or hesitation. So, what say you Joab?"

Still digesting the shock, Joab took a deep breath before answering, "If I want to continue to live, I must agree with your demands, and so too, if I see you on the battlefield, you are a dead man. I cannot and will not follow a half-Gershurite usurper in favor of David, God's chosen anointed king. Let us get on with this nasty business before I have a change of mind and try to carve out your traitorous heart."

And with that the two cousins, once best friends, were now hated enemies. They silently proceeded to the portico to face the army of Israel. As was fitting and proper, Absalom, the aspiring leader, was the first to step into the sunlight, followed close behind by a scowling Joab. The crier gaveled the anxious assembly into order and announced Absalom as the rightful claimant to the throne of David. Trying to appear regal and in command, Absalom began his address, "Army of Israel, as you have witnessed, there has been a leadership change. My father, David, abandoned Jerusalem as well as Israel and Judah. The elders have agreed to support me and my new regime of justice, and prosperity. My father, the king, needs to make an account of his dereliction and is hiding to avoid justice. I will need every man to assist me in reclaiming the greatness of Israel. In the spirit of new beginnings, Chief Captain Joab, and for health reasons, has nominated Amasa, son of Ithra, to be your new chief captain." You could hear the faint snapping of banners as the army of Israel collectively stopped breathing. Absalom continued, "Come forth, Amasa ben Ithra." Amasa then stepped up to receive the baton of command from Joab.

As it was fitting, the departing commander addressed the troops, "Men of the army of Israel, Absalom ben David is now the reigning authority in Israel, decreed by the provisional elders. As soldiers, we are obliged to follow orders from our commander. Your new chief captain is Amasa, and you must follow him as you have followed me. The newly recognized regent is Absalom, and to him, submit your allegiance."

Joab then proceeded to hand his baton of authority to Amasa with a nod of respect before calling forth his devoted cadre and leaving Jerusalem without any further fanfare. After making his way through the gate, one of his trusted servants said, "Chief captain, I heard the whisper that David and his men were across the brook Kidron in the plain of the wilderness."

Pleased by the news, Joab responded, "That is where I would have gone to distance myself and seek a reprieve from Absalom's assault. So let us be off to join the rightful king and see what we can do to right this wrongful grab for power."

CHAPTER THIRTY-TWO

Contradicting an Oracle of God

Ahithophel wanted to seize the opportunity of having the additional and skillful men that Chief Captain Joab unexpectedly provided. So, Absalom counseled, to which the thoughtful sage responded, "Let me now enlist twelve thousand battle-hardened warriors. I will arise and pursue David once they are in place. He would never have expected such an early and overwhelming attack. I will come upon David while he is weary, weak-handed, and without warning thus making make him afraid. Then, all the people with him shall flee, and I will kill the king only. In this way, I will bring all the people back to you. The man you seek will be no more; all the people will return to you in peace, and you will be their undisputed king."

Liking the sage's plan, Absalom and all the elders of Israel were pleased with limiting the killing and avoiding a pro-longed civil war while disposing of David only, whom they had despised for a long time. They all knew they had gone too far and could not turn back now. Undoubtedly, they were all dead men if David returned and regained the upper hand.

An evil spirit of uncertainty overcame Absalom, saying, "Let us call the cunning Hushai and get his learned opinion on Ahithophel's hastily conceived strategy."

Then, laying out in detail Ahithophel's plan to Hushai, he rejected it entirely and said, "The counsel of Ahithophel is not good at this time, and I will tell you why. Your father and the men with him are mighty men of valor. They are enraged and will fight like cornered dragons. Your father is a man of war and will not lodge with the people. He will be hidden in some pit or place that is not easily found, more than likely an easily defended high ground. In the first strike, your people will be overthrown and massacred. When this news goes abroad, people will say, 'There is a slaughter among the people who follow Absalom.' Even your most valiant men, even those with the heart of a lion, will melt in fear, for all of Israel knows that your father and his mighty men are invincible."

Being emotionally moved by the vivid description, as if defeat was a certainty, Absalom stiffened his backbone in defiance and said, "The strategy of Ahithophel will be my undoing. What do you suggest Hushai as a winning plan to defeat the army of David?"

"I propose that you gather all of Israel, from Dan to Beer-Sheba. Gather a force larger than the number of grains of sand by the sea. With you, Absalom, at the head of a vast army with your hair poled, clad in the king's armor, your majesty will strike fear in the army of David. We shall discover his hiding place and fall upon him as the dew covers the ground. We shall destroy him and all the men with him, leaving no one alive. Furthermore, if David escapes our first assault and seeks refuge in a city, all of Israel will bring ropes to that stronghold, and we will draw down its walls into the river below until not one small stone rests upon another."

The strategy of Hushai gratified the ego of Absalom and also pleased all the elders of Israel. They all agreed as if with one voice that the counsel of Hushai was better than the counsel of Ahithophel, "For the Lord himself had appointed Hushai to defeat the wrongful course of Ahithophel, intending that the Lord might bring evil upon Absalom."

Now in a hurry and losing not a moment, Absalom sent out militia recruiters from Dan to Beer-Sheba, as was Hushai's staling challenge. Hushai hoped to buy time for his master, King David, to recruit and organize.

After receiving rushes of praise and congratulatory back slaps from the elders of Israel, Hushai bowed out. Then, he rushed to the Tabernacle of the Congregation (or Mish-Kan) to advise Zadok and Abiathar, David's close friend and high priest, who was a direct descendant of Eli, the high priest or (kohen gadol) at Shiloh. David had advised Hushai that the two priests were sent back to Jerusalem with the Ark of the Covenant to honor God, keep a wary eye, and spy for the king to convey the plans and designs of Absalom through their sons,

Jonathan and Ahimaaz.

Hushai detailed all that leaked out of everyone's mouths and advised the priests, "Have your sons go quickly, for the king's life depends on the stealth and swiftness of travel. Tell David not to lodge in the plains of the wilderness but speedily pass over the Jordan. Inform him that I had overthrown Ahithophel's counsel to pursue David immediately. He said he could swallow up the king and all the people while they remained shorthanded and unprotected on the open plain. But I cannot say with certainty that he will not have a double mind and send twelve thousand seasoned warriors and kill the king only on this very night, as was the sage advice of Ahithophel."

"Thank you, Hushai, you have done well and have exceeded the king's commission," praised Abiathar before adding a warning, "Unfortunately, Jerusalem is in a partial lockdown, and everyone is detained at the gate and questioned about their purpose, limiting travel and insider information."

Zadok conspired with Abiathar, "We must get this knowledge to our sons hiding in the shadows of En-Rogel or the fountain of the traveler. It is maybe only a thousand yards from the city wall westward. But we will certainly be stopped if we try to leave as we are known as friends of David."

"Let us send Shiphchah, the serving wench. She loves David and can be trusted to deliver this urgent message to our sons in En-Rogel."

Shiphchah was called, and Abiathar prepared her, "My dear girl, service to God and Israel has presented itself with a task that only you can fulfill."

"Speak on, high priest."

"I have a critical warning that needs to be relayed to our king, who is in severe danger. I need you to go to En-Rogel and secretly deliver that message to Jonathan and Ahimaaz so they can, in turn, alert David, who rests vulnerable in the wilderness of the plain, before it is too late…"

"I will gladly do this thing to help save the king," Shiphchah replied.

Abiathar then went over all the details and had her repeat it to him word for word until it spilled from her lips perfectly.

However, unknown to Abiathar and Zadok, they were being watched by one of Absalom's informants as he was unsure of their loyalties to the new king, thus deciding to keep a close watch on their dwelling place.

It was late in the day when Shiphchah approached the western gate shadowed closely by Chakham, a cunning lad incredibly skillful in stealth and stalking.

Swiftly stopped at the sentry post, she was questioned. "What is your business outside the walls so late in the day?"

Thinking quickly, Shiphchah replied, "I am to harvest mushrooms for the evening's meal that only grow in En-Rogel. I must depart right now to return before I am locked out for the night."

The guard paused for a moment before announcing, "Go on then, and you better be quick, or you will spend the night outside these walls and be prey to four and two-legged predators."

Upon overhearing that Shiphchah's destination was the hamlet of En-Rogel, it piqued the ears of Chakham, the spy.

He followed her, for he was suspicious of her weak mushroom excuse and sensed a conspiracy unfolding. So, he stayed out of sight, darting behind trees and blending easily into the landscape.

It was a little over half a mile, and En-Rogel was nestled between one of the seven hills. At the Wayfarers Inn, in the shadow of Jerusalem's high tower, Shiphchah found the two young men drinking wine. They were known to her as she was known to them. She beckoned them outside for the sake of privacy. Jonathan inquired, "My father must have sent you urgent news. Is this not true?"

"Yes, and it is dire." She rehearsed every word she had learned, adding nothing while leaving nothing to the imagination. Then, Ahimaaz suddenly looked up and caught a faint glimmer of a distant figure diving into the underbrush.

"Were you followed?" he demanded.

"I did not see anyone, but I must confess that I felt eyes upon me every step of the way."

Jonathan was alarmed, "We cannot take any chances. King David must know all that has transpired because this timely knowledge is about life and death. Retaining a hold on his kingdom hangs in the balance. We still have daylight. Ahimaaz and I will take the road to Bahurim, and you, Shiphchah, need to get back to Jerusalem before the gates are locked down for the night. Before we leave in a rush, I thank you for your service to God and Israel."

And with that, the two young men were off in a run while Shiphchah doubled back to Jerusalem. Relieved that his cover wasn't blown, Chakham followed Shiphchah to witness her starting place and report back to Absalom before the night closed in.

She went straight to Abiathar's house, where he and Zadok waited. There, she confirmed the source of the treacherous disclosure to Chakham, who discovered that their sons Jonathan and Ahimaaz were the traitorous couriers. Chakham went straight to Absalom and told him all that had happened. Absalom growled in fury at the news, "We must find and kill those young men before they can warn David. Accordingly, I will send my best men to Bahurim and search every house until those two rogues are discovered and destroyed."

The two messengers of redemption managed to reach Bahurim at sundown. Johnathan knew of a man who was a friend and loyal to the king. An insistent knock brought Chavera, a former comrade, to the door. The door creaked open but only to a crack. "Who dares disturb my rest? Speak up or be gone!"

"I am Jonathan ben Abiathar and Ahimaaz ben Zadok, and we seek refuge in the name of David ben Jesse, king of Judah and Israel. Are we welcome here?"

"Well, why did you not say so sooner? Come out of the chill and the gloom, rest, and partake in food and warm milk. So, what brings you to my door so urgently at this hour? I am sure it must be very important sensing your exhaustion."

Jonathan replied, "We carry a great secret for the ears of King David only. We are being ruthlessly pursued. I am sure a cadre of destroyers have already picked up our scent, and if they find us, we will forfeit our lives."

Abela, Chavira's wife, overhearing the disturbing conversation, said, "Let us see if we can ensure that the breath of life continues in your mouth so that you can deliver your great secret to the king of Israel. But of course, if it is as you say, you must be hidden away before your trackers discover your whereabouts. They might already be closing in on our farmhouse. Unfortunately, if they find you in our company, we are doomed to execution. We have a courtyard well that has nearly dried out from the seasonal drought. Therefore, I propose that you two escapees from the grasp of Absalom's vengeance hide in the well until the danger has passed. I will cover the mouth with two flat stones and spread it all with wet barley nodes to dry out when the sun comes up."

It was not a moment too soon when a band of pursuers pounded menacingly at the front door. Finally, Abela, still with barley node dust on her hands, grabbed a rag after wiping off the telltale sign. She opened the door, stepped outside onto the crowded porch, and demanded, "What is wanted so urgently that you hammer at my door?"

The one-eyed captain Lobar, growled in response, "We are searching for two spies and traitors to King Absalom. Where are Ahimaaz and Jonathan? Do not lie if you value your lives. We have tracked them to your house."

"King Absalom? Is King David dead?"

"As good as dead, madam, but never mind about that. I will ask one last time: where are those two men? Do not lie to me, for your life will stand in forfeit."

"They were here, but only briefly. But they did say they

were headed for Brook Kidron. I am sure they have passed over to the plain of the wilderness by now. My husband is inside, and you are welcome to ask him. But unfortunately, he is in bed with the pox, so enter at your peril. But please, in the meantime, search the place till your heart is content and you are convinced that I hold nothing back for fear of slayers such as yourself."

The youngest guard was ordered inside. He covered his mouth with a rag the best he could. But only to confirm that the man was in bed and looked ill unto death, he hurriedly withdrew with no one else detected.

They investigated high and low and combed every nook and cranny but found no signs of the two men hiding in the stalls or the underbrush. So, they finally gave up, sparked their torches, and returned empty-handed to Jerusalem.

When the coast was clear, and the searchers had given up and were well on their way, Jonathan and Ahimaaz climbed up and out of their hiding place. First, they thanked their hosts for their lives, loyalty, and quick thinking. They then scurried as fast as their legs would take them and eventually found David. On arrival, an alert outpost guard questioned the two vagabonds, "Who are you? You are dead men short of having a legitimate reason for being here."

"I am Jonathan, and this is Ahimaaz, the sons of Abiathar and Zadok, the priests. We are trying to inform the king of the newly hatched plot designed to kill him and all the people on the plain of the wilderness."

Surprised by the information and accepting the urgency,

the guard said, "Come with me!"

The men were brought to David's wilderness camp tent, where they bowed, and David recognized them immediately. "You two could not be more welcome if you came down from heaven. I prayed that the plans to inform me of Absalom's intentions, Ahithophel's counsel, and what traps lay before me would come good, so tell me all that you know. Whether you know it or not, God protected your flight."

Jonathan began, "Arise, great king, and all the people with you and pass over the Jordan. Ahithophel has counseled against you. He plans to attack you with 12,000 battle-hardened warriors while you are weak-handed. Absalom has replaced Joab with Amasa as commander of the army. Joab got away with his life and is also inflight seeking the king. Hushai overturned Ahithophel's plan to give the king more time to organize. But Abiathar was afraid Absalom might have a double mind and concede to Ahithophel's immediate attack strategy and kill the king only."

Considering his options, David responded, "I can see the wisdom in Abiathar's caution; if I am caught out in the open, with little or no defense against such an onslaught, all would be lost." So, David gave the order, and all passed over the Jordan. A full moon lit their path through the shallows. By sunrise, not one was left behind on the shore of the plain.

CHAPTER
THIRTY-THREE
The Death of Intellect

Lobar, the captain of the trackers, had an unsettling report. He came before Absalom and Ahithophel, bowing with his eyes fixed to the ground, "Lord, despite our best efforts to locate and detain Jonathan and Ahimaaz, the two priest's renegade sons, and before they could relay to David the mind of Absalom, we could not locate them. Unfortunately, they remained one step ahead of us and escaped capture. We must assume the worst because we do not know what they might have disclosed. Yet, with growing confidence, I believe David is fully aware of your plans and who the enemies are that stand against him. It has been made glaringly apparent now that he has increased his defenses by distancing himself."

The cunning of Hushai the Archite convincingly countered

Ahithophel's perfect counsel. Ahithophel could see the writing on the wall written by the will of God's unstoppable hand. He knew that, once David became aware that he had turned against him, his former prime minister, he would be vilified and made to suffer public humiliation and forced to endure a traitor's death. Ahithophel took his leave and saddled his ass and went to his ancestral home in Giloh and set his house in order. Reflecting on his course, he resolved to seek his own life and avoid the judgment of his former master, David Ben Jesse. A man whom he had admired and loved as a friend who, in the end, caused him great pain and distress. He set about rationally composing his final thoughts.

'I, Ahithophel, meaning brother of foolishness, which is the dark side of great wisdom, and with that a great sorrow. Though, I have been blessed by God to see beyond the mark. God's glory is intelligence, so I have been made an heir to the outreach of intellect. This gift has been both a boon and a bane. It has brought me wealth and position if I sought to serve my fellow man.

Grandchildren are the jewels in an old man's crown, and so was my granddaughter Bathshua, meaning daughter of wealth. My son Eliam, one of King David's Mighties, and his precious daughter. The heartache came with her unfortunate tryst with Horite the Hittite, ending in an unwanted pregnancy. As the alleged father, he did the honorable thing by converting to the Hebrew faith and took the name, Uriah, meaning 'God is light.' Bathshua agreed to marry him to make the baby legitimate and avoid a grievous scandal and, by doing so, took the name Bathsheba, meaning daughter of the covenant. She vowed that all her children would be brought up as Hebrew. Unfortunately, her pregnancy terminated early, leaving her to endure a loveless marriage.

David purchased my adjacent lot to erect the king's mansion of cedar. Bathsheba was on my roof taking her Mikvah bath of rainwater seven days after her issue of blood stanched. My deceased wife had cisterns installed for just such convenience. David witnessed her nakedness on one fate-filled evening and was smitten beyond reason. An illicit affair ensued and again climaxed in an unwanted pregnancy. Her then-husband, Uriah, was at war in Ammon. David tried to avoid fatherhood from the adulterous affair. After several attempts, he was unsuccessful in luring Uriah into his estranged wife's bed. David was fearful that Bathsheba, his soulmate, and his unborn love child would suffer the judgment of Israel and be stoned to death. His only choice was to conspire with his nephew and Chief Captain Joab and use Amnon's sword to arrange Uriah the Hittite's death. The excuse was that the sword of war devours one as well as another. It was not personal, but the unpredictable turn of fate, chance, and bad luck.

All went well until the judgment of God, and my great-grandson died seven days after birth, and he did not receive a name or the promise of circumcision. I held David liable and did all I could to orchestrate his undoing. I have failed on each attempt. God protects his anointed at every turn, and I am left to kick against the pricks, the unbreakable bundled sticks, the laws of God. I seek to find peace at the rope's end.'

Ahithophel was buried in the sepulcher of his father.

CHAPTER THIRTY-FOUR

Gideon Times Three Revisited

Extremely aware of his perilous position, David and his people fled to the safety of Mahanaim, a secure, high-walled city in the wilderness of Gilead. Meanwhile, Absalom took his time and gathered his forces from all over the realm.

Then, finally, his army was deemed vast enough and ready to encounter David, his Mighties—and the fleeing king's hastily recruited militia.

After passing over the Jordan, the army of Israel followed after Absalom, who was clothed in all his spectacle finery. However, he soon grew weak from his overdone royal armor and the oppressive heat requiring the army to pause for refreshment. Absalom eventually turned north and continued to pursue David, who was moving faster than expected.

Absalom's army had left Jerusalem unprepared for such

an extended campaign and all too soon needed to rest and forage for food. They pitched their tents south of the Jabbok River in the Gilead wasteland. Losing track of David's retreat, scouts were dispatched to determine the enemy's strength and location.

David's past kindness was about to bear fruit. The greatest foe of any army is hunger. Not the enemy's slings and arrows but famine that gnaws at the backbone and can quickly turn strapping hulks into quivering shadows.

An unexpected bounty came from the house of a former enemy turned benefactor. After conquering Rabbah, David installed Shobi, the brother of Hunan, as the regent and governor of Ammon. With gratitude for the elevation, Shobi arrived with two other wealthy men of standing bearing badly needed provisions. First came Machir, son of Ammiel of Lo-debar, the fuller or the place of cleaning, and then came Brarzillai, who provided for David's household. Neither man requested favor or repayment because they believed in righteous David. They brought beds, basins, earthen vessels, wheat, barley, beans, lentils, and parched pulse. David, overwhelmed with their generosity, bowed down with gratitude. When he looked up, yet another caravan stepped up, this time carrying honey, butter, and the sweet cheese of kine, cows that had never known a yoke or plow. Following behind was a flock of fat baaing sheep, prime for the roasting. Finally, Brarzillai said, "This is for you, King David, and all the people with you, so they can eat and regain their strength. Your followers are hungry, thirsty, and weary; the wilderness is sparse and can be unforgiving."

David was grateful for the provisions, and this gave him time to organize his army and set forth a winning strategy with the help of God.

As a man of war, David was well-versed in military protocol. First, he numbered the people that were with him. In this way, he could assess his strengths and his weakness. Then he set captains over tens, fifties, hundreds, and finally captains over thousands.

Being greatly outnumbered, David prayed for inspiration. "Lord God Adonai, please lift my mind and confound my adversaries. Please give me the sword of Your indignation. Fill the hands of the righteous with the weapons of war. Let fear and trembling cover my enemies like a blanket. Make their feet slip out of place and let the ground fall out beneath them, dropping into deep hollows and bottomless pits. Whip them with brambles and briars and have the dark woods swiftly swallow the wickedness of my enemies. Do this so all might know that there is a God in Israel. Amen."

Finishing his prayer, David thought he heard the faint echo of a shofar horn far off in the distance. His thoughts then turned to an ancient hero, Gideon ben Joash. Was it, not Gideon that divided his small army of three hundred into three armies of one hundred men each, seemingly converging from three different directions?

Joab had finally found his uncle and presented himself. "Greetings, uncle. I was relieved, dismissed, and lucky to be alive. But unfortunately, your son has turned into a venomous viper. I am ready for a fight to set all things right. I await your command, sire."

The insulted former chief captain now hated Absalom for taking away his army, charring his barley field, and duping him to regain power in his uncle's kingdom.

With the cunning of forethought, David separated his people, a third under the hand of Joab, his middle nephew, and his former chief captain. A third under Abishai, his oldest nephew and veteran of many wars, Joab's older brother, and a third under Ittai the Gittite, a Philistine who had captained David's six hundred from Gath.

Suddenly, a forward scout named Lamar, the Egyptian who had converted and married a Hebrew woman, came running with vital news. "Absalom and Israel have encamped on the open plain adjacent to the wood of Ephraim, named after the defeat of the Ephraimites in the time of Jephthah. Ephraimites often fed their cattle there because Joshua gave them a grant and a place close to the waters of Jordan. So, they would drive their cattle over the river to the lush pasture on the eastern bank.

David then laid out his inspired battle strategy, "A surprise attack will afford us the best opportunity for success. We will confront the forces of Absalom just before dawn and on three fronts. First, Absalom's warming campfires will be our guiding light once we come within striking distance of their sleeping encampment.

First, Ittai and Abishai will flank to the right and the left like the horns of a bull. Shofar horns will strike fear and terror in the sleeping army. Second, Absalom will arise in confusion and reinforce both ends, thus leaving him weakest in the center. That's when Joab, who was holding back, will attack full-on and exploit the thinly guarded middle. Third, we will refuse Absalom and the army of Israel any quarter while denying them time to regroup or to counterattack. Fourth, pursue Absalom relentlessly, and you will have him trapped with his back to the Woods of Ephraim is where God has laid his deadly trap. Finally, you can make short work of Israel's army, unable to organize or form a defensive line in the underbrush, thus causing them to break ranks and flee for their lives. Are there any questions, you three chief captains? If so, now is the time to express any concerns or misgivings. The fate of Israel rests in your hands." A hollow silence took up the space until Joab finally nodded, looked over at his fellow commanders, and said, "Brilliant." All were impressed, and not another word was uttered, ending the discussion.

Then, showing confidence in his men, his plan, and his God, David announced to all within hearing, "I will go forth with the people into battle."

But the people then responded as one, "You must not go out to fight. Your loss would be too grievous! If we are forced to run away, so be it, for no one cares about us. Even if half of us should die, none will notice. But you, our king, are worth ten thousand of us. Consequently, please protect and support us as we remain vulnerable strangers in this life-and-death engagement."

David knew his mere presence gave the people hope and a sense of security in the wilderness. Besides, he had three tried and true, seasoned captains and a divine plan that God had outlined. If he abandoned his people now, it would mean unrest and dissension, and the three captains would look to him for direction instead of trusting in Adonai for His heavenly intervention.

David humbled himself and proved he was a man of the people, saying, "I agree with what you think is best. So, I will remain behind and stay among you, honoring the people's will."

David stood by the side of the gate as his three armies passed by him in hundreds and thousands. But first, he gathered his three commanders within the hearing of all the people and said, "Treat gently for my sake, the young man Absalom." All the people heard the king's heartfelt plea and were moved with confusion and compassion, lacking understanding of the depth of a father's abiding love for a son, no matter how reckless or malicious that child had become.

The first watch began when David's three armies departed the Mannheim gate. The three cohorts marched in a long line north with the setting sun to their left and west. A well-seasoned Egyptian scout knew the route like the back of their hands. It would soon get dark, and each man was warned of the dangers under their feet and to avoid crevices and potholes. However, Lamar, the Egyptian scout, had a trick up his sleeve to help keep the army heading in the right direction at night over uneven ground. He had made an Egyptian army standard that could be lifted to a needed height consisting of a brazen bowl filled with directional fire placed at the head of the column. It would keep the army of David on course as the blanket of night closed in. The Egyptian military was known for traveling in a long, single line of tracking chariots that snaked through dunes and high desert wastelands. At night, the brazen bowl had a fire, and in the day, oil-soaked cotton was used to create a pillar of smoke that could be seen for miles, keeping the route organized, avoiding misdirected travel, and guiding back lost stragglers.

CHAPTER THIRTY-FIVE

The Aftermath of a House Divided

The new moon was a dim silver crescent, deepening the darkness and reducing the enemy's field of view. The first gray light of dawn found a thick fog obscuring the ground. A cloud from heaven had fallen upon the earth, adding stealth and confusion to the pending battle. Silently approaching Absalom's base camp, David's three armies took their assigned positions.

David's people were poised and about to give Israel a well-prepared surprise. Once all were in place, a shofar horn loud enough to wake the dead signaled the attack.

Israel was caught napping as both flanks were attacked at the same time in an attempt to roll up the whole of the encampment.

Ittai took the right wing while Abishai took the left. The strike began with the echo of two shofar horns, signaling that both ends were engaged. Joab waited until Chief Captain

Amasa reinforced the overrun outer edges. This coordinated move would weaken Absalom's center, making it vulnerable to an overwhelming assault.

Amasa, as predicted, sent reinforcements to both ends and hoped to hold back the flanking offensive. Then, with another Shofar blast, Joab attacked the lightly defended center corp.

Overcome, the army of Absalom retreated to the thicket, hoping for a reprieve from the onslaught. The low-lying fog obscured the edges of cliffs, chasms, and the clefts that dotted the wooded landscape. Many soldiers were gobbled up in the wood of Ephraim, and the rest could not coordinate an advance or form an effective defense. Some fell into blind crevices and were wedged into ditches. Many frequently howled, dropping down into bottomless pits, while others got hopelessly tangled in vines, bushes, and brambles. The servants of David slew the army of Israel. There was a great slaughter that day of twenty thousand men. The battle raged and was scattered over the face of the countryside. The wood devoured more than the sword that day.

Unable to rally Israel, Absalom realized that complete defeat was inevitable. Attempting to flee, he mounted his she-mule in the hope of evading his fate and avoiding death, capture, and even worse, embarrassment.

Jockeying around a tight corner and passing under a pistachio tree, Absalom looked back over his shoulder, relieved that no one was pursuing him. Then, hearing a hissing sound, he looked down, and in a blur, a saw-scaled viper released its coil and struck his mule's tender fetlock. The animal then reared up and gave a mighty kick that launched Absalom high into the air. Coming down, his long hair wrapped around a prickly limb of a low-lying branch, and the she-mule ran away—braying, bitten, and frightened. Hanging helplessly between heaven and earth, Absalom reached up, desperate to untangle himself. He continued to struggle but to no avail. His hair was longer than his reach, and his sword had run away with the terrified beast.

A man in Joab's command who was hot on the heels of some fleeing Israeli deserters rounded a bend in a winding road where he was startled to see a man stricken and hanging by his hair. He cautiously approached to take a closer look. To his surprise, it was Absalom, a prince of Israel, dangling helplessly from a tree and flailing in desperation. He thought it best to report to his captain before taking any action.

Finding Joab, he reported, "I saw Prince Absalom alone and defenseless, hanging by his hair from a pistachio tree."

"You saw him, and he is our enemy! So why did you not kill him, and cut him down to the ground? I would have gladly given you ten shekels of silver and a girdle of authority."

The humble soldier rejected Joab's offer and said, "Though I receive a thousand shekels of silver, even a king's ransom, I could not put my hand against the king's son. For I heard the king command you, Abishai and Ittai, saying, 'Beware that none harm the young man Absalom.' So, I could not be in good conscience to disobey the king's plea for compassion. Besides, the king eventually finds out everything, and you would have also gone against me in that defiant disobedience."

"Very well, and as you wish. Now take me to the place of the hanging prince."

Joab and ten of his armor-bearers were immediately led to the pistachio tree. Joab turned to the finder, saying, "You must leave and be on your way. We have a different mind regarding what is fair and proper to set right my vengeful insults."

Joab then took three sharpened darts and addressed Absalom, "Well, cousin, you seem to be up a tree! I told you I would kill you if I found you on the battlefield. But before you meet your maker, I have three sharpened points I need to express now that I have your undivided attention. The first point is when you had me concoct a scheme to bring you back to Jerusalem and void your punishment of banishment for murdering your brother Amnon." Joab hefted the first dart, pulled his arm back, and let the torture weapon fly, piercing Absalom's liver and raising a blood-curdling cry that confirmed his exquisite pain. Joab waited until a dark red puddle of blood formed below Absalom's feet. Then, once again, he relished his revenge. Joab rebuked, "My second point is when you burnt my barley field and forced me to entice your father into allowing you to see his face, and so began your plot to take over his kingdom." Joab pumped back his arm, and the dart hit its mark in Absalom's privy parts, resounding in a high-pitched shriek, his pallor turning ashen and his hands desperately trying to protect his manhood from further damage. Joab was enjoying every moment but still needed to address a final insult, "Luckily for you, cousin, this is my last and sharpest dart; it is for when you relieved me of my command and took away my army, forcing me to fight against men that had been loyal to me through countless battles." Driven by Joab's hatred, the last dart took flight. It struck just above the fifth rib and near Absalom's broken heart. Straining for breath, Absalom spurted his curse as rivulets of life's blood soaked the roots of the pistachio tree.

"You are nothing but a brazen child… that has never grown up and will remain forever… in David's shadow… And at his end… he will most certainly… have you killed for… crossing him… one… too many times… without regard… to consequence."

Joab then ordered his ten armor bearers to surround Absalom and slay him.

When the ghost departed from Absalom's eyes, Joab blew the trumpet, and the servants of David returned from pursuing Israel, holding back any more slaughter and preserving as many men as possible to thwart the ongoing Philistine menace.

Absalom was taken down, his body placed in a deep pit and covered to the brim with stones. After that, all of Israel went back to their tents.

Absalom had no living sons, so he erected a pillar in the king's dale soon after his sons died so that his memory would not fade from the knowledge of legends and heroes of Israel.

CHAPTER THIRTY-SIX

A Hollow Victory

The king's enemies were soundly routed, and the following jubilation was overwhelming. Ahimaaz, a young man, could not contain himself. He needed to stretch his legs and spread his wings by informing the king of their triumph. Being the first to carry the good news to David would be an honor beyond his imagination—the privilege to run back to Mahanaim required permission from Joab, his chief captain.

Joab had a serious problem, and he knew there would be a row with his uncle after ignoring the king's pleadings to 'Deal gently for my sake with the young man Absalom.' Instead, he contradicted David's wishes, brutalized and then killed the young man viciously. Joab hoped the news of his triumph over David's enemies would soften the blow. Joab was playing for time when Ahimaaz came begging for his permission to carry the glorious report to the king, "Let me now run and bear good tidings that the Lord has avenged the king of his enemies."

Still unsettled, Joab curtly replied, "Not today, perhaps another day for the king's son is dead."

Wrestling with his torturous thoughts and dreading the king's reception, Joab reflected, 'Best to face the inevitable, get it over with and stop fighting with myself and forgo the second-guessing. Perhaps I can compose a note to explain the murder.' Then, seeing dark-skinned Cushi, plodding and purposely slow of foot, Joab said, "Go tell the king what you have seen, the flight of Israel and our decisive victory." Cushi bowed for the honor and ran as if his life depended on his swiftness.

Ahimaaz, witnessing Cushi's departure again, pleaded with Joab, "Let me also run, for in the mouth of two witnesses, the matter shall be established."

Joab interrupted, "You have no tidings ready?"

"I know what to say to the king. Let me run and be done with it."

Joab relented, "Run!"

Ahimaaz proceeded to run a grueling course and even overtook Cushi.

Waiting anxiously at the Mahanaim gate, David scanned the horizon for a messenger telling him whether he had retained his crown or his head was forfeit.

The watchman went up to the roof over the gate, looked far and wide, and yelled to the king below, "A man approaching and running alone!"

The king uplifted and said, "If he is alone, there are tidings in his mouth."

The king's curiosity sharpened when the watchman hollered, "Another runner in pursuit; he too has pressing news."

The lookout answered, "I recognize the first man. It is Ahimaaz, the son of Zadok, the priest."

The king felt momentarily encouraged and said, "He is a good man, and he surely comes with good tidings."

Without missing a step, Ahimaaz called out to the king, "All is well," He fell to the earth upon his face doing homage before the king and spoke. "Blessed be the Lord thy God, which has delivered up the men that lifted their hand against my lord the king."

Addressing the main concern, David asked, "Is the young man Absalom safe?"

Ahimaaz tactfully molded his answer, not wanting to be the bearer of grievous news, and said, "When Joab sent another of the king's servants and asked me as well, your servant, and upon departing, I heard a great uproar, but I am unaware of the aftermath."

Sensing that there was more to the story, David ordered Ahimaaz to stand aside and wait.

Cushi came running and hungry for air. Then, after catching his breath, he said, "Tidings, my lord the king. The Lord has avenged you this day and all those that revolted against you."

Still feeling like something was amiss, David blurted out, "Is the young man Absalom safe?"

Cushi soulfully replied, "The enemies of my lord the king, and all those that rose against you to do you evil, have answered for their treachery with their lives and have come to the same end as the young man Absalom."

The king was stricken by the news and held back his tears. He went up to his chamber over the gate and wept in solitude, seeking communion with God, and as he went, he said, "O, my son, Absalom, my son, my son, Absalom! God, I would have died for you, O, Absalom, my son, my son!"

Meanwhile, filled with confidence and bravado, Joab was sharpened by the destruction of all the king's enemies. But unfortunately, he scorned David's weeping and mourning and acting like a sentimental old washwoman.

The glee for such a decisive victory was turned into mourning for Absalom in support of the king's heartache. Though triumphant, the people stole back into the city downcast and ashamed as one who deserts the field of battle. David covered his face to hide his tears of loss and longing from the people, but so grief-stricken, he could not contain his emotions and, in a loud voice, cried out, "O, Absalom, my son, my son!"

Joab entered the city expecting cheers and well-wishers, only to find the people disheartened and sullen. So, he went straight away to confront the king. Entering the house, he found David with his head hung down, unkempt and pathetic, saying, "You have shamed this day the faces of all your servants who would have gladly traded their lives to save your own and the lives of your sons, daughters, your wives, concubines, and all that you hold dear. In that, you love your enemies more than the loyalty of your friends. I recognize that you have no regard for either princes or servants alike. If Absalom had lived and all the rest of us had died, it would have pleased you and joyfully framed your mind. Now rise from your woeful state and go and speak comforting words to your servants who were valiant in their resolve to protect and defend their king. I swear by the lord, if you do not go and speak gratitude and honor to their hearts, I will not abide with you this night."

Joab's anger heightened to outrage, and he threatened David with harsh retaliation, "I will make your life worse, even greater than all the evil that has befallen you since your youth until now."

Taking to heart his battle-weary servants, David arose and sat at the gate in a sign of praise and rejoicing to the multitude. Word quickly spread, saying, 'The king sits at the entrance and rewards his people with his presence.' Soon, the people came before the king, and all were satisfied that Israel, their former enemy, had fled every man to his tent, the official end to Absalom's trespass.

CHAPTER
THIRTY-SEVEN
A Beloved King Returns

All the tribes of Israel were opposed to recalling David, for the people feared retaliation. The elders voiced their nervous concern, "The king saved us from all our enemies and conquered all the nations on our eastern borders. He delivered us out of the hands of the Philistine and now has fled, forced out of the land by the will of his son Absalom. The same prince we anointed to rule over us has died while battling his father for absolute power. We have not yet invited the king to cross back over the Jordan. We need to repent, humble ourselves, and ask for mercy. David will be back, with or without our blessing."

King David sent for Zadok and Abiathar, his two loyal priests, and told them, "Speak to the elders of Judah and ask them, 'Why are you the last to invite the king back to his house?

All of Israel has spoken and welcomed me back. But Judah, my brothers, you are of my bone and flesh, and it is where the insurrection took root and fermented. Is this why you are the last to bring back the king, your kinsman, and brother?'"

This brought to David's remembrance of his Judean heritage and his unsettled issues with Joab. The brutal killing of Absalom, his bitter contempt, and neither begging for forgiveness nor extending the comfort of solace. This prompted David to call forth Amasa, his nephew, a fellow Jew, and chief captain appointed by Absalom, saying, "Are you not of my bone and flesh? Therefore, may God punish me, and even more so, if you will not remain commander of the army and so take the place of Joab permanently."

The reconciling act of promoting a Judean traitor to chief captain, instead of levying a deserved death sentence softened the hearts of all the men of Judah, even as the soul of one man was gladdened. The elders felt safe and sent word to the king, saying, 'Return with all of your servants.'

Now that all of the required invitations were extended, David and all his people passed over the plain of the wilderness and came to the Jordan. The Elders of Judah came to Gilgal on the plains of Jericho. Shimei, Gera's son, a Benjamite from Bahurim, hearing of the approach, hastened and came along with the men of Judah. A thousand men of Benjamin attended with Ziba, the servant of the house of Saul, and his fifteen sons with their twenty servants. They crossed on a floating barge to carry back all the king's household. Ziba thought it was best to lighten the king's burden with honor and foresight.

As David first set foot on the far shore and home soil, Shimei ran and fell before the king, his face to the ground. Then, Shimei, the cursing running dog, began, praying that his words would shield him from the king's vengeance, "May my lord not consider me guilty, nor call to mind what your servant did wrong on the day when you went out from Jerusalem so that the king would not take it to heart. Your servant knows that I have sinned, a great sin, so I have come to be the first from Joseph's house today to meet my lord the king by my loins and my knees begging for mercy, not justice."

Abishai stood on the left hand of David, his oldest nephew and trusted co-commander, and growled, "Will not Shimei be put to death because he swore against the Lord's anointed?"

David's objective was to heal the nation's wounds and seek neither retaliation nor vengeance but instead peace and acceptance, the handmaidens of prosperity and strength.

Israel still had many enemies, so every man was needed and considered essential for the kingdom's survival. David conceded that allegiance and obedience were greater than his need for retribution, thinking, 'Reprisal will come, but in God's time, not mine.'

David barked at Abishai, "What does this have to do with you, son of Zeruiah? That today of all days, you have decided to be my unruly adversary. Furthermore, no man will be put to death in Israel today. For I know this day, I am king once again."

The king then turned to assure Shimei, "You will not die while I am alive. I do so swear."

As if the tension was not intense enough, Mephibosheth,

the lame son of Saul, came down to meet the king entering Jerusalem. He was barefoot; to make matters worse, he had not yet trimmed his beard or washed his tattered clothes. He swore, 'That he would remain unkempt and filthy in protest until the king returned in peace and honor.'

Addressing Mephibosheth, a true prince downgraded to the appearance of a beggar, David questioned, "How is it you did not come with all the people and me when we fled the invasion of Absalom and Israel?"

"My lord, my king, my servant Ziba deceived me. I had him saddle assess with needed provisions for the king and his people. I also told him to saddle an ass for me, so I could come to the king. Ziba hastily departed and abandoned me, a lame man unable to travel. I have heard that Ziba slandered me, coming to the king with my goods to curry favor. But to me, the king is an angel of God and can discern good from evil. Therefore, do to me whatever you deem that is just and proper in your eyes. Most of the men of the house of Saul are dead men, and my lord, the king, is aware of this thing, and you have set your servant among them. Although you, my king, have invited me to eat at his table. Even though you know all this, what right do I have to cry injustice any longer to the king?"

Having had enough of this trivial infighting, David scolded, "Why do you continue to worsen the matter? As I said, you and Ziba must divide the land equally."

In fear of annoying the king, Mephibosheth humbly conceded, "Yes, let him take all the property. It is enough for me that the king has returned to his house and proper place in peace."

In solidarity with the king, Barzillai approached. He was a very aged man, even fourscore years old. He had provided the king with provisions when he needed them the most while he was laid up in the wilderness of Mahanaim. Besides the fact that the king favored him for his timely support, he was highly esteemed in his own right.

When the king saw the great man, he beckoned him, "I want you to come with me to Jerusalem so that I may honor you by feasting at the king's table."

The man answered, "If I were younger and livelier, I would reveal in the honor, but how long do I have to live that I should go with you to Jerusalem? I am eighty years old today and can distinguish between good and evil. But, unfortunately, I can no longer taste what I eat or drink. I can no longer hear the voices of singing women. Therefore, I will be more of a burden to my lord than a blessing. But I will go a little over the Jordan with the king, but there is no reason for him to give me such a reward. So then, if you would be so kind, I pray let me turn back so that I may die in my city and be buried in the sepulcher with my father and mother. But in exchange, and if you wish to honor me, let my trusted servant Chimham go the rest of the way over the Jordan and grant him anything you see as good as you would have honored me."

David replied to the old hero, "Chimham shall go over with me, and I will comply with whatever he requires in your honor." All the people went over with the king, and David kissed Barzillai with a holy kiss and blessed him, permitting him to leave, and immediately he returned home.

The king went on to Gilgal, and Chimham went with him, and all the people of Judah conducted the king and half the people of Israel.

The men of Israel felt deprived of the king's attention, so they came to him grumbling and claiming favoritism, "Why have the men of Judah stolen you away and have brought the king and all his household and his men over the Jordan?"

The men of Judah answered the men of Israel, "Because the king is near kin to us. But, foolishly, you are angry about this matter. We have received no special treatment or benefit from the king."

To which the men of Israel answered, "We have ten parts in the king, as we represent the ten tribes, and so we have more right to the king than you. So why do you despise us in our advice that we should have been first to bring back our sovereign?"

The men of Judah were fiercer with their words than the men of Israel. So, a contention was brewing, seeking a voice of revolution.

CHAPTER
THIRTY-EIGHT
An Ill-Conceived Insurrection

Amid the clamor for rights and privileges, a seditionist rascal named Sheba cried out in humiliation. He was a skillful and noted orator, a Bichrite of the family of Becher, the second son of Benjamin. He blew a trumpet to gain the ear of riotous Israel and thundered, "We have no part in this Judean David, neither do we have an inheritance in the son of Jesse. The tribe of Judah has possessed the king for themselves and will not allow us any share in him; let them, therefore, enjoy him alone, and let us seek out a new king. Let us all give up this unthankful chore of bringing the king back over the Jordan. Let us go each to our homes, that we may consider our best course of action, and then meet in private or public to choose a new king from our inherent lineage!"

The men of Israel heeded Sheba's words and withdrew in

bitterness, leaving David in the middle of the river. But the men of Judah held unbroken to their devotion and escorted the king from Jordan, across the plain of the wilderness, and safely into Jerusalem.

The gossip of washwomen had reached David's ear in Mahanaim, describing the grievous insult of Absalom's debauchery. In that, Absalom knew his father's concubines and uncovered their nakedness in the sight of all Israel. So, David came to his house, gathered the ten concubines, and prepared a feast to feed them. He sat them all down at the communal table. Each woman's eyes were cast down to the ground in shame and humiliation. None could look at David, fearing what he was about to say, "Gentlewomen, you all have given me countless hours of pleasure and comfort, especially when the world was roaring outside my door. I would find a welcomed reprieve in the bliss of your loving arms and warm caresses. My wayward son, Prince Absalom, had spitefully ravaged you, and he is no more. I do not hold any of you accountable because, as far as you knew, he was the new sovereign, and you did what was expected of you in having a good conscious. As far as Israel is concerned, you are deemed tainted women and no longer fit to suffer my embraces. I will not cast you out, though, or diminish you to harlots, nor sell you to slavers in the open market. But you will be shut up here and live in widowhood while all your accustomed luxuries will be provided for as long as you live." Standing up, he nodded in farewell and said, "Fair flowers of Israel, may you seek God's will so that He may restore your peace of mind in due time. Adieu."

Keenly aware of the building momentum of the insurrection and the rebel rousing power of Sheba's speechmaking, David knew it had to be quashed straight away before it had the chance to grow tentacles and reach the walls of Jerusalem.

Reasoning that it was time for him to prove himself, David called Amasa, his recently appointed chief captain, and ordered, "Gather the men of Judah for me and do it with all speed. You have three days to recruit and organize. This is essential to blunt the insurgent's drive before this boil festers beyond lancing and spreads to all the outlying tribes. I need you ready and back here without excuse or delay with the news of this rabble-rouser's demise."

Doing as ordered, Amasa departed to assemble the men of Judah. Regrettably, he found that there was an unexpected reluctance. The men of Judah had followed Absalom and were still licking their wounds and had no desire to engage in further armed conflict. Consequently, it required prodding with threats of violence to obtain submission. The time allotted to Amasa had expired, to the point where his loyalty was questioned.

Troubled by the deployment delay, David called upon his oldest nephew Abishai, a proven commander, and warned him, "Now, because of our inaction, Sheba can do us more harm than Absalom. Take my servants and pursue Sheba before he gets behind the secure walls of a fenced city and escapes us."

Still stinging from his demotion, former Chief Captain Joab gathered behind his brother. With no prompting, he had been assembling a sizable makeshift force, including the

Cherethites, the Pelethities, and all the mighty men on his own initiative. They all departed from Jerusalem in one long line to punish Sheba, if necessary, to the ends of the earth. The pursuers met at the great stone in Gibeon found on the borders of Benjamin, where Sheba was sure to go. But low and behold, Amasa was already there. He had gathered his legion and immediately pursued the defectors. He thought it prudent to proceed after Sheba and save time by not reporting back to David in Jerusalem.

When Joab came upon Amasa, he was wearing Joab's chief captain's garment and upon it the golden girdle of authority that Joab had been stripped of twice in favor of this traitor. Attached to Amasa's girdle was a magnificent sword fastened loosely upon his loins in a trailing leather casing. As Amasa approached to discuss strategy with Abishai and Joab, his sword awkwardly slipped out and tumbled to the ground with a clank. Joab slyly scooped it up and, while approaching Amasa, kindly inquired, "Are you in good health, my brother?" questioning his adversary's unsure gate. Then Joab unexpectedly took Amasa by the beard with his right hand and kissed him deceitfully. But Amasa took no heed to the sword in his left hand, and Joab struck, stabbing him between the fifth rib, leaving his bowels to fall to the ground. Joab took pleasure in another vengeful killing of a competitor. Amasa was shocked and taken completely by surprise, suffering the death of a fool by mistaking the viciousness of a hidden rival as honorable.

Amasa lay in a puddle of blood in the middle of the highway. His people stood still, unknowing and confused about what to do next. Finally, Joab had Amasa's body taken off the roadway and laid in the adjacent field. Joab then covered the gore with a piece of cloth, and everyone who came by stood still, honoring their short-lived leader. Just then, one of Joab's men stepped up and said, "He that favors Joab, and he that is for David, let him stand firm and follow Joab."

Without hesitation, all the people supported Joab in his dogged pursuit of Sheba. They were quietly glad for a more seasoned field commander of the royal family.

Chasing after Sheba, the army of Joab was relentless. Joab needed a victory to soothe the ire of David and regain even the smallest amount of favor. Not only had he murdered the king's son Absalom in cold blood, but now also Amasa, his newly appointed chief captain.

Joab went through all the tribes of Israel from Abel to Beth-Maachah and all the Berites of Benjamin, recruiting volunteers as they passed towns, villages, and even the smallest crossroad hamlets. His growing militia stalked Sheba and his every move. Sheba's traitorous followers were now growing disillusioned and weary from the unrelenting pursuit. He even began to lose recruits as they realized their cause was misguided and futile.

Sheba begged for refuge in Abel of Beth-Maachah and hoped its walls would stall the determined advance of King David's slayers of blood. His plea was met with an open gate and the promise of sanctuary was extended.

Abel was governed by female chieftains and had been so from the beginning. They avoided conflict in place of practical common sense and what was best for all their people.

Joab and Abishai approached the gate with a white flag, hoping to parley with the lever of diplomacy. Yelling out, Joab identified himself, "I am Chief Captain Joab, ben Seraiah, agent and nephew of King David of Israel, and I am on a mission to kill or capture Sheba, the Bichrite of the family of Becher, for rebellion. I have chased him to your door, and I will have him. It is up to you to surrender him peacefully, or I will take him by force by knocking down your walls and killing everything that breathes, whether it be sheep, cattle, or children. Or you can throw his head over the wall, and I, and all my men, will go home and bother you no more. What say you?"

The governor, a wise old matron, replied, "Many here are Benjaminite, and so the family of Sheba, and they have pressed me for mercy for one of their own, and in turn, I have granted him refuge behind our unconquerable walls. These stones have repeatedly kept us safe from invasion over countless attempts, making your threats hollow. We are well-provisioned and are prepared to try your patience in a lengthy siege or repel any death-defying storming of our ramparts. So, go back from whence you came and leave Sheba and us in peace and save yourself wasted efforts, squandered lives, and wrenching grief."

Joab turned and said to Abishai, "The old crone is bluffing. So let us begin our siege in deadly earnest, pull down their walls, and hold them accountable for knowingly harboring a fugitive from justice. In doing so, they will know with certainty that we have come a long way and will not abandon our quarry because of some old woman's idle warning."

Joab's army built a bank of dirt against the city wall. The arrows flew, the rocks fell, and Joab's men held fast. They withstood the deadly hail in their deepening trenches. The people of Joab battered the wall to throw it down. A prolonged siege of slow destruction would ultimately mean death to the city by sword, disease, or starvation.

Once it was evident that Joab would not be discouraged now that his army was steadily gaining entrance, the calls to surrender Sheba increased to a howl that echoed off the ramparts.

An ensign signaled it was time for calmer heads to prevail, and discussion was better than death and devastation.

The wise woman cried out from the walls, "Joab! Come near so that we may speak of dangerous and deadly things that reason may prevail and we can seek a resolution to this turmoil." The woman was contrite, seeing that Joab would not give up the fight or be deterred by stone walls. She appealed again, "Will the chief captain hear me out?"

Sensing the upper hand, Joab agreed, "I do hear you, madam, speak on."

"We will have peace, prescribed by ancient law, in that Joab should offer peace to strangers, much more than to a city of Israel, and if you do this, we shall soon bring things to an agreeable conclusion, for we are a peaceable people. I will ask our counsel so that we can end this matter. I am friendly and faithful to Israel. I was initially hostile to the same authority, which now pleads for an equitable solution. Yet, you seek to destroy a city and a mother in Israel. Why would you knowingly swallow up the inheritance of the Lord?"

Joab sensed the bulwark of defiance starting to crumble and answered again, demanding, "Far be it from me that I should swallow up or destroy. This deadly matter was neither taken up recklessly nor was it ill-conceived. But it is about a man from Mount Ephraim, Sheba, the renegade, who has lifted his heel against King David. So, in good conscience, I ask again, deliver him only, and I will spare the city and depart, causing no further harm or destruction, even though now you deservedly so should reap the whirlwind."

The lady called out in response, "I will present your terms again to the council and the people, and if they agree, we will go one better and throw his head over the wall, saving you the trouble of a bothersome execution."

In her wisdom, the woman went to all the people, and by a loud accord, they slew Sheba and cast out his freshly severed head over the battlements. It took a bloody bounce before making a cushy hollow thump, rolling around and finally resting at Joab's feet. He reached down, lifted the head by the hair, and placed it in a leather pouch that had been prepared earlier for transport. Joab then sounded the trumpet, signaling an end to hostilities and a total withdrawal from Abel of Beth-Maachah. The men retired from the city and went back to their own homes.

Victorious and in grand spirits, Joab returned to Jerusalem. Crossing Zion's gate, he hefted the severed head of Sheba several times, inciting the jubilant cheering crowd. Finally, he presented it to David, the king's favorite trophy of confirmation. In response, David reluctantly reinstated Joab as chief captain, demonstrating that success in battle goes a long way in mending fences no matter how terrible the offense.

Now, by cunning, murder, and another resounding victory, Joab had once again become the master of the host. For the good of Israel, David had put his personal feelings aside, at least for the time being.

CHAPTER
THIRTY-NINE
The Sins of the Father and
the End of a Bloodline

Swollen bellies and the cries of starving children cruelly announced the end of the third year of drought, creating a widespread famine that afflicted the covenant people of Israel.

Consequently, it fell to David to determine the unnatural cause of this blight. It weighed heavily upon the king's mind. The very length and severity of starvation felt like a supernatural punishment. But, as in times of peril and hardship, it was David's custom to seek the face of the Lord for heartfelt counsel.

Finding a quiet grove, the king dropped to his knees in supplication and prayer, "Wonderful God of creation, knowing the end from the beginning, hear the voice of your servant who seeks understanding for the plight of all his people in Israel, who are suffering from famine, distress, and death."

In a still, small voice that goes beyond understanding, the Lord answered his servant, "It is against Saul and his bloody house because he slew the Gibeonites, a remnant of the Amorites who had peopled the land soon after the flood. They sued for an accord and obtained a league for their lives and properties from the children of Israel. That day, Joshua made them hewers of wood and drawers of water for the congregation and the altar of the Lord, even unto this day, in the place he should choose. It was attested to and confirmed by oath and covenant by Joshua and all the elders. In time, they thought themselves bound to keep it and tied them down to that servitude of supplying, first for the Tabernacle and later to the house of God in Nob, with wood and water for sacrifice at the Lord's altar. They served the eighty-five priests who wore the linen ephod. These honorable people had renounced their idolatry and performed all the conditions of their promise."

In his murderous pursuit of David, Saul, the Lord's anointed king, killed Ahimelech, the high priest, and all the eighty-five priests for an alleged conspiracy to provide David Ben Jesse and all his men with Temple Shewbread to eat. David received a high priest's blessing of strength and was gifted the sword of Goliath. Saul believed it was to kill him. Saul then turned his fury on Nob, the peaceful Gibeonite village. He then had all his chieftains, and Doeg the oracle strangled everything that breathed: men, women, children, flocks, and herds. He did so to such a degree of guilt that he drew down divine judgment and wrath upon the land.

David was fraught with guilt, for he acknowledged his part in causing the massacre. He knew a hefty price had to be paid, perhaps even in blood, to balance the scales of divine justice.

After being made aware of the breach and heaven's judgment, David called for his nephew Abishai, known for his shrewdness in negotiating. The two immediately traveled to reconcile with the remaining Gibeonites. The king sought to lift the curse and relieve the people's suffering. David thought to console the former Amorite's unforgivable attempted genocide with silver and gold or whatever they deemed an adequate recompense in the king's power to grant. In as much that they would then pray to God, attesting that their need for justice has been satisfied.

David, his guardians, and diplomat nephew Abishai approached the Gibeonite stronghold. Abishai said, "The king of Israel wishes to speak to your tribal chieftain. It is a matter of utmost importance."

A slightly bent, hoary-headed man with an ancient, gnarled staff stepped out of the shadows and said, "I am whom you seek. My name is Akkadian, the Gibeonite chieftain and your humble servant, great king. I can only suppose you have come to my door because of this unending famine threatening to devour Israel. This has prompted you to journey; is this not so, great king of Israel?"

David replied, "Yes, it is so, Master Akkadian; I have come in good faith to right a wrong that has been left unattended for too long. The stench of evil has risen to the heavens, and God has affected divine judgment upon the land and demands a recompence to balance the scales of justice with an acceptable atonement decided solely by the injured victim."

Abishai interrupted, "Let us speak plain; we have gold by the talent and silver by the score. We wish to pay you for your dreadful loss the best we can so that you would pray to Adonai for our forgiveness that He may bring forth the rain and end this vexing dry spell before any more die of starvation. We will not diminish your loss with petty haggling. Name your price; we will move heaven and earth to satisfy your demands as far as it is in the king's power to do so."

David then added, "What shall I do for you, that you may bless the inheritance of the Lord?"

Listening to all the pleading, Akkadian stiffened and gave an unexpected demand, "We will have no silver nor gold of Saul's, nor anything from his bloody house. But, if we ask, will you kill any man in Israel for us?"

Sensing an end to the famine and once again being a hero, but before considering the potential consequence of such a kingly pledge, David said, "Whatever you say, I will do for you."

Having the king's pledge, Akkadian was prepared to lay down his demands with the assurance of the king's promise "The man Saul that had consumed us and devised evil against us that we as a people should become extinct in all the coasts of Israel. Let seven of Saul's sons be delivered to us, and we will hang them until dead unto the Lord here in Gibeah, the birthplace of Saul, and where the Lord chose him and anointed him king over Israel."

Beckoning to Abishai, David had made an impossible

decision and needed counsel. Abishai began, "That is a request I could not have imagined nor could I have conceived of such a challenge. How the people will view human sacrifice and destroying the house of Saul hangs on your judgment. On a positive note, it is politically practical; you will no longer have to struggle against any future claimants to your throne and vanish Saul's legacy forever. We can present it to the people that you had given the Gibeonites your word that you would grant them any request, and having done so, you are obliged to honor their demands without question or exception."

"Your appraisal meets the mark, nephew. I did give my word, and that is for certain. I can accomplish this murderous plot in good consciousness. We have just enough sons, and I can still spare Jonathan's son Mephibosheth the younger and keep the Lord's oath made between me and Jonathan, the son of Saul, to keep his son free from harm. We can take the two sons of Rizpah, meaning hot stone, Saul's concubine, that he had sired, Armoni and Mephibosheth the older. Fortunately, there are the five sons of Princess Michal, not of her body, but just as much by adoption. They are the five sons of her sister, Princess Merab, wife to Adriel, the son of Barzillai the Meholathite."

After finalizing the details with Abishai, David conceded to Akkadian demands, "We will accommodate your deadly request if you do not accept anything less than a human sacrifice. We will return with your hostages within a fortnight."

David had put Michal away some time prior, and all the boys she mothered were grown men now on their own. So, they would have to be rounded up and kept safe until delivery could be made. The only bright spot was that he would only have to deal with Michal after the fact, or if ever. But, on the other hand, Rizpah was a fiery wench and would not take the sacrifice of her only two sons lightly or without a fight.

Back in Jerusalem, time was becoming of the essence. People were dying of starvation in ever-increasing numbers. It was time to gather up the posterity of seven blameless sacrifices. "Listen up, nephew," David called Abishai to attention, "I want you to take a party of trusted guards and search out the five sons of Merab. First, you will have to trick Michal into disclosing their whereabouts. She will cast you out without help if she knew of your real intent. Next, approach her alone and make up some excuses; for instance, tell her I need a five-man trade delegation to Egypt who can negotiate because of their royal lineage. Take them one by one or in a group. Use the same ploy. If they resist, use ropes and chains if necessary. Next, I will deal with Rizpah. I will tell her I would like their company on a diplomatic mission to Gibeah to quell a growing resentment on an issue centered around their dead father King Saul's past exploits. If she denies me or they resist, they will be bound, and once in custody, I will reveal to Rizpah their intended fate; I owe her that."

All went as planned for King David, in fact even better than expected. One son was visiting Michal from a far country, and he was intrigued by the proposition, so much so that he went with Abishai to help locate the other four brothers. David sought out the concubine expecting trouble. Rizpah had never liked or trusted David because he always seemed to have a hidden agenda. So, David decided to take his guards to lessen the threat of violence. When approaching the cottage, luckily, Saul's two sons, Armani and Mephibosheth, the older, were working in their mother's garden. David told his men to keep an eye on them as he went in to speak to the royal courtesan. David stood in the shadow of the doorway. With the light pouring in behind him, it took a moment for Rizpah's eyes to focus on the intruder. After being taken aback by her recognition, she wryly exclaimed, "As I live and bleed, it's the king of Israel himself. What brings you here to my humble abode? I see danger is about to cross my threshold. I know trouble follows you like a wanton shadow, or do I suppose wrongly?"

Considering their long history over turbulent times, David decided to be forthright and hold nothing back, thus destroying her peace. "The Lord has cursed the ground for Saul's evil massacre against the peaceful Gibeonites, the servants of God. The famine brought about by the lack of rainfall is because the Lord has sealed the heavens and spoiled the sky, causing many to die."

"What has this to do with me and mine?"

"Not you, but your sons. The Lord will release his curse once the Gibeons have been made whole for their loss. Their demand is an eye for an eye, a tooth for a tooth, and a life for a life, as found in God's law. I gave them my pledge and a free hand to ask whatever they wished. They refused silver and gold and demanded seven sons from the house of Saul to hang until dead in Gibeah, the city of Saul. I need your sons' to help fulfill their savage demand to release the curse that ravages the land. "

Rizpah's feet fell out from under her, and she collapsed against the wall before shrinking to the floor in dismay and misery.

"How can you do such a thing? They are all I have and my reason for living."

David insisted, "My duty is to God and a greater Israel. Some must die so others might live. I fear this decision is final; peaceably or forcefully, they are coming with me. I can allow you to go with them if you promise no outbursts, screaming, or disruptive behavior. I am, after all, on the Lord's errand, which requires acceptance and a measure of decorum. Do you abide, madam?"

Having little choice, Rizpah was forlorn but agreed, "I do abide, my heartless King."

And so, the seven sons of Saul were delivered into the hands of the Gibeonites, who had already built sturdy gallows that would accommodate all seven of them. In doing so, the sound of their collective death rattle would be heard in heaven.

Comforting her two sons and the five sons of Princess Merab, Rizpah brought food and provided comfort by her singing. But her son Armani could not be consoled; Rizpah asked him, "What can I do to ease your mind, dear son of mine?"

"I am not afraid of dying because everybody dies; is that not so, Mother?"

"It is my son, and then gathered in the arms of the almighty and to know such happiness and peace that surpasses understanding, you will ask yourself why you fought so hard to stay alive in this harsh, cruel, and uncertain world."

"But it is in this manner, hanging, and soon after, with the birds pecking out your eyes and the wolves and jackals feasting on your feet."

"Be not concerned, my son, for I will stand guard so that no winged or footed creature will touch your body. I will comfort you in death as I comforted and protected you in life. I swear, by all mighty God."

On a hill overlooking Gibeah and in full view of God and all the people, the seven sons of Saul fell together and were put to death on the first day of harvest.

Rizpah, true to her pledge, took sackcloth and spread it out for herself upon a rock from the beginning of the harvest until the water dropped out of heaven upon them all. As promised, she suffered that neither the birds of the air nor the beasts of the field disturbed the dead men. Rizpah, with her sapling staff, smote the crows and ravens. She battered Griffon vultures, the king of birds, from sunup to sundown. The jackals were relentless, and the foxes cunning as they darted out from nowhere, avoiding stones and arrows in the process. The wolves came at night, but she kept them at bay with torches and spears.

David gathered Saul's seven sons and laid them to rest with the bones of their father and brother Jonathan in the sepulcher of Kish, the clan patriarch in Benjamin.

After that, God blessed the land, and once again, the windows of heaven opened. The rains came, the earth blossomed, and Israel flourished.

CHAPTER FORTY

The Best of Friends, the Worst of Enemies

A recount of David's past exploits

Prince Achish, the prince of Gath, was once David's benefactor and loyal friend. But, unfortunately, the love and respect they once shared had soured, and they had now become sworn mortal enemies. For the longest time, David had cleverly deceived Prince Achish and made him look like a fool in the eyes of the other four princes of the Philistine.

The Philistine town of Ziklag, once the province of Achish, was gifted to David and his six hundred vagabond armies of malcontents, misfits, and debtors. These men were neither farmers, merchants, nor tradesmen. Instead, David had taught them war and the resulting rich bounty that comes from pillage and plunder; the piracy trade was very well received.

After years of being chased from one stronghold to another or the next distant campaign, wanderlust had lost its magic, for some had had enough now that they were offered a permanent home in Ziklag. This prompted some to take wives and raise a family. But, like always, to do so required money. Some settled for farming, but even that needed treasure for livestock and seed. Most were, by disposition, soldiers of fortune and remained restless for the adventure of the next conquest. So, engaging in their well-practiced profession seemed like their best option. It was time to find vulnerable villages, towns, and hamlets ripe for the picking.

The six captains of hundreds and the high priest Abiathar sat down with their commander David ben Jesse to consider their best course of action. David began, "Ziklag is a prime location; we can make inroads to many Canaanite and Judean towns as well as villages alike, and none will be the wiser. I cannot, in good conscience, hurt our people even though we are still hunted by Saul, who remains busy preparing for war against the Philistine realm. We are safe here only if we stay in the good graces of Achish. Therefore, I propose that we loot the Canaanites only. Regrettably, it must be done with the utmost ferocity, as no one can be left alive. Men, and if we kill the women, what is to be done with the children, who will grow up to seek our deaths for retribution's sake? The little ones must be put to the sword without pity or exception. We can leave none alive to tell our tale of murder and betrayal. Besides, we are killing enemies and future enemies of Israel and Judah. I will tell Achish that we plunder only Judeans, and he will receive his share of the bounty. In his heart, he will decide that my people hate me, and I will be his servant forever."

David's view of Achish's ready acceptance depended upon

his share of the regular and generous bounty, thus reducing his need for questioning. Achish was so convinced of David's loyalty that, on the eve of the largest Philistine invasion of Israel, he invited David and his army to participate against his old master, King Saul. David and his men complied and appeared in full battle order but were speedily dismissed by the other Philistine princes as untrustworthy and unreliable, and that he, David, could easily turn against them in a critical part of the battle, as it turned out, this was rightfully so. David made a hasty withdrawal back to Ziklag while his head was still on his shoulders and his army remained intact. The impassioned plea of Prince Achish barely dissuaded the princess of the Philistine from capturing and executing David and his six hundred Hebrew mercenaries.

In time, David became king of Judah and then king of all of Israel. Though, politically, he remained on good terms so that he was able to enlist the Philistine chariot army in the conquest of Syria.

Israel and Judah, under the guidance of David, grew ever more powerful. He was conquering all his eastern borders, releasing the king's trade highway from the Euphrates to the Egyptian border, thus establishing the empire of Israel. Israel's wealth and power began to threaten Philistia and their ever-shrinking Canaanite legacy.

The death of King Maoch left a vacuum of authority; typically, it would have been filled by his son, Prince Achish, without dissension or rancor. But recently, and mostly by accident, a Canaanite man in his cups told an amazing story that held spellbound the denizens that haunted Gath's Black Raven tavern. The stranger began, "I was a lad, no taller than a broom bush. My mother heard a shrieking of terror and an uproar of commotion. She had me run and hide in the underbrush. I covered up until I was no longer visible. After the screaming quieted, I curiously parted a branch and looked out only to see my mother slaughtered, my house ransacked and then put to the torch. The flames turned into a holocaust. Some men with their swords drawn came poking and searching for anyone hiding. They came so close that a blade almost nicked my shoulder. But I cowered down deep and stopped breathing and evaded detection. As the gang of them finished filling their wagons and gathering up the livestock, one man caught my attention as he seemed to be their captain. He was giving orders and directing the action. He was different, beautiful, and ruddy. I heard one man yell, 'David, we are ready to depart; all the carts are full, and the herds and flocks have been rounded up.' I then heard the man with the red hair yell, 'Let us make our trail home to Ziklag before nightfall.'

"I waited until the next morning to uncover and search through the smoldering wreckage. There were no bodies, only scattered bones and piles of ashes. Eventually, I made my way to the roadway and was soon picked up by a traveling band of Amalekite raiders. I told them my story, and their leader, Lotan, intrigued by the revelation, began planning a reprisal. It was not so much for the destruction a fellow pirate caused but the opportunity to gather a horde of ill-gotten gains he felt was rightfully his. Lotan realized that a poacher was invading his territory; now he knew who and where the treasure could be found. Ziklag was on the outskirts of Philistine territory and the village where all the spoils were likely gathered for easy removal and transport. All he had to know was when David and his men were out on some adventure, leaving the village undefended."

A servant of Achish was in attendance, and he was sure the prince would need to hear this incredible story. The problem was that this tale would be repeated with the speed of bad news on the feathery tongues of gossipmongers. It would be a short time before the retelling would overstate this fantastic tale and soon would be common knowledge and challenge the standing of Prince Achish, who would be the rightful king.

Hearing the fantastic account made the prince's blood run cold with icy hatred for David, his Judean vassal's brazen deception. His once trusted servant had made him look like a fool. When the other four princes got a hint of this embarrassment, they looked narrowly and questioned his ability to govern. It was said that 'Achish might be entitled by blood but not by his disposition to be king.' The final decision had to be with the full consent of the ruling council.

Achish acted sovereign upon his father's death but was not yet installed as the permanent monarch. So purposefully, he needed to show some initiative to regain the respect of his fellow princes.

Achish stepped forward and launched his plan before a word could be uttered against him, "I believe I have a winning strategy to be successful in a new war with Israel." He confidently looked each prince in the eye, waiting to be challenged by one of his peers. Finally, Prince Axel of Gaza and Philistia's chief captain took the floor, "Please tell us, prince, who would be king? What ingredient have we missed all these years to vanquish our sometime friend and often mortal enemy, King David of Israel?"

Achish gladly responded, "In a word, giants and sharpened iron swords."

That piqued the assembled members' attention when Axel curiously questioned, "Speak on, prince, and leave us not in suspense."

Now that the attention of the leaders was fixed on him, Achish continued, "I have recruited four giants that have pledged to kill our nemesis, David ben Jesse, king of Israel. If we kill him, the flame of Israel will be extinguished, and their will to fight as a people will be greatly diminished. Therefore, I have recruited four giants: first, Ishbi-benob, or 'his dwelling is on the height,' the son of Rapha, and one of the Rephaim. He has the strength of ten men in his arms. I have forged a special iron sword to bring his colossal power to bear. In addition, I have obtained a Kenite sandstone to sharpen an edge that separates the flesh from bone, and with his spear of the three hundred shekel weight of brass, he is sure to be our avenger of past insults."

Axel again asked, "And how do you propose to lure David and the army of Israel into the arena of conflict? David is getting on in years and may neither rise nor be so inclined to accept your invitation to war."

Achish responded, "We will lay a trap for the aging David.

He will believe that he had discovered our secret plans to invade Jerusalem and that we have gathered all our forces at Shephêlah as a decoy, where we will seem to be the most vulnerable and see if he takes the bait."

"You said you had four giants, Achish."

"No, not to field them all together, but to keep three in reserve. Then we can slowly wear Israel to a nub, one battle after another, until we destroy them and David's legend. In such a manner, it will be a pleasure to watch our hated rival squirm and burn until we are victorious. We will let slip our invasion plans by making it a loosely guarded secret. David's spies will do the rest. We will gather all our five armies and stage our forces at Shephêlah. The soft-sloping rolling hills between the Judaean Mountains and the Coastal Plain. It will also give us the advantage of the high ground. David will try and avoid an invasion of Israeli borders. He will rally his army and attempt to surprise us in the open.

CHAPTER FORTY-ONE

One Giant and One War at a time

If you wish to make a secret a rumor, tell your listeners that it is confidential and for their ears only. Then, the mystery will soon travel in back alleys, over the hanging lines of washwomen, and into the ears of camel drivers.

Consequently, one of David's many informants sped the bad news back to Jerusalem that Achish, the acting regent, had put Philistia on a war footing. After receiving the disturbing dispatch, David summoned Joab and Abishai, his commander and co-commander nephews. Typically, Abishai was the first to arrive, showing his uncle his due respect, bowed to the king and said, "I pray the king is in good health. Your messenger said it was urgent, and I came on the run. Sadly, Joab is ill and not available and sends his regrets. So, tell me, uncle, what is your need, and how can I serve the king?"

David grimly stated his concerns, "One of my informants has confirmed that Achish, my former benefactor, is now the provisional king of Philistia. He has told the council of princes that he is qualified to rule permanently and aims to prove it by going to war with Israel. Achish claims he has found a way to conquer us, their old adversary. The messenger was not sure, but it was something about iron giants. He is preparing five armies at Shephêlah in this very moment. So, I deem it prudent to rally our forces and attack while the enemy stages for their invasion, and we can catch them napping."

"I hear and obey, great king. That is a winning strategy. We will encounter them on the plain of Shephelah or as they attempt northern travel on the King's Highway. As it matters not, they will be disorganized and vulnerable to attack. Therefore, I will assemble the army and give them their marching orders. We will be on the move and the hunt before sundown tomorrow."

The army of Israel proceeded to stretch their strides and was soon on the coastal plain of Shephêlah, where they faced five mighty Philistine legions in full battle array. Achish patiently waited on the high ground for his formal vassal turned archenemy, David, king of Israel. As Achish had predicted, David took the bait and fled headlong into his trap.

Looking up at a man standing on the crest of the ridge and casting no shadow, he called out below to the assembled Hebrew division, "David ben Jesse, my former and errant vassal, welcome to your ending. Patiently, I have been waiting for you. As you can see, we of the mighty Philistine hold the high ground, and dislodging us will be deadly and costly. There is little likelihood that you will not overcome the climb of aimed stones and tumbling boulders. However, you are free to attempt such a foolhardy adventure. But, I have a proposition to save you much gore and grief. Do you wish me to continue, or are you ready to try your luck in storming the heights?"

Ever ready for a challenge, David hastily replied, "Speak on, prince; there is unfinished business raging between us."

Achish was pleased by the response and proceeded to offer his compromise, "I propose single combat, one-on-one, and man-to-man. The victor takes the field with honor for his race and his people. The loser dies, and his people go home in disgrace but alive. No quarter will be asked or given until the last breath of one or the other has been expended. If you are too old to compete, David, king of the Jews, and wish to refrain, we are ready to battle you from the plateau and hope you enjoy watching the slaughter of your fellows."

After listening carefully, David stepped purposefully into the light at the base of the rise. The people of Israel drew back behind their king, giving him enough room to fight. He ungirded the weight of his armor that was hampering his stretch and stride. David defiantly wielded his sword over his head, falling to one knee and striking the earth menacingly. He raised, pointed the tip of the blade directly at Achish, and shouted his acceptance of the challenge, "To the death then, prince; I look forward to separating your bulbous head from your skinny neck. I await your royal presence."

Achish, flushed with hatred, took a breath and restrained himself. Then, mockingly, he replied, "You misunderstand; I would not lower myself to engage in a brawl with you, shepherd boy, son of Judah. Instead, my champion, Ishbi-benob, will act on my behalf. Unless your word is hollow, and you have become a fearful coward."

David replied, "Send your worst, even Satan, if he will tolerate your presence; the God of Israel is with me."

Stepping forward was a giant of a man with a spear with the weight of three hundred shekels of brass and an iron sword that easily weighed twice again. The superb iron blade boasted a handle and tang made of jasper and jade. He leaped down to the plain and onto the flat ground at the skirt of the hill. The giant eyed David and drooled spittle, hungry for combat. Ishbi-benob hefted his spear and magnificent sword and growled, "Was it not you, David, king of the Jews as a youth, who knocked senseless my brother Goliath of Gath with a sling and a stone? Then you brutally cut his head off with his fallen sword while he lay lifeless and helpless. He was a pure son of Rephaim and a mountain of a man. He was bigger and stronger than I, but he could not move fast enough to avoid your childish weapon. I am the son of Rephaim, but I can run and jump twice as fast as any of my race."

Crouching down in a battle stance, David chided the giant, "I can see the family trait of long-windedness. Were you planning to talk me to death? Let us get on with it, for I have an empire to govern."

David was as tough as ever. But, even though his age was a factor, he still had the heart of a lion, and fear was as far from him as the moon is from the stars.

Ishbi-benob ran out of words and cocked his arm, letting

go of his mighty spike, more in anger than accuracy. The giant attempted to make his point loud and clear as his brass spear whistled past David's ear and dug a deep furrow in the hard, unforgiving ground. Then, as it was in David's nature, he charged at the greater adversary, lion, bear, or Philistine colossus. The behemoth's polished iron sword glinted in the sun, and the glare obscured David's sight momentarily with the flash. The king pressed on, ignoring the blinding peril, before lunging and nicking the hip of the agile titan. David suddenly felt a loss of strength. He faded and stumbled. Watching on, Abishai became troubled by his uncle's struggle to remain vital and alive, fearing the light of Israel would be extinguished. So, he climbed to an outcropping above the fray. Once there, he pulled his dagger and waited until Ishbi-benob was directly beneath him. He then sprang down like a wildcat on the hunt. Abishai came down full force and stabbed the giant's neck until the blood spurted out with every pump of his heart. Doing his utmost to remain upright, Ishbi-benob's legs finally buckled, and he fell dead at David's feet. It was all too close to a disaster, and David's men swore to David, saying, "You shall not go out with us to battle anymore, that your death would quench the light of Israel, and we cannot and will not abide your loss to the nation."

True to his word, Achish and the Philistines withdrew, but the war was a long way from being over. All that was gained was that David survived his last battle with a giant and had won this day's reprieve from the Philistine entrapment.

David knew that his time had come, and his warrior days had ended as they had begun, battling giants in the noonday sun.

CHAPTER FORTY-TWO

Twilight of the Titans

Furious at his embarrassing defeat against an aging David, Achish was not finished with him or Israel's ever-growing threat. Because of the failure in Shephêlah, Achish remained a figurehead with no real power without consent from the governing council. Achish addressed the princes, "I was surprised and dismayed at the determination of the aged David. All would have gone as planned until his nephew, Abishai, climbed up and then jumped down upon

Ishbi-benob. In doing so, he bled his neck and opened a vein, causing death in sight of all present. The dying throes of our titan, our symbol of power, disheartened our people that the fight had gone out of them. But, as I had bargained, a withdrawal seemed our best and most honorable course of action."

Prince Axel then asked, "Do you have a plan, or have you gathered us here to reminisce about your past failures?"

Ignoring the slight, Achish continued, "I think we have

taken a faulty approach in bending Israel to our will. The way to overcome David and the Zionists is to disrupt their money supply, specifically the trade routes that afford them swords, armor, and soldiers. Fortunately, there is a place where they are the most vulnerable. A small village called Gob. It is just outside Gezer at the crossroads of the trade route linking Egypt with Syria and ongoing to Jerusalem and Jericho. Conveniently it is on the road from Ramleh to Yalo. We can mount a barricade and pillage the caravans as they come to the crossroads and make their turn on a blind curve. I have enlisted Sippai, son of Rephaim and Goliath's bigger brother. His presence will threaten and frighten the merchant processions. Consider that each train will be hauling vast amounts of treasure, ripe for the taking. We can then enslave or hold for ransom the wealthy merchants.

"Certainly, by the time David is aware of the raiding and begins to organize, we will have gathered a vast amount of gold, livestock, and camels. Then, when Israel finally deals with their losses, we will have been well rewarded and have fattened our coffers. Moreover, the profits will allow us to enlarge our military enough to repel and humiliate Israel, our archrival."

The plan intrigued the princes; even Prince Axel applauded it, calling for a united vote. Then, with the council's permission, Achish called forth Sippai, the giant, and a legion recruited from each of the five princedoms.

Once the Philistine soldiers were hidden behind trees and boulders, Sippai, like a giant colossus, blocked the crossroads, rendering them impassable.

The first caravan that emerged from a bend and came upon the menacing giant stopped firmly in its tracks. They were immediately set upon, pillaged, and enslaved; those who resisted were hastily slaughtered. This scene repeated itself many times over. There was so much loot that the Philistines needed a baggage train that stretched back to Gath.

Piracy was common and considered a business cost, but the losses soon became extreme. First, it was the complaints of the local merchants, but it became glaringly apparent when emissaries from Syria and Egypt protested to David about their overwhelming losses.

The outcry that reached David was undeniable. So, he called forth Sibbechai or Mebunnai the Hushathite, one of David's Mighties and captain of the eighth provisional forces.

Sibbechai fell on his face when entering the king's presence. David began, "Sibbechai, I long to see my old friend's catching smile; do not hide it from the king." Sibbechai then stood up, and David inquired, "Ah, that's better. Tell me, how is your health, and can you take on an assignment that requires fielding your army?"

"I am as fit as any man in my command. I lead by example. I do not ask any man in my militia to do something I am unwilling to do myself. Therefore, I am gratified to be called by you, my lord, to serve him and the nation. Tell me, what service can I perform for the greater good of God and Israel? All that is left for you to do is command me, great king."

"Very well, there has been a widespread outbreak of piracy on the King's Highway. From sketchy reports, it is somewhere in the Judean hills. We have narrowed it down to the crossroads between Gezer and Gob. It has been said that the Philistines are behind the crimes, yet no victims have come back alive to verify who the culprits are, and it is rumored that giants may be present."

"As you command, my lord, I will gather up my men and be on the hunt in three days. Consider the bandits erased, either Philistine or Amalekite brigands. It does not matter. After that, the robbery and murders will come to an end."

As promised, the army and Captain Sibbechai were on the King's Highway, which remained cautiously empty of traffic. Merchants now feared losing their wares, camels, men, and lives. The Eighth cohort passed through Ramleh and was halfway to Yalo between Gezer and Gob when a forward scout came running and shouting, "Philistines and a giant standing by a felled oak blocking the roadway!"

Calling his lesser captains for a strategy session, Sibbechai questioned his forward scout, "How many Philistines and giants did you see?"

"One giant for certain and hundreds of Philistines. But looking at the vastness and condition of the encampment, there are many more, and they had been there for a season."

Sibbechai then addressed his men, "They will not reveal the vastness of their host, not until we challenge them at their barricade. So, I will approach with a small cadre. The rest divide in a long line on the high ground, blotting the horizon. This will make us appear to have a greater strength of numbers."

Doing so, he approached the titan guarding the fallen oak. Sippai growled, "What is wanted here, puny Israeli?"

The yelling aroused the sleeping encampment. Since all the caravans now chose a less direct route to avoid the King's Highway at all costs, the Philistines lay idle, awaiting further orders to return to their tents. But now, the host rallied at the stump to support their symbol of power and repel Israel, their sworn enemy.

Captain Sibbechai heckled the giant, "Your size and idiocy support each other, just another overgrown running dog of the Philistine's crumbling empire. Your numbers are vanishing like a hoary frost in the noonday sun. Today is a good day to join your brothers in the afterlife."

Enraged, Sippai threw his spear, missing his quarry and splintering a nearby sapling. Sibbechai recovered the lance and charged the giant who had climbed upon the felled oak. When Sibbechai was close enough, the behemoth flung himself with all his might so that he might crush his foe with his fury. Bracing himself, Sibbechai planted the giant's javelin tightly in a rocky crevice. Once in flight, Sippai could not retreat or rethink his hasty leap. Instead, he impaled himself, like a dumb brute beast, in full view of his Philistine marauders.

The Philistine looked out on the horizon only to witness a wall of warriors as far as the eye could see controlling the high ground. They were outnumbered, and there was no benefit to battle. This crossroad, without its giant, was no longer profitable. The order was given, and the group returned to Gath empty-handed.

Reporting back to Achish on the death of Sippai, the giant, the intrusion of Israel, and the pause of caravan traffic at the crossroads at Gob had an unexpected and opposite reaction. Achish chuckled, "The operation was a success, better than I had hoped for or imagined. We have gained a great store of wealth, but unfortunately, at the cost of one giant. But all in all, a satisfying result." He accounted for the extent of wealth accumulated over the past few months to the council. They grew quiet from the loudness of the numbers.

"I propose we wait until caravan traffic resumes their regular course of travel. They will be wealthier prizes because of a delivery interruption filling an unsatisfied appetite. The merchant's confidence will strengthen as their cargo is delivered to its destination safely and without delay. Fortunately, so will the size of the baggage train, and frequency will double, thus increasing our rich plunder. I suggest we wait three months, giving time for the merchant's trust to be restored."

CHAPTER FORTY-THREE

Pillaging for Giant Profits

Still, after three months, Achish still lacked the full faith and confidence of the council. Achish proposed a second round of caravan piracy and subjecting the King's Highway to disruption, "We have increased our treasury and will soon be able to arm and equip Ammonite and Syrian mercenaries with iron weapons. This seizure of wealth will enable us to end Israeli supremacy. We suffered the loss of Sippai, but that was only because the dumb brute leaped before he looked. Now we have Lahmi, the more formidable brother of Goliath the Gittite, who can put a spear the size of a weaver's beam to flight."

Prince Axel then asked, "What will you do differently in this instance to ensure a favorable outcome?"

"We are limited to the Judean hills for an ambush between

Gezer and Gob at the high mountain way station. I propose two moveable barricades—one in front and one behind to stop anyone from fleeing. In addition, we will enslave people and kill the rest of any potential troublemakers. After that, the trains will again vanish into thin air. In this way, no alarm is prematurely sounded, thus increasing our harvest time until our plot is discovered."

The princes wagged their heads in acceptance.

Axel spoke for the majority, "All right, Achish, let us continue to fill our coffers with the seizure of plunder. But I warn you, if you bring destruction upon us, you will be held liable with your life and crown."

As foretold by Achish, the caravans started up again, carrying even larger and richer baggage.

The stage was set as the first movable barriers were put in place. Upon turning a blind curve on the King's Highway, the caravan master suddenly faced Lahmi, the giant. The colossus stood menacingly on the thoroughfare, dripping spittle and wielding a weaver's beam-sized spear, greater than eight cubits, point, shaft, and heel.

The wool, cotton, ivory, spices, jewels, fine teak, and mahogany furniture continued filling the Gath warehouses. Donkeys and camels gathered into herds of saleable pack animals. But there, too, was a ready demand from Egyptian slavers. The unsold old or injured were brutally slaughtered, avoiding any possible escapes that could lead to a troublesome discovery.

In time the outrage was again felt in the halls of the king's palace. Merchants and emissaries demanded protection from the mounting losses of men and treasure. It was not hard to imagine that the Philistines were up to their old tricks again. David called forth Elhanan, the son of Jaare, a fellow Bethlehemite and a trusted servant of David. He was known for his cunning and agility in battle. David had promised to make him one of his Mighties, but first, he had to prove his value and make a name for himself as a valiant warrior with some remarkable feats of bravery.

David cautioned, "Elhanan, as I had promised, an opportunity for greatness has presented itself. I believe the Philistines are pillaging the trade convoys between Gob and Gezer because it is the most exposed stretch of highway, and they are doing it a second time right under our very noses. My senses tell me they are amassing wealth to stage a major offensive by hiring mercenary armies and advanced weaponry. I want you to take a legion and stop any further pillaging. I suppose that by now, they are running out of giants."

"Thank you for your confidence, great king. I will return steeped in honors and resolve the Philistine menace once and for all, so help me, God. I have considered a plan to surprise our nemesis and wish your thoughts on my strategy."

"Speak on Elhanan son of Jaare."

"It is best to approach the Philistine ambush if disguised as a wealthy caravan of slavers. I also propose that all wear the rover attire. We will be directly followed by a company of fighters posing as enslaved people walking close behind a weapons-laden cart hidden under the animal fodder. All eyes will be on us while the rest of the militia will follow within striking distance. We will hold our own until relieved by the advancing column. Once we put the enemy on their heels, we will pursue and discover where they have cashed their mountain of treasure. However, putting the needed pieces together will take a week, perhaps two. In the meantime, we will cleverly drip the news of the vast wealth headed in the direction of Gezer. The Philistines will be salivating at their good fortune."

David was noticeably impressed by what he heard, "Your plan has merit, even brilliance. Tell me whatever you need, and I will put it at your disposal forthwith."

Costumes and camels were made ready. The strongest fighters wore rags, and quick-releasing ropes were affixed to their ankles and wrists. The advance guard left before daylight, so the casual eye could not connect the two parades. The stage was set as the procession left the gate just after sunrise. The rendezvous took place when the train reached the Judean hills, and they changed places. The supporting warriors then took a position two miles behind the clandestine caravan.

Turning a fate-filled corner, Elhanan, dressed as the caravan master, spied Lahmi, the giant towering over a heavy dew-covered grassy patch. He was blocking further progress while wielding his colossal javelin and growling death-defying commands. "Your journey has ended, and you will go no farther, not alive anyway. All who refuse to dismount, run, or struggle will forfeit their lives. But oblige, and you might survive and live to tell your grandchildren of your encounter with Goliath's bigger brother."

While the giant attempted to instill fear, the Philistines filled both sides of the ravine and barricaded the rear to prevent any escape. Then, dismounting and undoing his headscarf from his turban, Elhanan shouted back, "What gives you the right, you oversized pirate, to obstruct the King's Highway?"

Outraged by the refusal to comply and the oversized slight, Lahmi threw his spear with all his might in Elhanan's direction. Agile and quick, Elhanan dodged the huge projectile, hitting his exposed camel broadside instead and toppling the beast off its feet. Brandishing his sword, Elhanan charged the colossus. Lahmi pulled out his monstrous blade and opened his stance, bracing himself for a downward strike. Feeling the slickness of the dew and running full tilt as he came within just feet of the giant, Elhanan dropped to his knees and slid under the titan's legs just as Goliath's blade swished passed the back of his head. Elhanan thrust his sword upward and stabbed the monster in the groin. An agonizing howl of sharp pain echoed through the valley, forcing all within earshot to suck in an imagined gasp of agony. With a ground-shaking thud, Lahmi fell to his knees. Thinking quickly, Elhanan rose and sliced above the monster's ankles. The giant bled out and would rise no more to terrorize Israel.

The disguised enslaved people then leaped into action, releasing their binding chords and retrieving their hidden weapons. Luckily, a shofar hidden among the fodder was recovered and brought to a high plateau. It was powerfully blown with the passion of Gabriel's last call, rousing the closing battalion to speed to the rescue.

The Philistines closed in for the kill, going back and forth in the narrow gap, but the disguised warriors held the line until the trailing troop appeared not a moment too soon and caused a breakthrough. Then, flooding in and hollering their war cry, they cut, stabbed, and sliced their way into the fray, turning the tide and routing the Philistine marauders.

The retreating Philistines and the army of Elhanan fought a running battle from the Judean foothills and across the Shephelah. A ten-mile stretch of the coastal plain, a rolling cluster of grassy foothills to the gates of Gath, the Philistine capital.

The alarm sounded as the last heathen scurried through the closing portal, and the parapets bristled with archers. Two huge oil cauldrons hinged over the gate and had their heating fires ignited.

Gath was the bridle of the Philistine empire and had to be conquered by stealth and cunning. The fear was that, if it were attacked, the other four princes would come to Gath's rescue, taking all of Israel's strength and most of her allies to subdue the stronghold. Elhanan was aware that he was overmatched in attempting to overthrow the well-fortified citadel. His only viable option was to retrace his steps, bury his dead, and see to the needs of the wounded before reporting back to the king.

Lifting his arm and signaling for his men to withdraw, an errant enemy arrow found its mark and struck Elhanan in the armpit. It was not at first fatal but disabling. He had lost the use of his arm and had to travel back to the location of the ambush and then on to safety and Jerusalem.

As they entered Zion's gate, David met Elhanan and his battered but walking wounded, the remnants of his clandestine caravan and battalion.

David began, "Welcome home, warrior of Israel. I can see that you are wounded. Let us first call upon my physician. We can talk as your wound is dressed."

Elhanan was uplifted to see the king and handed him the giant Lahmi's sword, saying, "I thought this prize would be befitting since you had once captured the sword of Goliath, and now I present you with his brother's weapon, so now you have a matching set."

David beamed, knowing his ruse was successful and glad for the exceptional trophy. Elhanan's wound was cleaned and dressed in ointments and herbs, and his arm was put in a sling to aid healing. Once the healer left the room, David needed to know all the details as he was strongly advised not to participate in combat for the sake of the nation. Instead, he would get vivid pleasure in hearing the harrowing tales of battles, heroes, and giants.

Elhanan gave an accurate account of the incident of the fall of Lahmi, the brother of Goliath. He spoke of the intervention of the trailing battalion and the running battle to the gates of Gath. He left nothing out, neither skimped nor glorified, and stressed, "Sire, I believe all the wealth that has been stolen is behind those guarded walls, and nothing less than an all-out invasion will allow us to retrieve all that has been stolen."

David thoughtfully responded, "You have done a man's work this day, and the nation and I are eternally grateful for it. However, I must think of the proper response, in the cost of lives and treasure. I must question whether it is worth an all-out invasion and what we might accomplish to strengthen our borders. But I do need to instill confidence back into the hearts and minds of merchants, both near and foreign. It is the king's burden, but I will seek out the council of men and, in the end, the will of God."

CHAPTER FORTY-FOUR

The Least Likely of Men

Laurels were liberally dispensed, encouraging a renewed patriotism. Gratitude to the heroes of Israel was forthcoming. But God was afforded the greatest reverence for his grace and strength in overcoming the enemies of Zion, which makes all things possible.

The celebration of the victory was short-lived, for King David had made a difficult decision to either refrain or implement an invasion. So, he called upon Hushai the Archite, known for his clever mind and practical reasoning. Did he not refute the wisdom of Ahithophel and, by doing so, save David's life and kingdom?

Hushai approached the king with his face to the ground, saying, "You have sought me, sire. Your faithful servant came without delay; say the word, and I will move heaven and earth to obey your wishes."

"Rise, Hushai. I seek your wisdom and knowledge, nothing more."

"It is a privilege and an honor to serve the light of Israel. Speak on, great king."

"The Philistines have gone on a war footing once again. Achish is king in name only, once a friend who has turned bitter against me and is now a seething enemy. His power comes from the council of princes and total consent. In the kingdom of Philistia, their wealth and power weaken as Israel prospers and grows stronger, causing fear and resentment at the highest levels. They have been reduced to pillaging treasure on the King's Highway. They need funding for foreign militias and advanced weaponry to launch an effective invasion of Israel. That plunder is now an ample cache in Gath. My concern is that, if I attack Gath to reclaim our lost treasure, the other four princes will come to Achish's assistance and attempt to repel a full-scale invasion of their dominion. The cost of lives and treasure will be far greater than the Philistine plunder. What are your thoughts on this matter, Hushai?"

Pondering the gravity of his advice, Hushai reflected long and hard on both sides of the argument. Sitting long in silence, David was becoming impatient for an answer.

Finally, Hushai revealed his thoughts, "Your majesty, I do not see any other alternative but to strike while the enemy is unsure of your next move. Suppose we return lightning-fast to Gath before the other princes can organize an intrusion. Then, hopefully, you can recover the stolen goods, men, and livestock and return them to Jerusalem. Once the seizure is accomplished, I do not imagine the Philistines will attempt a poorly provisioned invasion. I must believe that the other princes will cease all piracy when offered a peaceful accord of toll in the disputed territory."

"Very well, Hushai, well spoken. After all that I can do, I will seek God's will, that I might cross the last bridge of understanding with his blessing."

Retreating to his hiding place, David called upon God for direction. Then, while praising God with gratitude and heartfelt longing, he heard a still, small voice utter, "Jonadab." David's first thought was, 'That was not my voice.' The only Jonadab that came to mind was Shimeah's son, also called Jonathan. He was known for his subtle shrewdness. David knew he was Amnon's best friend but did not know he had coached Amnon in the seduction and rape of Tamar, his half-sister: David's daughter and Absalom's loving virginal sister.

David knew that God does His work, His strange work, and brings to pass His act, His strange act. David had suffered from questioning the will of God, no matter how fantastic or impossible the task that presented itself. He learned to trust in God without hesitation or reservation.

Summoning Shimeah, Jonadab, and Elhanan, with his arm still in a sling, David discussed the treachery of Achish and the urgent need to invade Gath to free the caravan masters and drovers and recapture the stolen wealth. This had to be done before the other princes could rescue the city of the bridle with a legion of chariots.

David addressed the gathering, "Elhanan's wound prevents

him from fighting, and age has overtaken me. I am no longer permitted to trade blows with the enemies of Israel. I have no fear, but the nation insists that I refrain and not take the chance of quenching the light of Israel. Therefore, I have sought God and his infinite wisdom and am impressed to send Jonadab to lead the Gath expedition. This must be organized and launched immediately before the Philistines discover our intentions. What say you, Jonadab?"

Jonadab looked to his father, Shimeah, meaning 'that hears,' who heard of his son's sordid advice to Amnon, which caused turmoil and upheaval and killed the rapist prince. Shimeah thought this would be a perfect way for Jonadab to redeem himself in the eyes of God. So, he looked not at, as much through, his son and nodded his acceptance at the honor being bestowed and encouraged him to do likewise. Jonadab did not like the prospect of armed combat, where every man must face himself with death tugging at his shoulder. But mustering a false bravado, he rallied, "Thank you, great king, for the honor. I will make you and my family proud."

Shimeah looked knowingly at his baby brother, David, king of Israel, and both men grinned, recognizing the young man, genuine or feigned, was committed to fulfilling his destiny.

David turned to Elhanan, "Tell us what you saw and guide us on how you would attack the Philistine capital."

Elhanan advised, "The surest travel is along the King's Highway. Achish will no longer be scouring the horizon for trade traffic. He would not expect an army to approach in such a manner to attack his stronghold. I would leave the roadway and proceed south using the Judean foothills as a screen. Then turn east and cross the ten-mile Shephelah plain to Ziklag. We can rest there in relative safety." In his excitement, David exclaimed, "Ziklag, that is where some of my men decided to raise crops and a family and give up the uncertain life as roaming mercenaries."

Elhanan, smiling and confidently nodding to the king, asked, "If I may continue, my lord?"

Reminiscing momentarily, David applauded the cunning, "Yes, please go on. I am intrigued."

Elhanan continued, "Then I would turn north and attack Gath from the south. It would be best to arrive at the darkest hours and well before dawn while tower guards are in a drowsy stupor, slipping in and out of slumber. The key to the invasion of Gath is their stout wooden gate and the two hot oil vats protecting the entrance. I would secure the makings of climbing ladders and send a squad of fighters to scale the walls with a liar's stealth to slit throats and then switch uniforms. This must be accomplished before the end of the fourth watch. Once secure on the battlement, slowly pour a kettle of oil to soak the wooden planks. Then, using a war helmet lifted from one of the dead guards, douse the pulleys and the fixing ropes. Bring a white banner and signal to launch the fire arrows, and a consuming blaze will ensue. An alarm will be sounded, and the ramparts will flood with fighters. In the narrow space, you will withstand them until the cables snap and the doors swing open. Then, you can storm the city, reinforce the battlements with archers, secure the high ground, and prepare for battle.

Elhanan's proposal was met with delight and acceptance. David was generous in his praise, "Well done, Elhanan; I would venture to say that you have replayed this invasion in your mind a thousand times. The devil might be in the cracks and crevices, but God is certainly in the details, and you, sir, have proposed a well-coordinated attack. Even though your plan is well-considered, it is good to remember that combat is fluid, and the unexpected often rears up at the worst possible moment. I advise you, Jonadab, that you have the final decision on approaching and achieving your strategy as the expedition's commander. But, being a former field commander, I would urge Elhanan's scheme, which has a real possibility of success. I would also suggest that your legion start nestled between two separate and well-timed caravans. If spotted by any roaming Philistine spies, it will be assumed you are a security detachment. This will shield your true intentions until you depart the King's Highway and use the Judean foothills to screen your southern route."

All those present were confident in the approach. Jonadab exclaimed, "I believe this well-thought-out plan has given me sureness in completing my objective. Once we breach the gate, I will locate and detain Achish as my hostage. I will free the prisoners and gather the livestock and wagons before carting back the stolen plunder. Then, with your permission, great king, I will offer a path for Achish to save face and quell the certain retaliation from my invasion. I will explain that Israel wishes no further hostility and that we will concede to the disputed section of the King's Highway as Philistine territory.

Furthermore, I will extend the offer in the king's name for the Philistine empire to exact a toll tax of up to one-tenth of all goods crossing through their domain. That will allow Achish to maneuver a peace treaty with the ruling council and avoid further bloodshed."

David was pleased and said, "Now I know why God would have you as the point of my sword and head of my spear. You have my blessing and my permission, Captain Jonadab. If there is no other discussion, let us prepare for a successful conclusion to these constant outbreaks of giant hostilities." All present chuckled at David's lighthearted wordplay.

CHAPTER FORTY-FIVE

The Enterprise of Surprise

A well-provisioned and highly capable legion was hastily prepared for a combat mission. A necessary second-in-command was at the field commander's option.

David questioned Jonadab, "Have you considered a candidate for adjutant? I have found it best to exchange your thoughts on strategy, sieges, and breaches, as a second mind often reveals hurdles and missed opportunities. But realistically, you are going into combat, which I deeply miss. The intensity of living on the edge heightens one's senses like no other endeavor. Being that close to death purifies life's breath. When a moment is an eternity, your only thought is to vanquish the enemy, whatever the cost. Holding nothing back, faith replaces fear, and you become focused on destroying every obstacle. It is quite freeing, as it dispels all other concerns as trivial. As the leader, you are the most sought-after prize. If you fall, someone else must pick up the baton, rally the men, and urge them to victory."

"I agree, lord king, and I have thought hard and long about a relatable deputy. Therefore, I recommend my friend and your tenth son Solomon, also known as Jedidiah. We have split many a wineskin together, and our natures complement each other's thinking. He is quick-witted and always lands on his feet."

Encouraged by Jonadab's selection, David commented, "I am pleased with your choice and obvious insight. It is about time that Solomon tasted the hardships of a soldier's life and confronted leadership decisions. Let us invite Solomon to these proceedings to acquaint him with our proposition and what is expected of him. At this time of day, he will most likely be at the Three Swans Inn, eating and drinking with questionable comrades."

Solomon was none too pleased to be pulled away from his favorite pastime. But when the king's sons are summoned, the command is enforced by the determined, strong arms of the king's guardians.

Coming forth, Solomon bowed, respecting his kingly sire. Then, he questioned, "You called me, Father. I listen and obey. How can I please the king this day?"

"Welcome, Prince Solomon, my brilliant son. You who are fleet of foot in the pursuit of women and insatiable in the draining of vintage tubs. But fate has intervened in your becoming a seasoned warrior instead of drowning in excesses of pleasure. We will now witness how you fare in the cauldron of battle. You have been nominated by your friend Jonadab as his second-in-command for a surprise attack against Gath, the

Philistine capital. It has already been decided. I have purposely agreed that you will participate in this operational conflict."

"I see you have made up my mind for me, Father, and all that is left is for me to concede to the king's wishes. When do I leave on this expedition?"

"You and Jonadab are to prepare immediately. The sooner it is done, the safer it will be before Philistine spies uncover our plans and designs. I will leave it to Captain Joab to provide the details," the king replied.

Taking Solomon aside, Joab laid out the strategy for freeing the captives, livestock, and pilfered caravan merchandise. "Consequently, if we can subdue Achish, we are to propose a political compromise to quell a bloody Philistine uprising."

Jonadab half-joked, "Besides, cousin, when I heard that there would be a wagon full of wineskins, you were the first person that came to mind."

"I do not know if I should be pleased for the honor or insulted by the complaint. It feels more like the latter."

"Your fertile mind and quick wit will come in handy when it matters. Our long-term familiarity also prompted my decision to invite you to our military invasion."

"Ok, then, and thank you for soothing my sensitive ego. One refinement I would propose is to bring a battalion of skilled archers and a wealth of arrows."

"Consider it done, cousin."

Men at arms were assembled with provisions and marching orders.

The first caravan left the gate earlier that day while another was preparing for departure the next morning. It was finally time for the stealthy cohort to nestle between the two fleets of wealth-laden dromedaries.

After several grueling hours, the hot desert sun blazed orange on the horizon. Finally, the horn sounded to pitch back and make camp. Outpost guards were assigned, and wineskins were generously supplied to fortify against a chilly night. The water casks had a stale taste of iron but were used to fill the emptied skins once the last trickle of the tasty elixir vanished.

Warming fires dotted the landscape, and a lucky few got to enjoy roasting a fresh kill.

Meanwhile, the two co-commanders settled on an overlook in full view of the encampment.

Swigging down his fill, Solomon gave an empty belch as he spied Jonadab's nearly full wineskin, only drained of a mouthful. Solomon anxiously questioned, "Are you going to finish that? If not, give it here. Even a drop arouses my thirst, and a craving for more becomes an unscratchable itch."

"No, cousin, I am no longer in that frame of mind. You are welcome to my portion. The aftermath of my last jaunt and its dire consequences has lessened my appetite. But I see that your fondness for the grape has only intensified since our younger days of unbridled revelry."

With a slight smile, Solomon replied, "For good or for ill, that is quite true—my spirit soars when wine washes over my gums and tickles my tongue. It sends fire down my throat, and my belly smolders. My face flushes, and my mind rushes to a fevered pitch. Yet, an overwhelming sense of ease and comfort saturates my soul. I feel confident and invincible; I can even talk to women, all shyness and uncertainty melt away, and my dancing takes on a joyful abandon. I know you might think this absurd, but I feel a wholeness with God. Yet, some undeniable demand compels me to chase these elusive feelings. My only answer is that more of the same will help me attain a more blissful state, verily a oneness with the divine."

"That, my dear cousin, was an intriguing description of wine's cunning and baffling power. Unfortunately for you, the skins are empty and filled with water to keep them from sticking together, and besides, water will be more valuable than gold where we are going. We will need life-giving water in our winding trek south, east, and north to approach Gath from the wilderness wasteland. You will be glad for the cool, wet quench when you are on the coastal plain and parched from the winds that whip through the hot and dry dunes," Jonadab assured.

"There will be no ability to satisfy my thirst for wine. That is why my father was so glad of your nomination. It gives me a needed break from my continual drinking. It will strengthen me physically by enduring a soldier's hardship and mentally concentrating on life-and-death decisions under combat conditions."

The night quickly passed without detection or interruption, but it dragged on in a restless sleep for Solomon. He woke soon after midnight in a sweat. Try as he might, the ground was hard and unforgiving. Meanwhile, Jonadab slept like the dead and had to be roused after the fourth watch ended.

Jonadab called forth his captains of tens and hundreds and laid out his battle plan, "We are ten miles from Gath, and if we make a direct approach, we will be in full view of tower lookouts. Consequently, this will allow the Philistines to catch us on the open plain without an adequate defense. I do not doubt that a legion of chariots will pour out of the city to overwhelm us. Unfortunately, there are too few of us to withstand such an engagement. Therefore, our main weapons are our surprise, stealth, and subterfuge. Their war wagons are useless when bottled up in the city and unable to maneuver, and that is where I intend to keep them. I believe that, so far, we have managed to go undetected. Let us keep it that way. There will be no more warming fires to give away our presence. We will continue our southern route using the Judean hills to conceal our travel and drop below Gath for six miles, and then we'll cross over the Shephelah coastal plain and cover the ten miles to Ziklag, King David's first capital. Many of his six hundred are still there from the old days, those who put down the sword and picked up the plow. We will find rest there without causing alarm or fear of discovery. After a brief reprieve, we will turn north at nightfall, journey six miles, and approach Gath from the south at midnight."

The captains nodded along as Jonadab continued, "This is when the real work begins: scaling the walls with stealth and siege ladders, overpowering the guards, and putting on their vestments. It will require twenty men to control the battlements. Our timing is critical, and it must be done within one hour and no later than two hours after posting the fourth and final watch. Those guards roused from a deep slumber and peering out into the darkness will flutter in and out of consciousness. Once we have silenced the tower guards and have taken charge, I will start dousing the connecting cable pulleys and release the locking pin. Then, slowly tip an oil cauldron to cover the planking thoroughly. Your signal is the white flag being waved from the battlements and that the oil has been spread, awaiting a spark. Then, let the fire arrows fly to their mark. The gate will quickly be engulfed and burning hot. An alarm will be sounded, and the parapets will flood with guards attempting to douse the inferno and regain control. The securing ropes will take time to burn, but once one gives way, the other chords will release their tension, and the doors will open as if by magic. Prince Solomon and the remaining detachment will storm the entrance, holding nothing back. Meanwhile, a company of archers and swordsmen will quickly be dispatched to the battlements and support my covert warriors against a furious Philistine onslaught. By now, Gath will be fully roused, and unorganized groups will attempt to push us back out of the city. But remember, without their chariots able to maneuver, we retain the advantage and the high ground from the ramparts."

He then paused to take a look at all in front of him before continuing, "Please, commanders, this is the time to question and bring forth any doubts or misgivings." Not a single utterance was sounded, to which Jonadab responded, "Good. Let us get on with it, knowing God is our guide, buckler, and high tower. Please do not make a mistake and take this invasion lightly, as we are about to attack the Philistine capital."

CHAPTER FORTY-SIX

The Grasp of Twelve Fingers and
the Speed of Twelve Toes

The winding sixteen miles to Ziklag found the army of Jonadab in good spirits. Solomon was ready to put down his water-filled wine skin and taste the pleasing and refreshing local vintage.

The people of Ziklag were still loyal to David, their former commander, and gladly shared their food, wine, and the delicacy of insider information.

The legion entered Ziklag with King David's banner to ensure a welcoming reception. The mayor named Rosh, meaning greater, rushed to meet the two commanders.

"Greetings, commanders of Israel. Please feel at ease as you are among friends. Whom do I have the pleasure of addressing?"

Jonadab began the introduction, "I am Chief Captain Jonadab, also known as Jonathan, son of Shimeah, and this brilliant fellow is Prince Solomon, also known as Jedediah, son of David and my esteemed co-commander."

"Welcome, lords. I am Captain Rosh, master of Ziklag village and former soldier of David, and I remain a loyal follower of Zion. I can provide men, labor, and materials for your mission, whatever is needed. However, one thing I need to insist on is that our help is not mentioned. If word returns to Achish and the other princes that we assisted you in your mission, we will be held accountable in a day of reckoning. Living here on the border is only permitted because we have married Philistine women and raised mixed heritage children. So, we dutifully pay our tribute promptly, keep to ourselves, and cause no trouble avoiding Philistine ire."

Jonadab was pleased with the offer of support, "Thank you, Chief Rosh. I am sure King David will remember you with admiration and kindness, and I assure you that your assistance to our cause will not go abroad."

Jonadab continued to speak of needful things, "I require four trustworthy forty-foot ladders to scale the walls of Gath, enough food, wine for my men, and oil rags for my fire arrows. But even more valuable is information about the capital's daily comings and goings."

"All your ladders will be completed, requiring a two-day effort. But I must warn you that a six-fingered and six-toed giant named Segitiga guards the entrance. He is well-appointed with unique weapons."

This intrigued Jonadab, who questioned, "Unique weapons? Speak on."

"On each finger is a ring with a curved blade resting just above the knuckle. When he makes two fists, there are twelve cutting claws in all. Each of his toes is fitted with a sharp penetrating blade. When he kicks, each foot can splinter an oaken board. He makes up for what he lacks in height and girth with speed and strength. He is the brute that protects Prince Achish and the compound with the ferocity of a storm. Make no mistake; you will encounter this seething demon once you cross the city's threshold. Segitiga mourns his kin, who is now the last of the Gath goliaths, and would take vengeance on Israel for killing his brothers. Living this close to Gath, a near lair of giants, I have learned that seventy-five arrow strikes are among the few ways to kill these monsters."

The two days of training, along with good food and stout wine combined, produced the needed effect. Every man knew his place and what to expect. The ladders were sturdy and well-constructed, and Jonadab's men were keen for the challenge. The prize was a horde of pilfered treasure, and each man was entitled to an equal share of the bounty. But first, it had to be recaptured and transported back to Jerusalem to obtain the king's blessing.

A new moon signaled to Jonadab that the timing was perfect and God had his hand in the operation.

A dim silver crescent screened by fast-moving clouds put a chill on the six-mile overland trail to Gath, the fortified capital. Four men were needed to carry each ladder. It was awkward and only accomplished through hours of practice with a neck and shoulder harness. Progress on the open ground was treacherous, especially in the dark. A misstep that resulted in a twisted ankle or broken leg could hamper a well-coordinated attack. Quivers were crammed full, and each bowman had a helper to heft the extra arrows.

Chief Rosh, true to his word, provided all the essential materials. But he remained a bit sullen due to missing the glory days of personal combat. Ignoring his age, he still craved to join the battle. So he offered to scout the route, ensuring the speed and safety of the army of David, "If you accept my guidance, Chief Captain Jonadab and Prince Solomon, I know of a well-traveled goat path that will put you and your army within striking distance of the city walls, without being detected."

Considering Rosh's offer, Solomon said, "You sound like your former commander and my father, King David. He is aged but still itching for a fight. Some men rail against the loss of vitality and youth but mindfully remain strong and formidable. So, I agree to your guidance through the wilderness, but only on the condition that you refrain from combat and stay far from harm's way. Besides, if you are spotted among us, Ziklag will suffer and burn in retribution."

"You make a stern point, prince. However, even though I wish to take part, for the safety of Ziklag, I will hold back and promise to remain in the shadows."

Jonadab then called his ranks to order, "Men, we have practiced our assault, and every man knows his position. The darkness is both our ally and nemesis in our travel through the wilderness. Keep your eye on where the man before you steps, and avoid potholes, cracks, and crevices. Since we count on surprise and stealth, refrain from talking as your voice may carry on the wind. An errant cough or sneeze could signal death if we are accidentally discovered. I pray that God goes before us, for our cause is just, and our mission ordained."

A muted chorus of "amen" were the last voices heard. Then, a long line of men set out silent as the grave on the dimly lit coastal plain, challenging the six-mile trek to the citadel.

The slap of muted sandals proved the only sound on the three-hour sure-footed travel, while the torchlight from the Gath battlements provided a beacon in the pitch-black surroundings.

Solomon quickened his pace to catch up with Jonadab. Movement on the parapets signaled the changing of the guards and the beginning of the fourth watch. Jonadab quietly questioned his adjutant, "Have there been any injuries, and are the ladders ready to be deployed?"

"None, no, and everyone is in their assigned position, eager and waiting for your orders."

"Very well then, in one hour or when you observe stillness and the snoring from the guards becomes noticeable. Next, we will silently launch the ladders and secure the walls by cutting throats. Then, I will tip the oil vat, douse the pulleys, and burn the securing ropes. The Philistines have graciously provided torches to spark the flames. Your fire arrows will rapidly increase the blaze. Remember that if all else fails, you are to launch at the first sight of fire or the white flag. We will hold the gatehouse until the locking cables break, and then you storm the opening and relieve us on the upper balcony with archers and swordsmen."

"Understood, my chief captain."

It felt like time stood still while waiting for the guards to succumb to fatigue. Finally, a little over an hour had passed when the faint grunt of a snore penetrated the stillness. The order was whispered, and twenty men with four ladders led by Jonadab set off in the darkness with two ladders assigned on either side of the gatehouse. The ladders found a quiet rest cushioned by jute on the head and positioned without a sound on the stony ramparts. A quick wave and twenty men scurried to the top and jumped down on the narrow parapet, landing without making a sound. As expected, the guards were half asleep, leaning, slouched, or hiding in the corners. Jonadab and his men made quick work of them by cutting throats and putting on their girdles and markings. Once the gate was secured, men were deployed on each side to guard the narrow passageway against intrusion. It was now Jonadab's moment. He removed his enemy helmet, filled it with greasy fluid, and doused the pulleys, ropes, and locking pins. Unlocking the hinge on the first cauldron, he cranked until the tallow poured slowly down and covered the gate in the thick, slick liquid. They were still undetected when he reached for a nearby torch and set fire to the rigging. At once, Solomon's men lit their fire arrows and launched, sending the fiery darts streaking across the night sky and engulfing Gath's gate in a raging holocaust. The sleepy city was suddenly aroused by horns and men shouting fire. The ramparts immediately flooded with soldiers. Jonadab and his twenty were called to stand firm until the gates opened. They had a fire at their back and a stream of enemies fighting to push them aside and put out the blaze. Their saving grace was the narrowness of the walkway. One at a time or two abreast, they could not be rushed. If one fell, someone else could take his place. As if by providence, the gates opened sooner than expected as the securing cables were rotted.

Solomon and the rest of the legion rushed in to support Jonadab and his men, who were still holding fast on the battlements.

Pushing through the fleeing rabble, Solomon led his men to the palace entrance, hoping to capture Achish, who was still sleeping and unaware of the breach. Then, without warning, the notorious brute Segitiga, Prince Achish's bodyguard, appeared out of the dim first light, looking like a gigantic gray phantom. As reported, he had six fingers on each hand and six toes on each foot. Each finger had a ring with a raised curved blade, and each toe ring had an extended dagger. He jumped into the fray, swiping with clenched fists and tearing men to shreds in the process. Then, kicking and stabbing, he herded Solomon and the army of Israel back through the still-smoldering entranceway. Jonadab beheld the murderous giant destroying his legion from his vantage on the battlement. Immediately, he ordered the archers to shoot their arrows at the approaching monster. Unfortunately, they had little effect and could not even slow down his rampage. Soon, he would be at the gate and under the second cauldron that was now boiling from the fire. Jonadab dashed over and released the hinge with a smoking timber.

He could leverage the whole vat onto the giant as he passed underneath the opening. However, to do so, his timing had to be perfect. There was no time to think, just do it, and do it now. There would be no second chances. The cauldron and the boiling oil fell and hit their mark. In response, Segitiga let out a blood-curdling scream that shook the supports Jonadab was standing on. It caused spines to shiver and everyone to stop and stiffen in horror. Burning cinders handily fell and set ablaze the oil-covered hulk. He ran, only fanning the flames and screaming until he finally collapsed face down, smoldering dead as the sun peeked over the horizon.

Segitiga was burnt and brutalized in full view of the Philistine garrison, now cowering at Israel's menacing approach. Solomon and Jonadab, the two commanders, entered the palace without a challenge and found Achish calmly waiting in his parlor. After being told of Segitiga's gruesome death, Achish was not surprised at the armed intrusion into his private confines. He blurted out, "I assume you are here to take my head at the request of David, your king. You know my death will incite Philistia and the other four princes to move heaven and earth in retaliation against Israel."

Jonadab looked at Solomon, prompting him to answer the charges with a skillful rebuttal, one prince to another. "I am Prince Solomon Ben David, and this imposing fellow is Chief Captain Jonadab Ben Shimeah, my cousin." The briefest nods were exchanged in polite recognition.

Solomon continued, "Although we have never met until now, I know you from my father's stories and adventures in

Ziklag, fighting wolves, and your long-time friendship. But first, let me add my condolences for the recent passing of your father, King Maoch, and if fitting, congratulations on your rise to the throne of Philistia; hail, King Achish."

Completely confounded at the pleasantries, Achish responded, "Prince Solomon. You sound more like an ambassador than a warrior. I know you have something on your mind other than my severed head, and like most politicians, please come to the point before I die of flattery and old age."

"Yes, of course, mighty king, I will get right to it. My father, King David, wishes to end hostilities and begin anew. He proposes that Israel concedes the disputed lands that intersect the King's Highway trade route claimed by Philistia. You will be entitled to one-tenth of all treasure that passes through the disputed territory in place of your consent and protection from pirates and highwaymen. David believes this bargain would go a long way in securing your position with the council of princes and confirming you as the undisputed king. In the meantime, we will recover all retained from your previous sorties against wealth-laden caravans—the immediate release of all prisoners and funds enough to buy back all citizens sold to slavers. We will need carts and camels to haul back the seized goods. One-tenth will be yours to keep, and this downpayment of treasure will finalize our treaty in good faith. If you agree, we will leave you in peace. What say you, Achish King of the Philistines?"

"I do not doubt that you, Prince Solomon, are as cunning as your father. Besides, we are out of giants and options. So let us proceed with the Devil's own bargain."

CHAPTER
FORTY-SEVEN

With Many Or a Few, God Will Make Do

Pride is the most grievous sin to the Lord, for it disavows His existence or the need for Him thereof.

Israel and Judah basked in wealth and power and vainly relied on their own understanding and not on the Lord their God for guidance.

The king's trade highway was a golden river that showered strength and prosperity to all the inhabitants. As a result, the empire of Israel thrived and became the envy of many hungry despots who intently watched Israel becoming fat, lazy, and ill-prepared for invasion.

David was no longer permitted to engage in or even attend armed conflicts for fear of quenching the light of Israel.

His advancing age and resulting frailty heightened his feelings of weakness for himself and the nation.

Golden idols sprung up like mushrooms in the dark. Israel believed it was all-powerful.

The Lord was not pleased with Israel and Judah's prideful arrogance and would use David to awaken His disobedient children and once again seek His refuge in all things spiritual.

Like clutching fingers, a cold chill swept across the seven hills and entered the king's chamber. It brought with it a vivid dream that invaded David's restless sleep. Waking up with a start, he suddenly felt compelled to count the young men at arms in preparation for some dark, unseen force about to spring forth from the shadows.

David called Joab, chief captain of the host, who had apartments in the mansion, staying close to the king and was always with him for protection. "Nephew, I have just been prompted that Israel and Judah are in peril." Impatiently, he commanded his trusted general, "Go now through all the tribes of Israel, from Dan even to Beer-Sheba, and number the young men so that I might know the fighting strength of Israel."

Uneasy about the challenge, Joab attempted to ease the king's misgiving. "I see this action as needless and useless, for their numbering would not make them greater or lesser. God sets the number of them needed to protect and defend the stakes of Zion. Are not all the king's servants ready to obey you whenever you command them, whether numbered or not? God often accomplishes his ends with much less than expected, so there is no doubt that the victory is His, and the power pours down from heaven."

The king listened as Joab continued saying his piece, "It

could even prove to have a harmful effect. A great number could make the people feel invincible and dismiss the power of the Almighty as irrelevant and can only bring down the wrath of God upon them for their lack of trust. Or a lesser number would make them faithless and fearful. It will also be a troublesome and expensive undertaking. Surely, the king must cast his eyes for peace of mind and not find delight in trusting in the arm of man, but in God's omnipotent wisdom."

Despite his best attempts, Joab's argument fell on deaf ears, and as usual, David's self-righteous pride overruled all opinions to the contrary. The king's command prevailed against Joab and all his lesser captains, and concerning the Lord's anointed, they departed the king's presence to number the people of Israel as requested.

Joab's census brigade passed over the Jordan River and pitched their tents in Aroer on the rim of the Armon Gorge. It lies to the city's right and next to the wadi of Gad, a wadi that went from a trickle to rage in the rainy season and flowed north to the town of Jazer. The route was laid out to lessen time and effort. Some towns accepted the questioning, but some villages were reluctant and even hostile to the inquiry and complained of kingly harassment.

Then they came to Gilead and the land of Tahtim-hodshi or the lower ones of my new moon. They then continued with all due haste to Dan-Jaan and roundabout to Zidon, the place of fishing. This was followed by a show of force coming to the stronghold of Tyre, or the place of strength, and all the cities of the Hivites and Canaanites. Lastly, they turned south of

Judah, even to Beer-Sheba or the well of seven oaths.

Diligent and true to his word, Joab and his well-armed lesser captains took nine months and twenty days to complete their mission. They wearily returned to Jerusalem with their scribes and filled logs attesting to their painstaking accuracy with minimal bloodshed.

In a fresh uniform, bathed, trimmed, and perfumed, Joab addressed the king, who now seemed subdued, contrite, and regretful. Then, bowing in respect, he began, "My king, I have counted the strength of Israel as you had commanded, and the numbers are formidable."

In a curt tone, David underscored Joab's dedicated effort, "Speak on nephew, do not tarry, for I have more pressing matters."

Without further ado, Joab gave up the sum of the number of people to the king. "There are eight hundred thousand valiant men in Israel that draw the sword, and in Judah, there are five hundred thousand men."

Hearing the accounting and recalling Joab's warning, a dark spirit came over David, and his heart exposed his sin of vanity as the fear of God overtook him for numbering the people. In crushing distress, David called out to the Lord as if from the sorrow of the pit, "I have sinned greatly in what I have done. I implore You, O Lord, to take away Your servant's iniquity. For I have done very foolishly." David was met with a deafening silence. The Lord would not make his mind known directly. But would allow David a night of soul-searching before He would relay His displeasure through His prophet.

David's rest was fitful and disturbed. Harrowing visions of the underworld pulled him to and fro. He tossed and turned like a broken hinge upon his bed. His body rebelled with cold sweats and fevered chills, and his mind spun out of control. Then, finally, the morning light dispelled the dark clouds and gave David a momentary reprieve of peace.

The word of the Lord came to His prophet Gad and David's seer, saying, "Go and say to David that I offer him three punishments to balance the scales of justice for his insult and lack of faith. He can choose one of them that I may then do to him."

Gad came to David and spoke all the Lord's words, laying out the three penalty choices one by one, "Shall seven years of famine come unto the land." David considered the first proposal. He reflected on Joseph and the seven years of famine in Egypt, the extended swollen bellies, the hopelessness of men, women, and children, and the far-reaching destruction of hope. "Or you will flee three months before your enemies seek your life." All the years of running from Saul flashed before his eyes, his heart pounded, and his senses rebelled. Lastly, "Three days of pestilence throughout all the land." David chafed at a raging plague, but then it was for only three days. Gad then said, "Now advise me on what answer I shall return to He that sent me."

David said unto Gad, "I am in a great strait. Let us fall now into the hand of the Lord. For His kindness is large, and His mercies are great. Let me not fall into the hands of man."

David sealed the fate of Israel, and the Lord, true to his

word, sent a pestilence from that morning to the appointed time of the assembly.

The fierceness of God swept across the nation on the wings of divine punishment. His wrath laid low seventy thousand men counted as fighters from Dan to the far shores of Beer-Sheba. Through the mist, David witnessed the choking destruction and glimpsed the destroying angel wielding the sword of the Lord's retribution, striking the people with dark fury. David called upon the Lord, saying, "Lo, I have sinned and done wickedly, but these sheep, what have they done? Let your hand; I pray You to be against me and my father's house."

The Lord God heard David's plea, and out of the mist and the smoke, Gad the prophet spoke to David the words of the Almighty, "Go and rear up an altar unto the Lord in the threshing floor of Araunah the Jebusite." With faith, hope, and relying on God's tender mercies, He could be persuaded to stay His hand if David did as commanded.

But when the angel of the Lord stretched out his hand to destroy Jerusalem, the Lord felt sorrow for His chosen people's place of assembly. So, He restrained His retribution and called to His avenging angel, saying, "It is enough. Stay now thy hand. The angel of the Lord was by the threshing place of Araunah the Jebusite, where the wheat is separated from the chaff, a place of separation and revelation.

From afar, Araunah could see David and his servants coming up the hill to him and his threshing floor. So, he went out and bowed down to the king with his face to the ground, "Praise God, and long live the king of Israel. What honor has brought my lord to your humble servant's doorstep?"

"I am here at the Lord's bidding to buy your threshing floor and build an altar on this high place that overlooks the city and do sacrifice to end the pestilence that devours the people," David explained.

"My lord king, take and offer up what seems good and right. Then, witness for yourself, here are the oxen needed for the burnt sacrifice, and threshing implements, even the yoke and the wooden pens used by the cows and bulls."

All these things Araunah gave freely without price or favor, saying, "I pray that the Lord our God accepts these gifts."

"Nay, I have been challenged, so I cannot offer a burnt sacrifice that has cost me nothing and risk the further displeasure of the Almighty. But I will surely buy it from you for a fair price."

So, David obtained the threshing floor, oxen and all, for fifty shekels of silver.

Once the last coin was placed in Arunah's hand, David built an altar unto the Lord and offered both sin and peace offerings, and so the Lord was petitioned for the land's sake, and the plague was held back in Israel, and Jerusalem was spared.

CHAPTER
FORTY-EIGHT
The Chill of the Grave

The world's weight pressed heavily on David's aging shoulders, and a stiffening chill invaded his body. Even thick and plentiful woolen clothes could not produce the needed body heat. Warmth remained elusive and unattainable—even when standing near a roaring fire, close enough to singe garments.

Ebed, David's near and dear life-long servant, was still fussing over the king's welfare. Both men were rapidly approaching their twilight years. Yet, for nearly a lifetime, Ebed had become familiar with the needs and wants of his master and frequently provided long before the request was even uttered.

Taking a deep breath to boost the impact of his word, he petitioned the king for permission to speak freely, "Sire, if I might be so bold, I have an observation and a possible solution to your constant cold."

"Speak on."

"Since the insult of Absalom in uncovering the king's nakedness in the sight of all Israel, you have shut away your concubines and do not attend them, ever. It is also rumored that the king no longer visits his wives and that even Bathsheba, your most ardent and fanciful lover, goes wanting."

"Yes, all you said is quite true and correct. I have lost interest in such things. But I take it from the broad inquiries that you have discovered a balm to ease my suffering. So, hurry and get on with it before this deepening chill freezes my chattering teeth," ordered David.

"Of course, my lord. I will come to the point. Allow us to find for you a new love so that you might feel the surge of youth and vigor in your loins and again know the fire of desire. Perhaps an unsullied virgin beautiful in face and form—a blossoming young woman that can stand before the king in all her glory. Let her cherish you and allow her to lie in your embrace so that the lord my King may flush pink with passion."

"Very well then, Ebed. That sounds reasonable and has possibilities. It is worth a try as none of my physicians have offered me a solution, only that my end is nearing. My body is withering and preparing for its journey back to the earth, and my spirit is made ready to take flight."

Ebed petitioned Hushai the Archite, whom David had appointed as his prime minister, for the confounding of the advice of Ahithophel and thus saving David's life. Hushai was now the acting ruler and governed the nation during David's incapacity. He eagerly agreed with Ebed's suggestion that all efforts should be put forth to sustain the light of Israel.

A commission of the king's trusted men noted for their appreciation of the feminine form was hastily recruited. Once told of the unusual mission, they eagerly volunteered. They were to search the coasts of Israel for a beautiful young virgin to heal the king and restore him to health and vitality. Eventually, after many failed attempts, the seekers became discouraged and were about to abandon their search and retreat empty-handed back to Jerusalem. In their retreat, they chanced upon a Shunammite village known for its hospitality. Needing to slake their thirst, they encountered a stunning beauty at the town well, hauling water buckets for her supper.

The striking radiance of this daughter of Israel captured the captain's attention. He began, "Please excuse my boldness, but we are on a quest from the king and so too from God. We seek a comely woman who can revive King David, the light of Zion whose life's flame has begun to diminish. He grows cold, and a youthful companion may create the spark to return the king to his former vibrant self. We have been tasked to seek out that lady ordained by God to help renew and sustain our monarch. I am compelled to believe you are that woman. What is your name?"

The woman replied, "I am Abishag, the orphan."

"I believe you, Abishag, may very well be the answer to our prayers. Tell us more about who you are so we can decide your suitability to be a companion to our great King David."

"I will, my lord, but my tale is common and filled with strife. My father died soon after my birth, and I was raised by my mother, who had recently succumbed by working herself to death to provide a roof over our heads and enough food to sustain life. I am alone and have been praying for a sign from God to know His will and what direction I should travel. I have been solicited to submit to a harlot's life or starve to death. You have come just in time to save me from a life of ruin. To be the king's concubine would be an honor."

"Very well, I can see God's hand in all things. Therefore, you will accompany us to Jerusalem and be presented to the ailing king, and forthwith, I will address you as the king's elixir."

The group approached Jerusalem's seven hills and proceeded through an unattended gate, avoiding little or no attention. Finally, they entered the mansion through a side door set aside for such occasions. When informed of the capture of a suitable damsel, Prime Minister Hushai hurriedly organized a bevy of servants to bathe and adorn the young maiden with exotic perfumes, revealing robes and fresh flowers in her hair.

Ebed, David's body servant, was summoned the moment the damsel was prepared for presentation to the king for his approval. The commander did the honors, "Ebed, this vision of loveliness is Abishag the Shunammite. She has agreed to try and beguile the king and heighten his fervor for life and living. We are praying she can return him to health and youthful vigor."

"Thank you, commander. Israel honors you for your efforts on behalf of the king. Now, I will take the damsel, Abishag, to the king's apartments and witness if her presence rekindles the king's absent passion.

Ushering Abishag through a long and winding hallway, Ebed took a moment to stress the importance of what was expected of her, "You have been selected, my dear, by fate and by God for this very moment of service to the nation. The king weakens, and his body sickens, and try as he might, the cold fingers from the grave now invade his bones. So, we need you to entice, seduce, and arouse the king and tease him back to life. Use your women's wiles, motherly instincts, and tender love."

"I understand what is needed of me, and I will strive to restore the king to health with all my feminine charms by making myself available to the king's wants and desires," Abishag insisted.

As usual, the king was in his chamber, covered in heavy woolen blankets. Even on the hottest days, he remained bundled. He napped much more often and always seemed tired; the bounce in his step was all but gone. Ebed knocked and knocked at the door, chancing the king's displeasure—but having such a delectable offering, he thought the risk was acceptable.

Near blistering, Ebed's knuckles reddened from the pounding. Finally, a croak came from behind the locked door, "Ebed, is that you, since no one else would dare to alarm the king in his dreams? What is so urgent—war or fire? If any less, you will feel my anger for disturbing my slumber."

"A thousand pardons, lord king, for the disturbance, but I have brought a superb surprise that I believe will return the king's zest for life."

The hinges suddenly creaked, and the door parted. In his nightshirt wrapped in a blanket, David beckoned in Ebed and the stunning youthful vision beside him. "Who is this lovely stranger that invades my bed chamber?"

"This is Abishag the Shunammite. As you can witness, sire, she is a vestal beauty offering warmth and comfort to her beloved monarch."

"Leave us, Ebed, so we might discover if she carries the spark that reignites my flickering fire."

Left alone in discreet privacy, the moment's awkwardness was soon cast off with the abandonment of Abishag's clothing. All she wore was the hint of a smile, and she relished her abandonment. Then, breathlessly, Abishag's chastity was about to be reaped by the legendary king of Israel, David the Unconquerable. She pleaded in a husky voice, "Allow me, lord king, to comfort you and arouse in you the youthful gallop of a wild stallion." David's blood coursed, and for a brief moment, he relished a soothing heat radiating from his loins. But all too soon, cold fingers tightened their grip, leaving no doubt that youth had departed and left frailty and wisdom behind in its wake.

Abishag captured David's attention by looking up with her innocent, almond eyes before whispering, "Do I not please you, sire?"

Looking down, David swallowed hard before replying, "Your youth and beauty are sublime, but I need sleep and body heat more than intimacy."

David then abruptly turned, shook his head, and sighed in frustration. He laid back on his bed and proceeded to pull the covers over his head. Abishag could do no more, so she crawled next to the king and ministered to him with all the comfort she could muster. But the king knew her not. So Abishag's virtue remained intact and untouched.

CHAPTER FORTY-NINE

Caught On the Horns of Rebellion

David's health continued to decline. He was barely hanging on to life, with the last of his strength ebbing away. Until he named a successor and had him anointed and blessed with all the trappings of authority, the double crown prize would follow the lawful succession of birth rights.

Adonijah, meaning my Lord is Jehovah, was the son of Haggith and David's fourth son. Therefore, he believed that by birthright, he was the next in line and heir to David's throne on the day of his father's passing.

Amnon, the eldest, was murdered by Absalom because of the rape of Tamar, his half-sister. Chileab, the second son, also called Daniel, died innocently, never knowing a woman's charms. Finally, Absalom, the third in line, was slaughtered by his cousin Joab when his hair caught in a pistachio tree while escaping his failed attempted insurrection.

Adonijah exulted himself and prepared to receive the

mantle as the next anointed king of Israel and Judah. This would be the case if David did not name his successor before he departed this life. Unfortunately for Solomon, the king made no such announcement. David was content to let things play out naturally and secretly believed Adonijah would make a good administrator. Besides, Solomon was much too fond of wine and women, and the absolute power of a king could very well be his undoing.

Adonijah began to prepare before the fact and acted as if it had already been decided. This portrayal of power and authority was essential and would allow him to settle into the role of king without dissension or objection.

Whether traveling near or far, Adonijah imitated Absalom, the usurper, by riding in the king's chariot accompanied by regal cavalry in all their finery riding behind him, as well as having fifty men run before him, attesting to his greatness.

Jessie was David's aged father. He was a gentle soul, lacking scorn, mockery, or punishment of his children. He spared the rod and the correcting tongue and relied on God and fate to mold his offspring's temperament. Unfortunately, like his father, David was prone to refrain from disciplining his many sons. It was the same trap that Eli, the high priest at Shiloh, had fallen into by lack of consequences for his offending children, Phineas the younger, and Hophni, the mastermind, by ignoring their rampant delinquency to go unchecked and invoking the punishment of God.

David never disciplined Adonijah or questioned him or his other 18 sons. Neither their choices nor behavior, that freedom pleased Adonijah greatly. Adonijah was also a goodly man, easy to look at, strong, tall, and beautiful. The apple of David's eye did not fall far from the family tree. His mother, Haggith, bore him only a few hours after Maacah delivered her son Absalom. It seemed like at the time that the two women competed to be the first to provide David with a son and heir. The women were straining and stressing, pushing with all their might to bring life through the divine matrix. But David was delighted to have two healthy sons born to his body on the same day in Hebron.

David's life is now hanging by a thread. Knowing this, it was a crucial time for Adonijah to recruit allies to secure his ambitions. He considered the military's control and over-whelming power to be essential to his cause. The first on his list was his cousin Chief Captain Joab, his aunt Zeruiah's middle son. He sought out Joab to entice his allegiance with the promise of a permanent captaincy and a warning of his father's vengeful need to balance the scales of justice, even from the grave.

Adonijah proceeded to Joab's house outside the city walls, seeking his pledge of support and warning him of the dire consequence of Solomon's ascension to the throne. Adonijah began, "Greetings and salutations, chief captain."

Joab politely responded, "It has been too long since I have enjoyed your company. What brings you out here? It must be important to tear you away from Jerusalem and your father's rapidly worsening condition."

"We need to speak in private as some delicate matters need discussion."

"Certainly, in my private study, we will be safe from prying eyes and curious ears. The penalty in the military for spying is death. So be assured your words will go no further than these walls." Joab signaled an aid to provide wine and two bowls.

"So, tell me, cousin, why are you here?"

"I need your army's unwavering support before David takes his last breath. Your recognition of my birthright to the throne will make for an easy transition. Consequently, for your support, I pledge that you will continue as chief captain for as long as I live. There are other rumblings that you should be made aware of. David has been rumored to seek an eye for an eye, a tooth for a tooth, and a death for death or some insult he harbors as and goes to his grave unsatisfied. Unfortunately for your cousin, you are at the top of his hit list due to your killings of Abner, Amasa, and Absalom. This could very well be your penalty if Solomon reins in Israel. They will be quickly and quietly dispatched to the afterlife as soon as I am anointed. What say you, chief captain for life, Joab Ben Seraiah?"

"You are compelling, my lord king. Long live Adonijah, king of Israel!"

With the backing of the army, Adonijah knew the religious community was the group he next needed to recruit. David's long-time friend and his high priest, Abiathar Ben Ahimelech, was the great-great-grandson of Eli and the only survivor of the massacre at Nob. He would be the last high priest from the House of Eli because Jonathan, his son, had no interest in the Levite mantle. Abiathar was aware of David's unwilling-ness to name an heir because he wanted the law of birthright to prevail. Truth be known, David favored Adonijah, as he was a man of numbers and is accounted as having a sensible, mature nature. Moreover, he would be an ideal administrator for the vast wealth from trade on the King's Highway that poured in daily.

The tabernacle of the congregation overflowed with the penitent seeking salvation through sacrifice. Adonijah sought out Abiathar amid the departing crowd scurrying to get undercover before sundown.

Adonijah said, "High priest, I need your support and blessing to be the next king. I will require your holy anointing. My brother Solomon makes growling noises and would challenge my birthright to the throne. His mother, the adulteress Bathsheba, pressures my father on his deathbed to name her son Solomon king and heir. What say you, priest? Can I count on you as a friend to upend this usurper?"

"I know Prince Solomon well. We have downed many a wineskin together. He is the only man who can drink more wine than I and discuss deep thinking without the slightest evidence or notice of impairment. He is adept at hiding his legendary appetite with logical reasoning and profound philosophy. If he is not drinking wine, he is chasing women, usually one fueling the other. Solomon as king would be an utter disaster for Israel. You are the best choice to be king by the law, education, and disposition."

However, scorn for Adonijah came from Zadok, the priest, Benaiah, son of Jehoiada, and Nathan, God's prophet. Even Shimei, who had cursed David, had a change of heart. Rei, an officer of the royal guard, and all the mighty men that belonged to David could not abide Adonijah's potential rise to power.

An elaborate feast of expensive meats was organized to celebrate the forgone conclusion that Adonijah would be king. All that was missing was the pledge from certain nobility and the anointing to make it legal.

CHAPTER FIFTY

Redemption For the Nearly Dead and Dying

A regal banquet in the scope and luxury only afforded by a reigning monarch was presented to sway any doubting holdouts. Adonijah slew sheep, oxen, and fat cattle by the stone of Zoheleth or the serpents steal. It was also known as the conduit stone. Which is by En-Rogel or the fuller's spring, the place of cleaning. He called all his brothers the king's sons and all the elders of Judah the servants of David, and some that required the confidence only found in the security of a like-minded crowd.

But Nathan, the prophet Benaiah, David's mighty men, and Solomon marked as a stumbling block and an adversary, was the only brother not invited.

Nathan was troubled that, unless David intervened, Adonijah would be king by general approval. The prophet of God needed to warn Bathsheba, the mother of Solomon, and said to her, "How is it that you have not heard that Adonijah, the son of Haggith, yours and Solomon's nemesis, now rules and reigns, if not in truth but certainly in the minds of powerful men, Therefore, do not be surprised while you are talking to the king. I will come in behind you and confirm your words, for it is written that the matter shall be established in the mouth of the second witness. Now take unto yourself my counsel that you might save yours and Solomon's lives. Go now while there is still time and go unto King David as he lies upon his deathbed and remind him of his promise that he swore to you that he would have Solomon sit upon his throne and rule. But with guile and cunning, Adonijah has assumed the king's mantle and reins in his stead."

Bathsheba scurried to the king's bedside as if her life and her son's life depended on the swiftness of travel.

Bathsheba stepped into the darkened room and did her homage, for the king was very old. Abishag the Shunammite nursed the king and saw to all his needs. The room had the creeping shadow of the grave, final and unyielding. Finally, Bathsheba blurted out, "I have come to save the king from the judgment of God."

David rallied, sat up with a start, and questioned his eighth and last wife, "What is that you say? Have you come to tie the final knot in a dead man's shroud?"

"No, my lord, I have come to save you from a broken vow you swore before me and God, now a stain in your tongue before you die. Did you not, my lord O king, swear to me and in the presence of God, saying, 'Assuredly Solomon, your son shall reign after me and shall sit upon my throne?' Do you wish to stand before God, the judge of all creation, with deceit on your lips?"

Her righteous judgment startled David, and he asked her, "What would you have of me, madam?"

"The king is unaware that Adonijah has set himself as ruler, waiting for the king's passing. He has slain oxen, sheep, and fat cattle in great abundance. He has called all the king's sons, Abiathar, the priest, and Joab, the host's captain, now giving him the army's backing. But Solomon was purposefully not invited. Therefore, all the eyes of Israel are upon you, waiting for you to name your successor. If you depart without naming a successor, the crown goes to Adonijah, which I believe you already knew. But you have not considered that Solomon and I will be counted as offenders and destined to embrace the assassin's blade. So, you will have sworn falsely and have our innocent blood upon your head."

At that very moment, Nathan, the prophet, approached, dismissing the shadows and burning with an inner light of his own. A servant announced, "Behold, Nathan the prophet." He came before the king and bowed with his face to the ground. Bathsheba turned to the prophet and took her leave, allowing the men to speak privately.

Nathan inquired, "My lord, have you said, 'Let Adonijah reign after me, and he shall sit upon my throne?' Today, he has provided a coronation feast with abundant trappings of fat cattle, oxen, and sheep. All the king's sons, Joab and Abiathar, the priest. They often toasted, saying, 'God save King Adonijah.' But I was not included; neither was Zadok the priest, Benaiah, the son of

Jehoiada, Solomon, and all the king's Mighties. Has your word done this, and you have not informed me, your servant, who will sit on your throne once you are gone?"

David was distraught with himself for forsaking the necessary and the obvious, "Call me Bathsheba." Her name rang through the corridors promptly, and she presented herself to the king again.

David began addressing Bathsheba with a contrite heart: "I swear, as the Lord God lives, you have redeemed my soul out of all distress. I swear to you by the Lord God of Israel, and I assure you that Solomon, your son, shall reign after me, and he shall sit on my throne. I will proclaim that decision this very day."

With that proclamation, Bathsheba's spirit soared because she was reprieved from a certain death sentence, and her son Solomon, whom she loved more than life itself, shall be king of Israel and Judah without further delay. Then, bowing in supplication with her face to the ground, she replied, "Let my lord king David live forever!"

Immediate action was required to seize the moment before Adonijah's rise to power was a forgone conclusion and accepted by all the people. David again felt vital and alive by facing his last challenge to organize and take charge. He would keep his sworn word and save the lives of his dearly beloved wife, Bathsheba, and her son, Solomon. The warning of the prophet Nathan continued to ring in David's ears, 'The sword will never leave your house.'

David rallied and ordered, "Call me Zadok, the priest,

Nathan the prophet, and Benaiah, the son of Jehoiada. The men that held fast and would not be swayed by Adonijah's posturing bluster."

Gathering before King David, he devised his plan to thwart Adonijah's attempted power grab.

David heightened as if preparing for battle and ordered, "Take my guards, the Cherethites and Pelethites. Take all the men you need to accomplish the deed. Have my son Solomon ride upon my mule and parade him down to Gihon and break forth the watercourse that fills the fuller spring of En-Rogel, where Adonijah entices the young men to mutiny.

"Once you have arrived, have Zadok the priest and Nathan the prophet anoint Solomon King over Israel, and immediately sound the shofar ram's horn and say to the heavens, 'God save King Solomon.' Then and without delay, escort him back to Jerusalem, where he shall sit upon my throne. For then, he shall be king, taking my place. None will doubt or dare to challenge that I, David, have appointed him to rule and reign over Israel and Judah."

Jehoiada's son, Benaiah, answered the King, saying, "Amen! The Lord God of heaven and earth says so as well. But, as God has been with my lord the king even so, he will be with Solomon, his son and heir, and make his throne greater than the throne of my lord King David."

As it was said, so it was done. Zadok, Nathan, and all the king's men escorted Solomon, riding on the king's mule above the place of Adonijah's feast and in sight of all of Israel. Zadok, the priest, took a horn of oil that had been separated and blessed in the presence of God for the anointing of kings and priests. It had been taken from the Holy place next to the veil in the Tabernacle of the Congregation.

Nathan, the prophet of God, anointed Solomon with a precious drop that dripped down from the anointing horn to the crown of Solomon's head, saying, "Solomon Ben David, with this oil that has been set apart in the household of faith for the healing of the sick and afflicted and the elevation of kings and the sanctifying of priests and saints. I bless you that your rule and reign will be with an eye single to the glory of God and that your cup runneth over in service of your people Israel." And all said, "Amen."

The shofar blew, the clouds parted, the pillars of heaven shook, and everyone screamed uproariously loud, "God save King Solomon!" All the people came up after him, piped, and joyfully rejoiced with so much noise that the earth trembled.

Meanwhile, Adonijah and all the guests with him heard the commotion and swallowed their last mouthful hard with growing concern. After hearing the last trump, Joab asked, "Why is the city in such turmoil?" While the question still hung in the air unanswered, Jonathan, the son of Abiathar, the priest, came in breathless. Adonijah asked him, "You, being a valiant man, do you bring good news?"

Jonathan looked down in despair and replied, "With certainty, our lord king David has made Solomon king in the eyes of God and man."

The men fell silent as Jonathan continued, "King David sent him with Zadok, the priest, Nathan, the prophet, and

Benaiah, the son of Jehoiada, and the Cherethites and the Pelethities, David's royal household guards. They made Solomon ride upon the king's mule in the sight of all the people. Zadok, the priest, and Nathan, the prophet, have anointed him, king, in Gihon. They came from there rejoicing at every step, reaching the gate, and the city rang out. That is the disturbance you have heard. Solomon sits on the throne of the kingdom. All the king's servants came to bless our lord Solomon, the anointed monarch."

Jonathan announced to the uneasy gallery the deathbed decree of King David that he proclaimed to all the people, 'God make the name of Solomon better than my name and make his throne greater than mine.' The king then bowed upon his bed and said, 'Blessed be the Lord God of Israel who has allowed The One to sit on my throne this day, and that I can see with my eyes before I die.'"

All the guests at Adonijah's banquet were afraid after hearing of Solomon's coronation and David's blessing, which was heartily accepted by all the people who said amen to the peaceful transfer of power. So, every man hurriedly went his own way, scattering like mice in fear of the butcher's knife.

Terrified and in dire straits, Adonijah scurried to the Tabernacle, seeking sanctuary. But, as expected, he went in and caught hold of the horns of the burnt offering altar. Where the animals were tied, awaiting sacrifice, and where blood was spilled and sprinkled.

Solomon was told that Adonijah feared retribution and had sought refuge in the Tabernacle. In desperation, he had caught hold of the altar's horns and would not let go until King Solomon swore he would not slay his servant with the sword.

Solomon considered his best course of action, and his brother's blood on such a holy day of elevation would not be fitting or proper and could even send the wrong message of vengeance rather than compassion.

Solomon sent his first decree as king, telling his brother Adonijah, 'If he shows himself to be a worthy man, there shall not be a hair of his that will touch the ground violently. But if wickedness is found in him, he shall die.'

So, the servants of Solomon conveyed the king's message before taking their master down from the horns of the altar.

Adonijah came and bowed himself to the king, who now had the power of life and death, and Solomon said to him, "Go to your house and trouble me no more."

CHAPTER FIFTY-ONE

Benefits and Punishments From
Beyond the Grave

Every day, David thought he would breathe his last, and every night, he resigned himself to eternal rest. But, · like any father, he wished to pass down wisdom and knowledge acquired from a lifetime of conflict and hardship while learning to revel in passion and triumph.

David propped himself up on one elbow. The air was thick with burning incense to comfort the ailing monarch. Oil lamp wicks began to sputter, fighting against the coming darkness. He called forth Solomon, for he had some choice words to impart before going the way of the earth. Confidently, he prepared to meet his maker with a clear conscience for honoring his covenants.

He charged Solomon, his son and heir, "I am about to depart this life. I can no longer hold you up or bring you down, so you need to be strong and show yourself to be a man. In all that you say and do, keep the commandments of the Lord your God and walk in his ways to keep his statutes, judgments, and testimonies as written in the law of Moses. If you do these things with an eye single to His glory and not rely on your own understanding, you will prosper in all your efforts. Wherever you go, put your hand in the Lord, and He will honor His word that He had spoken to me, saying, 'If your children take regard to the way they walk before me in truth and with all their heart and with all their soul, they shall not fail or fall. You are now the man that sits on the throne of Israel and heir to that promise, my son.'"

Feeling parched, David sipped some cool water before continuing, "Now, my son, hearken to my counsel and respect my final wishes before I succumb to age and the grave. I have some unfinished business that presses heavily on my heart and mind."

Solomon listened quietly to his father's words, "You know what your cousin Joab, the son of Zeruiah, has done to me and what he did to the two captains of the host of Israel. Abner, son of Ner, and Amasa, the son of Jether, whom he slew, shedding the blood of war during peace. He put the blood of war upon his sash and stained red the souls of his feet. I also cannot dismiss the pain I have endured over these many years from Joab's cruel torture and slaughter of your brother Absalom, who hung helplessly from a pistachio tree. He did this thing knowingly against my order and plea for compassion. I will leave the particulars to your wisdom and your pleasure, but if it were up to me, I would not allow his aged gray head to go down to the grave in peace without repayment for his dastardly deeds." David took a much-needed breath as Solomon waited patiently for his father's dying last words.

David then cleared the thickness in his throat and continued, "So too, Shimei, the son of Gera, a Benjaminite of Bahurim, cursed me with grievous charges of murder. He kicked up dust as if I was a mongrel dog and threw stones that pelted and insulted my company. It was the day I went to Mahanaim in flight from the insurrection of your brother Absalom and was already in despair. The scoundrel met me at the River Jordan, frothing at the mouth with hatred and evil intent. I swore to him in the name of the Lord that I would not put him to the sword. You are a wise man and hold him not guiltless, and you know what needs to be done. His gray head should be brought down to the grave with blood. But you are king, and it is given to you to decide what to do by having the power of life and death at your fingertips."

David took another pause before proceeding to continue with his wishes, "I would admonish you to show kindness to the sons of Barzillai the Gileadite and let them eat at your table, for they came to me with needed food and provisions when fleeing from the sword of Absalom, your brother," David said, showing gratitude.

"Finally, a warning from my self-imposed judgment. Nathan, the prophet of God, tricked me. He spun a tale of a rich man with flocks and herds and a poor man with one ewe lamb. The rich man took the poor man's one ewe lamb that was treated like family and dressed it for the stranger. It was a fable describing the taking of Uriah, the Hittite's wife. Nathan asked me for my judgment, to which I blurted out, 'I would have him killed and made him pay it back four times.'

"Nathan then condemned me, saying, 'You are the man.' I had judged myself and affixed my punishment. Nathan then assured me that God did not seek to forfeit my life. He then spoke for God and said, 'The sword should never depart from your house.' This is because you have despised me and taken the wife of Uriah the Hittite to be your wife. Thus, the Lord says, 'Behold, I will raise evil against you out of your own house, and I will take your wives before your eyes, and give them to another, and he shall lie with your wives in the sight of the sun. For what you did secretly, I will do this before all of Israel and in broad daylight,' sayeth the Lord of Hosts. Shamefully, by this adulterous deed, you have given great occasion to the enemies of the Lord to blaspheme. Therefore, the child that is born unto you shall surely die.'"

David looked sad as he considered these difficult past moments: "The male child, the fruits of our adulterous affair, died seven days after birth, so it was never named nor circumcised. Then Amnon, my firstborn, was murdered by Absalom's command. Then Absalom was slaughtered by Joab while hanging from the pistachio tree. So, I paid back three times, but four was the number I had demanded. So, beware, my son, of your brother Adonijah's thirst for power for the sword, still needs to devour another."

David's last thought was how his killing of Uriah to possess Bathsheba caused him to name his punishment. Was this how

God balanced the scales of justice by having man stand before Him, with perfect knowledge of his crimes, to judge himself and suffer a fitting penalty for breaking the commandments? At that moment, David, to his sorrow, realized that mercy could not rob justice.

The end had come peaceably in the night. David slept with his father. He was buried in the city of David, first known as Jebus, or lastly, Jerusalem.

David reigned over Israel for forty years. First, he reigned in Hebron, his Judean capital, for seven years and then thirty-three years in Jerusalem over all of Israel.

Solomon sat upon the throne, and wealth and power flowed from the Euphrates to the Nile Delta. His kingdom flourished and became greater than David's, and the days of Solomon will be forthcoming.

Selah.

Historically, these books are in a series, starting with 'Gideon, The Sound and The Glory,' 'David God's Chosen Crucible,' and "Second 'David, Trials and Tribulations. Each book stands alone. The last in the series will be 'Solomon—Wine, Women, and Song.' Stay tuned!

Milton Keynes UK
Ingram Content Group UK Ltd.
UKHW022000241123
433237UK00004B/86